2nd Edition

The BASIC

Handbook

Encyclopedia of the
BASIC Computer Language

by
David A. Lien

COMPUSOFT® PUBLISHING
A Division of CompuSoft, Inc.
San Diego, California 92119 U.S.A.

International Standard Book Number: 0-932760-05-8
Library of Congress Catalog Card Number: 81-67479

Printed in the United States of America   10 9 8 7 6 5 4

Preface To The 2nd Edition

When the 1st Edition of *The BASIC Handbook* was released in 1978, I was pleasantly overwhelmed by the response. It is with great pleasure (and a bit of modest pride) that I offer this greatly expanded and revised 2nd Edition.

In our fast changing field 3 years is a generation, and the BASIC language has changed in many ways. With each new computer came new words, and with each new word the need to update. Relying on what I believe is the most extensive BASIC language library in the world, plus assistance from many manufacturers, I've attempted to document and explain virtually every BASIC feature of virtually every computer in the world.

In this 2nd Edition, special attention was given to documenting the diverse BASICs implemented on the many new computers introduced (and about to be introduced) from Europe and Asia. In addition to filling gaps in the 1st Edition, a strong effort was made to continue documenting "disk BASIC", that misunderstood enigma which frustrates so many users. Since there are no standards for "disk BASICs", only common concepts, documentation follows the few identifiable trends.

Many kind readers offered suggestions for changes in format which they felt would increase The Handbook's usefulness. Many of those suggestions are incorporated, and to the correspondents I say "Thank You".

To fellow computer students of all ages, in all places, and at all levels of proficiency, I wish you the best in your BASIC programming endeavors. May *The BASIC Handbook* be your guide to success.

Dr. David A. Lien
San Diego --- 1981

Acknowledgements

In addition to the many acknowledgements in the First Edition, I would like to especially thank the following:

David Lunsford of San Diego, California, the Principal Researcher and Technical Editor.

David Gunzel of Ft. Worth, Texas, the Managing Editor and designer.

Introduction To
The 2nd Edition

The BASIC Handbook places at your fingertips authoritative information about the principal BASIC programming language words from "dialects" used around the world. Correspondence from all parts of the globe attest to the fact that *The BASIC Handbook* has become **The Standard BASIC Language Reference.**

This greatly expanded 2nd Edition documents BASIC as implemented on virtually every BASIC-speaking computer in the world.

Its creation was a monumental task. We hope it will be of great value to you.

A Perspective On The Language

The BASIC language is a rushing river, or a swamp, varying with its mood. Most manufacturers and language designers travel its wide "mainstream", staying in the channel. The mainstream is fed by tributaries, each adding a flake of gold --- or effluent.

Along the river are aspiring rivulets, most going nowhere. Some connect isolated ponds to form obscure networks --- pretenders to the throne of "BASIC".

To carry deeper traffic, some designers dredge the main channel, stirring up tons of mud and silt. Expanded beyond its flow, the river is still called BASIC.

Perhaps this drawing will help you visualize the terrain as we portage across the dry spots.

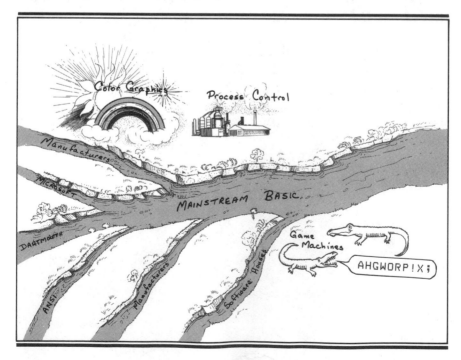

The Ground Rules

In preparing *The BASIC Handbook*, certain "ground rules" had to be established. For without setting boundaries, the job would never have been completed and no one would benefit from the information. The ground rules are listed here so you might understand the working concepts we used to create the Handbook.

1. The Handbook will be an encyclopedic type reference work --- not a dictionary or a textbook. It will be a precise and definitive reference suitable for accompanying a good BASIC language text, but will not attempt to replace it.

2. Top priority has been given to information that will help BASIC language users solve the problem of program incompatibility due to the existence of hundreds of BASIC dialects.

3. There is a large "mainline" core of BASIC words that is shared by most computers. Extensive treatment of that core is more important than extensive coverage of lesser used and obscure special-purpose words. To the extent that time and space allow, lesser-used BASIC words are covered. But like the universe, BASIC keeps expanding. We can only chase it --- but never catch it all.

4. BASIC is used in everything from pocket computers to huge mainframes. But since some small computers have vastly superior BASIC capabilities, size is unimportant. Priority will be given to documenting the language, not machines.

5. For ease of use, BASIC words will be treated in as uniform a manner as possible. Those words that are little used, or exclusive to only one machine with limited possibility for translation to other dialects, will be documented in an abbreviated format.

6. It is not as important to identify whose version of BASIC does what as it is to thoroughly document each important BASIC word. Tying specific capabilities to specific manufacturers will therefore be given low priority.

7. Large computers typically use compilers; small ones usually use interpreters. Since it makes little difference to the language itself, the words interpreter and compiler will be used interchangeably.

8. To hold down size and price, the book will refer readers to key central words rather than repeat the same information in many places.

9. There is little uniformity in BASIC control of peripheral devices such as disks, tapes and printers. Such control words stray far beyond mainline BASIC. We have made an initial attempt at documenting these words, but a standardized treatment will have to wait for that part of the language to "shake out".

10. The Handbook is not a substitute for the manufacturer's manuals that accompany each computer. It is a supplement.

11. Manufacturers change their BASICs, eliminating "glitches", frequently without acknowledging that a problem existed. No attempt will be made to document every known glitch, change, improvement or modification by manufacturers or software houses.

12. BASIC as implemented on "light and game machines" is generally not used for serious computer applications, nor did most of these manufacturers attempt to adhere to reasonable language standards. Since incidental computing is only one of their several capabilities, these "off-the-wall" dialects will be documented in relation to their importance and potential for adaptation to other computers.

Converting Programs From One Computer For Another

Some Handbook users are programmers who rewrite programs from other languages into BASIC. Many other users are computer students who need detailed explanations of BASIC words; what they mean, and how they do their job in different ways.

Judging from the mail, however, the greatest help The Handbook offers is to those converting a BASIC program written for one computer so it will **run** on a different one --- usually their own. A few words at this point might benefit the many readers performing such conversions.

Prepare For The Trip

To adapt a program to RUN on a different computer, you must have a thorough understanding of your own computer's dialect of BASIC. The computer's own reference manual (tho perhaps incomprehensible) is the starting point. At least try to figure out what the manual contains and where that good stuff is hidden.

If the manual doesn't have a good index, list all your computer's BASIC words alphabetically on a sheet of paper, along with a notation where the explanations are found. *The BASIC Handbook* can then become the "missing link" between the program to be adapted and your computer.

Untangle The Original, First

Untangle the original program so you can understand it, **before** trying to convert it. Sample Runs of the original program, if available, can be very helpful in determining the programmer's intent. Find those words which behave differently on the original computer and yours. *The BASIC Handbook* will show you alternate words and subroutines.

Long programs with multiple statement lines and no blank spaces make conversion unnecessarily difficult. Identify these lines, and also those having words foreign to your BASIC. Rewrite them, allowing only one statement per line. **Renumber** the program as necessary to make room for the additional lines. Keep copies of the program at each stage of conversion, so if (when) it "bombs", you can take one step backward and try again.

Table of Variables

If the original program is more than just a few lines long, prepare a table showing the **Allocation of Variables** within it. List each variable letter, string, array, etc. and briefly describe what that variable represents. This table will be invaluable as you untangle and convert the program.

Create a similar table for your own version of the program. The table can (preferably) be included at the end of the program in REM lines as part of its documentation, or, (if memory is limited) written on a separate sheet of paper.

A Word About Word-For-Word Conversion

Word-for-word program conversion is very inefficient and produces a poorly designed end product. It does not take advantage of the special features that are the strength of your particular machine.

Try instead to break the original program into small, functional blocks or modules. Sprinkle REMark statements liberally throughout, as tho you were explaining its operation to someone else. In other words, perform the program documentation which the original programmer probably ignored. Then, with the help of "The Handbook", determine how to accomplish the intention of each of those blocks by using the BASIC words and features that are part of your computer.

Always A String Attached

As a general rule, the most formidable differences between BASIC dialects are the ways in which they handle strings and external (disk or tape) files. Many BASICs require strings to be DIMensioned before use. Computers with this requirement generally manipulate substrings by use of subscripts. Example: A$(3,5) refers to the third thru fifth characters in string A$.

Other computers usually use MID$, LEFT$, RIGHT$, etc. to process substrings. Know which system is used by your BASIC and perform a "global" conversion, if necessary.

File It Down

File handling is the least standard feature of BASIC. If external files are part of the program, determine how they are used, carefully document that use, then redesign and rewrite those parts in accordance with your computer's filing system.

Is It An O Or A 0

An unfortunate carry-over from earlier days of computer programming is the problem of distinguishing an O from a 0. Originally, and for many decades in the electronic communication field, a / thru a 0 identified it as a zero. Since early computer programmers did not generally come from the ranks of radio hams or other communications types, they slashed the symbol O and used it to specify the letter ohh. Check any outdated programming text to see the confusion.

During the latter 1970's, a concerted effort was made by manufacturers of keyboards and printers to standardize on the slashed 0 to mean zero. A quick inspection of your program's line numbers will show which is which.

A matter not yet resolved is, which is which when **neither** uses a slash? Many printers use an O with squared off corners to mean the letter and an 0 with "pointy" tops and bottoms to mean the number. That's easy enough, but many other printers exactly reverse them. We're right back where we started! Again, the quickest way to tell is to check any line number.

Avoid use of either the letter or number 0 as a variable in your programs. **Avoid them like the plague!** We have enough confusion in this field already without providing more opportunities for errors.

Imbedded Special Keys

A few computers (e.g. the Commodore PET) allow their programs to contain special symbols indicating commands inserted by special purpose keyboard keys. These symbols represent moving the cursor on the screen, displaying characters in reverse video, CLEARing the screen, moving the cursor to HOME, etc. The symbols are contained in PRINT statements and are apparent by their very uniqueness.

Examples:

```
510 PRINT ":PRESS #RETURN# WHEN COMPLETED"
520 PRINT "#ENTER THE PROGRAMS ON SIDE"I
530 PRINT:P=P+1
540 PRINT "  PROGRAM #";P;"  JIBI";
```

In the lines below, the words "down", "reverse-field", "off-the-reverse field", "back", "up", etc. describe actions that are created by single keystrokes on the PET keyboard.

```
 900 PRINT "down, reverse-field";N$;"off-reverse-field, back, up";: GOTO 250
1000 PRINT "down, null-symbol, back, up";:N$="":GOTO 250
```

Except for printing the special graphics characters, accomplishing the intent of most other keys on another computer is simply a matter of substituting equivalent statements, when possible.

Goofy Printers

Some printers do not print standard character sets. As I write this, I'm looking at a set from a British magazine which prints a backslash instead of a $ sign, tho a $ sign is intended; and another, from an American magazine has something that looks like the footprint of a 4 toed animal to represent an *. Sometimes the accompanying text will point these things out. Don't let printer differences confuse you into thinking you are dealing with another dialect of BASIC.

Goofy Computers

Hundreds of thousands of TRS-80 computers print an up-arrow on the screen but a left bracket on most printers. Since the up-arrow is used almost exclusively in mathematical formulas, it is in formulas where this ROM "glitch" will usually be noted.

Goofy Programming

Some programmers think they have to define each variable by using an entire word instead of a simple letter variable. Such elegance is alright in simple programs, but can lead to very serious problems on computers that don't permit lengthy variables.

Worse, the reader may think the variable is some new and exotic BASIC word not included in *The BASIC Handbook*. The way to untangle this problem is to create a good **Allocation of Variables** table, then rename the variables.

PEEK and POKE Mean Trouble

If the program relies heavily on PEEKs and POKEs, translation to another computer is nearly impossible without memory maps of **both** computers --- plus knowing how to use the maps. This task is beyond the skill of the average BASIC language programmer. Determine the price you are willing to pay in terms of time and frustration to make a particular program RUN on your system. It may not be worth the effort.

Impossible?

In the final analysis, not every program can be converted to run on every computer. Within the context of "mainline" BASIC however, such programs are rare.

At this time in history, the toughest conversion problems involve programs from "color video game machines" which include a "custom" BASIC interpreter as a marketing afterthought. This and the problem of undocumented manufacturers' glitches are also discussed in the section titled **GROUND RULES**.

But Good Shall Triumph!

Your own keen interest, a good dose of organization and common sense --- plus *The BASIC Handbook* will solve most problems and make your programming time a lot more efficient and enjoyable.

How To Use This Handbook

The information about each BASIC word is broken into a number of parts. Study this example carefully to better understand what to expect from your *Handbook*.

① **The WORD itself:** It is a word found in a BASIC program, or used to control one. Words which are used for overall system monitor purposes, editor languages, and other computer languages are **not** part of *The BASIC Handbook*.

①A **Other words:** Abbreviations and alternate spellings of the word are placed here.

② **ANSI Standard notation:** If the word "ANSI" appears here, it means the word is part of the National Bureau of Standards American National Standards Institute minimum BASIC vocabulary.

③ **Word Category:** BASIC words are divided into 4 categories:

Commands: which tell the computer to do something with a program, like RUN, LIST, etc. Some computers allow commands to be imbedded in a program, thus also serve as a Statement.

Statements: words which actually appear within a program, and comprise the detailed instructions on which the computer makes its decisions and performs its duties. Example:

```
PRINT A,B,C
```

Functions: words which call forth pre-programmed machine-level "micro-programs". They perform relatively complicated "functions" such as finding a trigonometric value, a square root, etc., serving as part of a larger statement. Examples:

```
LET X = TAN(Y)          PRINT LOG(A)
```

Operators: non-word characters which perform in special comparative or modifying capacities. Examples: comma, colon, equal sign, etc.

In *The BASIC Handbook,* Commands, Statements and Functions appear in alphabetical order. Operators, not lending themselves to alphabetizing, appear in a separate section at the back.

④ **Introductory and Descriptive remarks** about the WORD, telling what it is and what it does. May include special notes relating to brands of computers which predominantly or exclusively use the word.

⑤ **TEST PROGRAM:** Allows user to enter a brief program into a computer to see if its interpreter or compiler recognizes the word and makes use of it.

⑥ **SAMPLE RUN:** Shows how the computer might be expected to respond to the TEST PROGRAM. Results will vary slightly from machine to machine, but the general pattern should not vary widely from the sample run.

⑦ **HELPFUL HINTS:** Sometimes there are programming techniques which greatly simplify achieving a high level of simplicity and/or reliability. They are noted here.

⑧ **ALTERNATE SPELLING:** When different spellings are used on different computers, the alternate spellings are noted here.

⑨ **IF YOUR COMPUTER DOESN'T HAVE IT:** Gives alternate ways to accomplish the same objective using other BASIC words, when possible... and it isn't always possible. In the case of functions, a sub-routine is usually included which is able to circumvent the absent intrinsic function. In the case of statements (especially PRINT), a simple re-writing of part of a program using other words and techniques allow program execution with the same or somewhat diminished results.

⑩ **VARIATIONS:** Variations in usage of the WORD; that is, how the WORD **itself** might be used differently by different computers. (Not variations in how the desired results might be achieved with other words.)

⑪ **ALSO SEE:** Rather than spend an inordinate amount of space duplicating information, words are sometimes "clustered" around a central word, and that central word is discussed in great detail. Related words then treat their specific purpose only, referring to other words for more detail as desired.

SEG$ extracts a segment of a string from a string variable. SEG$ has three arguments: the string variable, the starting position in the string, and the number of characters in the substring.

① SEG$ ②

1A SEG

Example: IF A$="COMPUTER", THEN PRINT SEG$(A$,4,3) prints PUT.

⑤ Test Program

```
10 REM * SEG$ TEST PROGRAM *
20 A$="CONTESTANT"
30 B$=SEG$(A$,4,4)
40 IF B$<>"TEST" THEN 70
50 PRINT "SEG$ PASSED THE ";B$
60 GOTO 99
70 PRINT "SEG$ FAILED THE TEST"
99 END
```

⑥ Sample Run

```
SEG$ PASSED THE TEST
```

⑦ SEG$ can be used to simulate LEFT$ and RIGHT$. SEG$(A$,1,4) is equivalent to LEFT$(A$,4), while SEG$(A$,LEN(A$)-3,3) is equivalent to RIGHT$(A$,3).

⑧ Alternate Spelling

A few computers use SEG.

⑨ *IF YOUR COMPUTER DOESN'T HAVE IT*

If neither SEG$ nor SEG is available on your computer, try MID$ in the test program. If that doesn't work, some computers that require a DIM statement for all strings (e.g. Hewlett-Packard) will accept A$(4,7) as the substring in positions 4 through 7.

⑩ Variations In Usage

None known.

⑪ Also See

```
MID$, LEFT$, RIGHT$, DIM
```

The ABS function determines the ABSolute value of a number or numeric variable. A number's absolute value is its value without a + or − sign.

Example: `PRINT ABS(-10)` prints 10.

ABS is capable of handling any number, large or small, within the limitations of the computer's interpreter.

Function

ABS

A N S I

A.

Test Program #1

```
10 REM 'ABS' TEST PROGRAM
20 X=35
30 PRINT "ABS PASSED THE TEST IF";
40 PRINT ABS(-435.28);
50 PRINT ABS(-.03245);
60 PRINT ABS(-X)
70 PRINT "ARE ALL PRINTED AS POSITIVE VALUES."
99 END
```

Sample Run

```
ABS PASSED THE TEST IF 435.28 .03245 35
ARE ALL PRINTED AS POSITIVE VALUES.
```

Most interpreters also allow use of the ABS function within arithmetic operations. This feature is valuable in programs which require a positive value from math operations that would otherwise produce a negative value.

The entire math operation following ABS must be enclosed in parentheses.

Test Program #2

```
10 REM 'ABS' MATH OPERATION TEST PROGRAM
20 A=18
30 B=58
40 PRINT "THE ABSOLUTE VALUE OF";(A-B)/2;"IS";ABS((A-B)/2)
99 END
```

Sample Run

```
THE ABSOLUTE VALUE OF -20 IS 20
```

Alternate Spelling

Some computers accept A. as an abbreviation for ABS.

IF YOUR COMPUTER DOESN'T HAVE IT

If ABS is not intrinsic to the computer, it can easily be simulated by the following subroutine:

Test Program #3

```
10 REM 'ABS' SUBROUTINE TEST PROGRAM
20 PRINT "ENTER A NEGATIVE NUMBER";
30 INPUT X
40 GOSUB 30010
50 PRINT "THE ABSOLUTE VALUE OF";X;" IS";Y
60 GOTO 20
30010 REM * ABS(X) SUBROUTINE * INPUT X, OUTPUT Y
30012 Y=X
30014 IF X>=0 THEN 30018
30016 Y=-X
30018 RETURN
30999 END
```

Sample Run *(using -35.5)*

```
ENTER A NEGATIVE NUMBER? -35.5
THE ABSOLUTE VALUE OF -35.5 IS 35.5
ENTER A NEGATIVE NUMBER?
```

Variations In Usage

None known.

The ACS(n) function is used in some BASICs to compute the ARCCOS of the ratio *n* in radians (**not in degrees**). A radian is approximately 57 degrees.

ACS

AC.
ACSD
ACSG
ARCOS

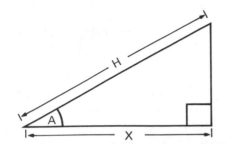

Arccos (ACS) is defined as the angle (A) of a right triangle formed by the hypotenuse (of length H) and one of the sides (length X).

```
A=ACS(X/H)
```

The opposite of ACS is COS (cosine). The cosine of an angle (whose measure is A radians) is the length of the side adjacent to the angle divided by the hypotenuse of the right triangle.

```
COS(A)= X/H
```

Test Program

```
10 REM 'ACS' TEST PROGRAM
20 PRINT "ENTER A COSINE VALUE (-1 TO 1)";
30 INPUT C
40 W=ACS(C)
50 PRINT "THE ANGLE WITH THE X/H RATIO OF ";C;" IS ";W;
   "RADIANS"
30999 END
```

Sample Run

```
ENTER A COSINE VALUE (-1 TO 1)? 0
THE ANGLE WITH THE X/H RATIO OF 0 IS 1.5708 RADIANS
```

To convert values from radians to degrees, multiply the angle measure (in radians) by 57.29578. For example:

```
40 W=ACS(C)*57.29578
```

There are some computers that will calculate the angle in degrees or in grads (100 grads = 90 degrees). These computers use ACSD for degrees and ACSG for grads. Substituting in Line 40 and using 0 in the sample run should produce 90 degrees and 100 grads.

Alternate Spellings

The Sinclair ZX80 uses ARCOS while the SHARP 1211 (TRS-80 Pocket Computer) uses AC.

IF YOUR COMPUTER DOESN'T HAVE IT

If your computer won't accept line 40 in the TEST PROGRAM but recognizes ATN (ARCTANGENT) and SQR(SQUARE ROOT), substitute

```
40 W = 1.5708-2*ATN(C/(1+SQR(1-C*C)))
```

If your computer doesn't have ATN or SQR, the following subroutine can be substituted. The subroutine program under ASN must be added to this one.

```
30000 GOTO 30999
30500 REM * ARCCOS SUBROUTINE * INPUT C, OUTPUT W
30502 REM ALSO USES VARIABLES S, X, Y AND Z INTERNALLY
30504 S=C
30506 GOSUB 30520
30508 W=1.570796-W
30510 RETURN
```

Finally, change line 40 in TEST PROGRAM to:

```
40 GOSUB 30500
```

To make the ARCCOS subroutine express the angle in DEGREES, add the following line:

```
30509 W=W*57.29578
```

Variations In Usage

None known.

Also See

```
COS, ASN, ATN, SQR, SIN, TAN
```

A.

AND is used in IF-THEN statements as a "logical math" operator.

For example, IF A=8 AND B=6 THEN 80 reads; if the value of variable A equals 8 AND the value of variable B equals 6, the IF-THEN condition is met and execution continues at line 80.

Test Program #1

```
10 REM LOGICAL 'AND' TEST PROGRAM
20 A=8
30 B=6
40 IF A=8 AND B=6 THEN 70
50 PRINT "AND FAILED THE TEST AS LOGICAL OPERATOR"
60 GOTO 99
70 PRINT "AND PASSED THE LOGICAL OPERATOR TEST"
99 END
```

Sample Run

```
AND PASSED THE LOGICAL OPERATOR TEST
```

A few computers use the AND operator to "logically" compare strings.

For example, IF A$="A" AND B$="B" THEN 80 reads, if the string variable A$ is equal to (or "the same as") the letter A AND the string variable B$ is equal to the letter B, the IF-THEN condition is met and execution continues at line 80. For more information see the operators + and *.

Test Program #2

```
10 REM STRING LOGICAL 'AND' TEST PROGRAM
20 A$="A"
30 B$="F"
40 IF A$="A"AND B$ >"B"THEN 70
50 PRINT "'AND' FAILED THE TEST AS A LOGICAL OPERATOR"
60 GOTO 99
70 PRINT "'AND' PASSED THE STRING LOGICAL OPERATOR TEST"
99 END
```

Sample Run

```
'AND' PASSED THE STRING LOGICAL OPERATOR TEST
```

Some computers use the logical operator AND to determine if the conditions are met in two relational operators. When the condition of both operators is met, AND returns the number -1. When the condition of the AND operator is not met, AND returns a 0.

For example, PRINT A=4 AND B=8 if A equals 4 AND B equals 8 the computer will print the number -1. If either condition is not met, the computer prints a 0.

Test Program #3

```
10 REM 'AND' LOGICAL TEST PROGRAM
20 PRINT "ENTER A NUMBER FROM 1 TO 10";
30 INPUT A
40 B=A > 4 AND A < 11
50 IF B=-1 THEN 80
60 PRINT A;"IS NOT GREATER THAN 4 AND LESS THAN 11"
70 GOTO 20
80 PRINT A;"IS GREATER THAN 4 AND LESS THAN 11"
99 END
```

Sample Run (typical)

```
ENTER A NUMBER FROM 1 TO 10? 2
 2 IS NOT GREATER THAN 4 AND LESS THAN 11
ENTER A NUMBER FROM 1 TO 10? 8
 8 IS GREATER THAN 4 AND LESS THAN 11
```

The AND operator is used by a few computers to compute the binary logical AND of two numbers using Boolean algebra.

Without presenting a complete course in Boolean algebra... it compares two binary bits to determine whether **both** are a binary "one". When both ANDed bits are a binary one, the computer answers with a 1.

For example:

```
1 AND 0 = 0
0 AND 1 = 0
1 AND 1 = 1
```

Therefore, when the computer ANDs one number with another, each number's bit value is logically ANDed with the other number's bit value, producing a third number.

For example:

DECIMAL		BINARY
3		0011
	(logical) AND	
5		0101
= 1		0001

In this example only the rightmost bit is a binary one in both numbers, so the resultant number is a decimal 1 (binary 0001).

Test Program #4

```
10 REM 'AND' BINARY LOGIC TEST PROGRAM
20 PRINT "ENTER A VALUE FOR X";
30 INPUT X
40 PRINT "ENTER A VALUE FOR Y";
50 INPUT Y
60 A=X AND Y
70 PRINT "THE LOGICAL 'AND' VALUE OF";X;"AND";Y;"IS";A
80 GOTO 20
99 END
```

Sample Run *(using 6 and 10)*

```
ENTER A VALUE FOR X? 6
ENTER A VALUE FOR Y? 10
THE LOGICAL 'AND' VALUE OF 6 AND 10 IS 2
ENTER A VALUE FOR X?
```

Alternate Spelling

A few computers (e.g. Britain's Acorn) allow A. for AND.

Variations In Usage

The AND (*p,q*) statement is used by the WANG 2200B computer to compute the binary logical AND of two hexadecimal values or two character strings. The first value, *p*, must be a string variable and the second is either a string variable or a 2-digit hex constant. The resulting value replaces the first of the two values.

For example, if P\$ = hex number 5A and Q\$ = hex number 3C, then AND(P\$,Q\$) sets P\$ = hex number 18.

	HEX		BINARY
	P\$ = 5A		01011010
		AND	
	Q\$ = 3C		00111100
then	P\$ = 18		00011000

When P\$ is a character string and Q is a hex constant, each character in the string is converted to its ASCII value and logically ANDed with the hex constant. The results are converted back to character form and stored in P\$. So string "EFG" ANDed with hex 43 results in string "ABC".

	E	F	G
ASCII	69	70	71
HEX	45	46	47
BINARY	0100 0101	0100 0110	0100 0111
	AND	AND	AND
hex 43	0100 0011	0100 0011	0100 0011
=	0100 0001	0100 0010	0100 0011
ASCII	65	66	67
so P$ =	A	B	C

Test Program #5

```
10 REM 'AND' TEST PROGRAM
20 DIM A$3 (Note: this line sets the length of A$ to 3 bytes.)
30 A$ = "CCC"
40 AND(A$,F1)
50 PRINT "AND PASSED THE TEST IF ";A$;"=AAA"
99 END
```

Sample Run

```
AND PASSED THE TEST IF AAA=AAA
```

IF YOUR COMPUTER DOESN'T HAVE IT

If you don't have the logical AND operator, its effect can be simulated with two IF-THEN statements. Replace line 40 of TEST PROGRAM #1 with

```
40 IF A <> 8 THEN 50
45 IF B = 6 THEN 70
```

The AND statement as used in the WANG 2200B computer can be replaced with statements that combine string handling functions with the logical AND operator. Example: Line 40 in the above test program can be replaced with the following statements:

```
40 REM 'AND' REPLACEMENT
41 N = LEN(A$)
42 FOR I = 1 TO N
43 C$ = C$ + CHR$(ASC(MID$(A$, I, 1)) AND 241)
44 NEXT I
45 A$ = C$
```

Also See

```
OR, XOR, NOT, *, +, =, <, >, <>, <=, >=
```

APPEND is a command to combine a program from external storage (e.g. disk or tape) with one already in memory. The line numbers of the program being brought in from "outside" must be larger than the last line number of the program already in memory.

For example, APPEND PROG2 will cause program PROG2 to be brought in from the outside and APPENDed to the end of the resident program.

Test Program

(For our example, we'll assume cassette tape storage.) To test APPEND, store this short program on tape as PROG2. (See CSAVE for information.)

```
1000 PRINT "THESE LINES ARE"
1010 PRINT "FROM PROG2"
1020 END
```

Then type NEW or SCRATCH to erase the program and enter PROG1:

```
10 REM 'APPEND' TEST PROGRAM PROG1
20 PRINT "THESE LINES ARE"
30 PRINT "FROM PROG1"
40 PRINT "    BUT..."
```

Then type APPEND PROG2.

When PROG 2 has been loaded, RUN (use your computer's naming method for SAVE PROG2 and APPEND PROG2, i.e. quotes, single letter names, etc.).

Sample Run

```
THESE LINES ARE
FROM PROG1
    BUT...
THESE LINES ARE
FROM PROG2
```

APPEND is often used to load large DATA files into a program. It may also be used to "append" a frequently used subroutine to a resident program (which is why all the major subroutines published in *The BASIC Handbook* have non-overlapping line numbers beginning above 30000).

IF YOUR COMPUTER DOESN'T HAVE IT

If your computer doesn't respond favorably to APPEND, try TAPPEND, MERGE or WEAVE. If none of them work, some computers can be made to append a program if the "pointers" to the present program can be located.

This gets a little sticky, so consult your computer's Manual. The following is the procedure used with a TRS-80.

Locate the pointer that gives the **ending** address of the program currently in memory. For the TRS-80 Model I, this number is stored at 16333 and 16334. Use PEEK to get the values stored there.

Subtract 2 from the **first** number (the one stored in 16333). If the difference is negative, add 256 to it and subtract 1 from the SECOND number.

In either case, POKE these 2 numbers into 16548 and 16549 without additional changes.

Now, CLOAD the program in from tape. Restore the values at 16548-49 with POKEs of 233 into 16548 and 66 into 16549.

The second program is now APPENDed to the first.

Also See

TAPPEND, PEEK, POKE, CSAVE, CLOAD, DATA

The ASC function converts a character or string variable to its corresponding ASCII decimal number.

For example, PRINT ASC("A") prints 65, the ASCII code for the letter A. PRINT ASC(A$) prints the ASCII code of the first character in string variable A$.

ASCII

Test Program #1

```
10 REM 'ASC(CHARACTER)' TEST PROGRAM
20 PRINT "THE ASCII CODE FOR LETTER A IS";
30 PRINT ASC("A")
40 IF ASC("A")=65 THEN 70
50 PRINT "ASC FAILED THE TEST"
60 GOTO 99
70 PRINT "ASC PASSED THE TEST"
99 END
```

Sample Run

```
THE ASCII CODE FOR LETTER A IS 65
ASC PASSED THE TEST
```

The next program tests the ASC function with a variable.

Test Program #2

```
10 REM 'ASC(STRING VARIABLE)' TEST PROGRAM
20 PRINT "TYPE ANY LETTER, NUMBER, OR CHARACTER";
30 INPUT A$
40 PRINT "THE ASCII CODE FOR ";A$;" IS";ASC(A$)
99 END
```

Sample Run *(using H)*

```
TYPE ANY LETTER, NUMBER, OR CHARACTER? H
THE ASCII CODE FOR H IS 72
```

Some computers which incorporate the ASC function can *accept* character strings longer than one character, but only the first character is evaluated and converted to ASCII code. To test for the ASC string limit, use the second Test Program and INPUT progressively longer strings until an error message appears.

Alternate Spelling

Some computers (e.g. DEC-10) use ASCII instead of ASC.

Variations In Usage

Some interpreters (e.g. MAXBASIC) use the format ASC(A$,X) which prints the ASCII code of the first X characters contained in A$.

Also See

CHR$, CODE, Appendix A for the ASCII code.

The ASN(n) function is used by the TEKTRONIX 4050 series BASIC to compute the ARCSIN **in Radians** (not in **degrees**) of the ratio n. A radian is approximately 57 degrees.

ASNG
ASND
ARCSIN

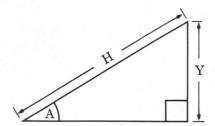

Arcsin (ASN) is defined as the angle (A) created for a certain **ratio** of the length of the side opposite it (Y) to the length of the hypotenuse (H) of the right triangle.

```
A=ASN(Y/H)
```

The opposite of ASN is SINE (SIN). The SINE of an angle is the ratio of the length of the side opposite the angle to the length of the hypotenuse of the right triangle.

```
SIN(A)=Y/H
```

Test Program

```
10 REM 'ASN' TEST PROGRAM
20 PRINT "ENTER A RATIO OR SINE VALUE";
30 INPUT N
40 W=ASN(N)
50 PRINT "THE ANGLE WITH THE Y/H RATIO OF";N;"IS";W;
   "RADIANS"
30999 END
```

Sample Run *(using .5)*

```
ENTER A RATIO OR SINE VALUE? .5
THE ANGLE WITH THE Y/H RATIO OF .5 IS .52359 RADIANS
```

Some computers calculate the angle in degrees or in grads (100 grads = 90 degrees). These computers use the functions ASND for degrees and ASNG for grads. Using .5 in the sample run should produce 30 degrees and 33.3333 grads when each is substituted in Line 40.

To convert values from radians to degrees, multiply the angle (in radians) times 57.29578.

Example: `D=ASN(A)*57.29578`

To convert values from degrees to radians, multiply the angle (in degrees) times .0174533.

Example: R=A *(angle expressed in degrees)* *.0174533.

Alternate Spelling

Some computers (e.g. Sinclair ZX80) use ARCSIN in place of ASN. Try ARCSIN in line 40 of the Test Program to see if your computer allows its use.

IF YOUR COMPUTER DOESN'T HAVE IT

If your interpreter has the ATN (ARCTANGENT) and SQR (SQUARE ROOT) capability, but does not have ASN, substitute the formula 2*ATN(X/(1+SQR(1-X*X))) for ASN.

If your interpreter does not have ASN or ATN and SQR capability, the following subroutine can be substituted:

```
30000 GOTO 30999
30520 REM * ARCSIN SUBROUTINE * INPUT S, OUTPUT W
30522 REM ALSO USES VARIABLES X AND Z INTERNALLY
30524 X=S
30526 IF ABS(S)<=.5 THEN 30556
30528 X=.5*(1-ABS(S))
30530 IF X>=0 THEN 30536
30532 PRINT S; "IS OUT OF RANGE"
30534 STOP
30536 W=X/2
30538 IF W=0 THEN 30554
30540 Z=0
30542 Y=(X/W-W)/2
30544 IF Y=0 THEN 30554
30546 IF Y=Z THEN 30554
30548 W=W+Y
30550 Z=Y
30552 GOTO 30542
30554 X=W
30556 Y=X*X
30558 W=(4.241734E-2*Y+2.399402E-2) *Y+4.552063E-2
30560 W=(((W*Y+.074947)*Y+1/6)*Y+1)*X
30562 IF ABS(S)<=.5 THEN 30566
30564 W=SGN(S)*(1.570796-2*W)
30566 RETURN
```

To use this subroutine with the TEST PROGRAM for finding the ARCSIN (in RADIANS) of a ratio (SINE), make the following TEST PROGRAM changes:

```
35 S=N
40 GOSUB 30520
```

To make the ARCSIN subroutine express the angle in DEGREES, add the following lines:

```
30566 W=W*57.29578
30568 RETURN
```

Variations In Usage

None known.

Also See

```
ACS, ATN, COS, SIN, SQR, TAN
```

Function

A.

The AT function is used with PRINT statements (TRS-80 Level I BASIC) to specify the PRINT statement's starting location. The AT function value may be a number, numeric variable, or mathematical operation. A comma or semi-colon must be inserted between the AT value and the string.

For example:

```
10 PRINT AT 420, "HELLO"
20 PRINT AT (420); "HELLO"
```

Both lines print the word "HELLO" AT location 420. The parentheses are optional.

Test Program #1

```
10 REM 'AT' TEST PROGRAM
20 PRINT AT 128,"2. IF THIS LINE IS PRINTED AFTER LINE 1."
30 PRINT AT 0, "1. THE 'AT' FUNCTION PASSED THE TEST"
40 GOTO 40
99 END
```

Sample Run

```
1. THE 'AT' FUNCTION PASSED THE TEST
2. IF THIS LINE IS PRINTED AFTER LINE 1.
```

The TRS-80 has 1024 PRINT AT locations (0 to 1023). If an AT value smaller than zero or larger than 1023 is used, the computer automatically calculates the difference between the out-of-range number and 1023 for the AT value.

For example, PRINT AT 1034 "HELLO" prints the word HELLO at location 10 (don't forget to count zero as one location).

Test Program #2

```
10 REM 'AT OVERFLOW' TEST PROGRAM
20 PRINT AT 192, "'AT' (OVERFLOW) PASSED THE TEST"
30 PRINT AT 1248, "IF ONLY ONE LINE IS PRINTED."
99 END
```

Sample Run

```
'AT' (OVERFLOW) PASSED THE TEST IF ONLY ONE LINE IS
     PRINTED."
```

The following program tests the interpreter's ability to use numbers, numeric variables, or mathematic operations in the AT function.

Test Program #3

```
10 REM 'AT VALUE' TEST PROGRAM
20 FOR X=1 TO 15
30 PRINT X
40 NEXT X
50 PRINT AT X*28+4, "'AT' PASSED THE TEST IF THIS IS LINE
   #8.";
60 GOTO 60
99 END
```

Sample Run

```
1
2
3
4
5
6
7
8 'AT' PASSED THE TEST IF THIS IS LINE #8.
9
10
11
12
13
14
15
```

Alternate Spelling

The @ operator is used by some computers (e.g. the TRS-80 Level II, Level III and Disk BASICs) for the AT function. See @ for specific constraints. Computers using Tiny BASIC also allow A. to be used for AT.

Also See

```
@, PRINT, TAB, HLIN, VLIN, DRAW, XDRAW
```

Function

ANSI

ATN

ATAN
ATND
ATNG
ARCTAN

The ATN(n) function computes ARCTANGENT **in Radians (not in degrees)** of the ratio *n*. A radian is approximately 57 degrees.

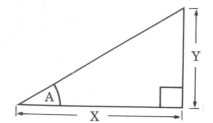

ARCTANGENT (ATN) is defined as the angle (A) required for a certain **ratio** of the length of the side opposite it (Y) to the length of the side adjacent to it (X). ATN means literally "The Arc (angle) of the TaNgent (ratio)."

```
A=ATN(Y/X)
```

The opposite of ATN is Tangent (TAN). The Tangent of an angle is the **ratio** of the length of the side opposite it to the length of the side adjacent to it.

```
TAN(A)=Y/X
```

Test Program

```
10 REM 'ATN' TEST PROGRAM
20 PRINT "ENTER A RATIO OR TANGENT VALUE";
30 INPUT N
40 A=ATN(N)
50 PRINT "THE ANGLE WITH THE Y/X RATIO OF";N;"IS";A;
   "RADIANS"
30999 END
```

Sample Run *(for input of 2)*

```
ENTER A RATIO OR TANGENT VALUE? 2
THE ANGLE WITH THE Y/X RATIO OF 2 IS 1.10715 RADIANS
```

Some computers calculate the angle in degrees or in grads (100 grads = 90 degrees). These computers use the function ATND for degrees and ATNG for grads. Substitute each of these functions in line 40 of TEST PROGRAM and run it. Using 2 in the sample run should produce 63.43495 degrees and 70.4833 grads.

To convert values from radians to degrees, multiply the angle (in radians) times 57.29578.

Example: `D=ATN(A)*57.29578`

To convert values from degrees to radians, multiply the angle (in degrees) times .0174533.

Example: R=A *(angle expressed in degrees)* *.0174533

Alternate Spelling

A few computers use ATAN for the ARCTANGENT FUNCTION. To see if ATAN can be used with your computer, substitute ATAN for ATN in line 40 and run it.

Some computers (e.g. Sinclair ZX80) use ARCTAN in place of ATN. Try ARCTAN in line 40 of the Test Program to see if your computer accepts this spelling.

IF YOUR COMPUTER DOESN'T HAVE IT

If your interpreter does not have the capability of finding the ATN (Arctangent), the following subroutine can be substituted.

The subroutine program you'll find under SGN must be added to this one to make it work (saves space not to duplicate it here).

```
30000 GOTO 30999
30570 REM * ARCTANGENT SUBROUTINE * INPUT X, OUTPUT A
      (RADIANS)
30572 REM ALSO USES B, C, D AND T INTERNALLY
30574 GOSUB 30080
30576 D=X
30578 X=ABS(X)
30580 C=0
30582 IF X<=1 THEN 30588
30584 C=1
30586 X=1/X
30588 A=X*X
30590 B=((2.86623E-3*A-1.61657E-2)*A+4.29096E-2)*A
30592 B=(((B-7.5289E-2)*A+.106563)*A-.142089)*A
30594 A=(((B+.199936)*A-.333332)*A+1)*X
30596 IF C<>1 THEN 30600
30598 A=1.570796-A
30600 A=T*A
30602 X=D
30604 RETURN
```

To use this subroutine with the TEST PROGRAM for finding the Arctangent (in Radians) of a ratio (Tangent), make the following TEST PROGRAM changes:

```
35 X=N
40 GOSUB 30570
```

To make the Arctangent subroutine express the angle in Degrees, add the following line to it:

```
30603 A=A*57,29578
```

Variations In Usage

Some (rare) interpreters convert everything to degrees automatically.

Also See

TAN, ASN, SIN, COS, ACS

A TRICK

This is very important! Most computers have only an ATN as their "inverse trig function". ARCCOS and ARCSIN are rarely found. This leaves ATN as the only "window" through which all angles can be calculated and returned to the "outside".

Now obviously, if ATN is to be used, the TAN must be known, or able to be determined, and that may be easier said than done. The following formulas will enable you to convert any ratio to TAN, and from there to the angle itself, via ATN.

$$TAN = 1/COT \qquad TAN = \sqrt{\frac{1 - COS^2}{COS^2}} \qquad TAN = \sqrt{\frac{1}{\frac{1 - SIN^2}{SIN^2}}}$$

$$TAN = \sqrt{\frac{1}{CSC^2 - 1}} \qquad TAN = \sqrt{SEC^2 - 1}$$

These formulas make use of relationships between the trig functions to give us ways of calculating each of the inverse functions. For example, to calculate A = ARCSEC(X) use

```
A = ATN(SQR(X*X-1))
```

The formulas for each of the inverse functions coded in BASIC are:

```
ARCCOS(X) = 1,5708 - 2*ATN(X/(1+SQR(1-X*X)))
ARCCOT(X) = ATN(1/X)
ARCCSC(X) = ATN(1/SQR(X*X-1)
ARCSEC(X) = ATN(SQR(X*X-1))
ARSSIN(X) = 2*ATN(X/(1+SQR(1-X*X)))
```

The AUTO command provides automatic insertion of program line numbers. The starting line number and the incremental value between lines can be specified in the AUTO command. For example, AUTO 100,5 sets the first line number at 100 and increments each successive line number by 5. This feature is very convenient when writing new programs.

If the starting line number and increment value are not specified in the AUTO command, the computer automatically sets the first line number at 10 and increments the line numbers by 10.

If the AUTO command generates a line number that is already in use, an asterisk may appear following the number. This cautions the programmer that information typed into the computer at that Line number will erase existing statements. The AUTO feature may be turned off to prevent this from happening. To turn off the AUTO feature, some computers require pressing the BREAK key, while others require typing a control C.

Test Procedure

To test the computer's AUTO feature, type the AUTO command and press the ENTER key (RETURN on some keyboards). If the line number 10 is printed followed by a prompt, then the computer successfully passed the AUTO command test.

Press the ENTER key again. The computer should print another line number increased in value by 10.

Type the command AUTO 10,5 and enter this program.

```
10 REM 'AUTO' TEST PROGRAM
15 PRINT "THE NEXT LINE NUMBER SHOULD INCREASED BY 5"
20 PRINT "PRESS THE BREAK KEY TO STOP THE AUTO FEATURE"
99 END
```

After the AUTO feature is stopped with the BREAK key, line numbers out of sequence can be entered (e.g. line 99).

Again enter AUTO 10,5 and line 10 should be printed, followed by an asterisk, indicating information is already stored in a line 10; if ENTER is pressed, it will be erased. New information can be typed in instead, or the original information can be saved by pressing the BREAK key.

List the program to check the contents of each line.

Variations In Usage

None known.

Also See

BREAK, LIST, MAN

The BASE statement is used in some computers (e.g. those with Control Data BASIC Version 3) to define the BASE (lowest) variable array element value as 0 or 1.

For example:

```
10 BASE 0
20 DIM A(5)
```

The BASE 0 statement defines this array as a six element array [A(0) to A(5)].

Many computers automatically establish array elements 0 to 10 (11 elements) without prior DIMensioning. The BASE statement allows this range to be changed from the normal 11 elements (0 to 10) to 10 elements (1 to 10), and back again.

Only one BASE statement may ordinarily be used in a program and it must be executed before DIM statements and before array variables are manipulated.

Test Program #1

```
10 REM 'BASE' TEST PROGRAM
20 BASE 0
30 DIM A(5)
40 FOR X=0 TO 5
50 A(X)=X
60 NEXT X
70 FOR X=0 TO 5
80 PRINT A(X);
90 NEXT X
100 PRINT "THE BASE STATEMENT PASSED THE TEST"
999 END
```

Sample Run

```
0 1 2 3 4 5 THE BASE STATEMENT PASSED THE TEST
```

A few computers (e.g. those using MAXBASIC) allow more than one BASE statement in a program and allow the BASE value to be defined as any integer value.

For example:

```
10 BASE 5
20 DIM A(10)
```

The BASE 5 statement defines this array as a six element array [A(5) to A(10)].

Test Program #2

```
10 REM 'BASE' TEST PROGRAM
20 BASE 3
30 DIM A(5)
40 FOR X=3 TO 5
50 A(X)=X
60 NEXT X
70 BASE 0
80 FOR X=0 TO 2
90 A(X)=X
100 NEXT X
110 FOR X=0 TO 5
120 PRINT A(X);
130 NEXT X
140 PRINT "THE BASE STATEMENT PASSED THE TEST"
999 END
```

Sample Run

```
0 1 2 3 4 5 THE BASE STATEMENT PASSED THE TEST
```

Variations In Usage

ANSI BASIC includes the OPTION statement.

Also See

```
DIM, OPTION
```

BREAK is used in a few computers (e.g. the Harris BASIC-V) to direct one or more program lines to stop execution and place the computer in the monitor or immediate mode, similar to a STOP statement.

The BREAK statement can be used to cause any line number (or line numbers) to stop program execution by placing each line number (separated by a comma) after the BREAK statement.

For example, 10 BREAK 50,70,100 stops the computer before executing lines 50, 70, and 100. Program execution is continued after each BREAK by typing **CO**ntinue.

BREAK also accepts a range of line numbers by placing a dash between the first and last line number in the range.

For example, 10 BREAK 50-100 stops program execution at the end of each line from 50 to 100.

Execution can be stopped before each program line by using the BREAK ALL statement. This allows the user to "step through" the program one line at a time, typing the CO command after each break.

Unlike the END statement which (in some computers) causes all variables to be reset to zero, values stored in variables are retained when the BREAK statement is executed.

Test Program

```
10 REM 'BREAK' TEST PROGRAM
20 BREAK 30,50,70-90
30 PRINT "THE COMPUTER SHOULD STOP EXECUTION AT LINE 30"
40 REM TYPE THE COMMAND 'CO' TO CONTINUE
50 PRINT "LINE 50"
60 REM THIS LINE NOT INCLUDED IN THE BREAK STATEMENT
70 PRINT "LINE 70"
80 PRINT "LINE 80"
90 PRINT "AND LINE 90"
99 END
```

Sample Run

```
THE COMPUTER SHOULD STOP EXECUTION AT LINE 30
LINE 50
LINE 70
LINE 80
AND LINE 90
```

Variations In Usage

Most keyboards have a BREAK key to allow manual interruption of the program.

Also See

STOP, CONT, END

GOODBYE

BYE is a command used to exit from BASIC. Most large, time-shared computers accept BYE as the sign-off command and terminate the user's job.

Several small computers (e.g. SOL and ATARI) enter the **monitor** level or the Disk Operating System when the user types BYE. BYE can be included as a program statement in Processor Technology's Extended BASIC.

Alternate Spelling

Time-share systems often accept GOODBYE instead of (or in addition to) BYE when a user signs off the computer. Check the user's manual for the sign-off procedure at your installation.

Variations In Usage

None known.

Also See

SYSTEM, the Disk BASIC Summary

The CALL(*n*) statement transfers program control to a machine-language routine that has an entry point at memory location *n*. The routine may be part of the computer's system software or could be written by the user. User-written machine-language programs can be entered via POKES from the keyboard, by a BASIC program, or using a "monitor/editor" program at the system level.

Example: CALL 18624 will cause a machine-language program stored at decimal address 18624 to begin execution. When a RETURN instruction is encountered in the machine language program, we are back in BASIC and the statement following the CALL statement is executed. To test the CALL statement, you must load a machine-language routine into the computer or locate the entry point of a resident subroutine. Check your computer's Manual for information on how to do this.

Variations In Usage

Some computers use the CALL statement to branch to a specific BASIC subroutine. In these computers, CALL can be used just like a GOSUB except a subroutine name is used instead of a line number. When CALL is used in this way, the subroutine begins with a SUB statement that contains the name and ends with a SUBEND.

For example, CALL TEST causes control to be transferred to subroutine TEST. Control is transferred back to the statement following the CALL statement when a SUBEND is reached.

Test Program

```
10 REM 'CALL' TEST PROGRAM
20 CALL TEST
30 PRINT "'CALL' PASSED THE ";A$
40 GOTO 99
50 SUB TEST
60 A$="TEST"
70 SUBEND
99 END
```

Sample Run

```
'CALL' PASSED THE TEST
```

Also See

```
USR, POKE, SYSTEM, GOSUB, RETURN
```

Function

CDBL is used to change numbers or numeric variables from regular "single-precision" to "double-precision". Variables used in the CDBL function return to their original single-precision status if they are used again without the CDBL.

Double-precision variables are capable of storing numbers containing 17 digits (only 16 digits are printed). Single-precision variables are accurate to 6 digits. Great care must be used to ensure that the numbers which are used to create a double-precision answer are also double precision. If not, the answer will be a big long lie.

Test Program

```
10 REM 'CDBL' TEST PROGRAM
20 X=2
30 Y=3
40 PRINT "CDBL CHANGES X/Y FROM";X/Y;"TO";CDBL(X)/CDBL(Y)
50 PRINT "AND BACK TO THE VALUE OF";X/Y;"WHEN REMOVED"
99 END
```

Sample Run

```
CDBL CHANGES X/Y FROM .666667 TO .6666666666666667
AND BACK TO THE VALUE OF .666667 WHEN REMOVED
```

Variations In Usage

None known.

Also See

DEFDBL, DEFSNG, DEFINT, CSNG, #, !, %, CINT

CH is a function in the Acorn ATOM computer that identifies the ASCII number of the first character of a given string. For example, PRINT CH"ACORN" will cause 65 (the ASCII value of A) to be displayed on the screen. Only the first character of a string is identified by CH.

See ASC for more information.

Test Program

```
10 REM 'CH' TEST PROGRAM
20 PRINT "THE ASCII CODE FOR LETTER A IS";
30 PRINT CH "A"
40 IF CH"A"=65 THEN 70
50 PRINT "CH FAILED THE TEST"
60 GOTO 99
70 PRINT "CH PASSED THE TEST"
99 END
```

Sample Run

```
THE ASCII CODE FOR A IS 65
CH PASSED THE TEST
```

Variations In Usage

None known.

Also See

ASC, CODE, CHR$, Appendix A for the ASCII code.

Statement

CHAIN is used to load a new program into the computer's memory from an external device (such as disk or tape) and execute that program without additional RUN commands. A program may CHAIN to any other program, including back to the starting one which may serve as a "menu".

The main advantage of CHAINing is that it permits consecutive execution of related programs automatically without needing to keep more than one of them actually in the computer at a given time. This is especially useful where there is a common file of DATA stored externally which can be accessed and manipulated by programs in the CHAIN. CHAIN finds its best application in systems large enough to have disk storage, with fast access times.

If the values of variables are to be carried from one program to another, a separate file must be created for them. Before such a program is allowed to CHAIN to another, it must save the values of its variables in this file so the NEW program can read them back in prior to **its** execution.

Some BASICs are able to pass the values of the variables used by the first program directly to the second. Microsoft BASIC 5.0, for instance, accepts the statement `CHAIN "PROG2", 150, ALL` which "chains" to a program on disk called PROG2. PROG2 begins execution at line 150 after receiving values of **all** the variables that had previously been defined by the calling program.

The new program's name must be included after the CHAIN statement. Some computers specify the new program's starting line number by a number following the program's name. If the starting line is omitted, the computer automatically starts at the new program's beginning.

For example, `10 CHAIN TEST,30` tells the computer to erase the program presently in memory and load a program called "TEST" from an external device, then start execution at its line 30. The external storage device can be specified in some computers (e.g. the DEC 10 BASIC) by placing the device name after CHAIN, followed by a colon.

For example, `10 CHAIN PTR:TEST,70` This tells the computer to load a program named "TEST" from the Paper Tape Reader and start execution at its line 70.

Test Programs

Save this program on disk or tape under the name "TEST".

```
10 REM *TEST* PROGRAM
20 PRINT "THE 'TEST' PROGRAM IS NOW RUNNING"
30 FOR X=1 TO 9
40 PRINT X;
50 NEXT X
60 PRINT "THIS PROGRAM SHOULD NOW CHAIN BACK
   TO THE MAIN PROGRAM"
70 CHAIN MAIN, 40
99 END
```

Now, enter the main program into the computer, and save it on disk or tape under the name "MAIN".

```
10 REM *MAIN* PROGRAM
20 PRINT "THIS PROGRAM SHOULD LOAD AND RUN THE 'TEST'
   PROGRAM"
30 CHAIN TEST
40 PRINT "CHAIN PASSED THE TEST IF THE 'TEST' PROGRAM"
50 PRINT "PRINTED A SERIES OF NUMBERS"
99 END
```

Prepare your disk or tape(s) to be read on command, then RUN.

Sample Run

```
THIS PROGRAM SHOULD LOAD AND RUN THE 'TEST' PROGRAM
THE 'TEST' PROGRAM IS NOW RUNNING
 1 2 3 4 5 6 7 8 9
THIS PROGRAM SHOULD NOW CHAIN BACK TO THE MAIN PROGRAM
CHAIN PASSED THE TEST IF THE 'TEST' PROGRAM
PRINTED A SERIES OF NUMBERS
```

IF YOUR COMPUTER DOESN'T HAVE IT

CHAINING can be accomplished successfully, if more slowly, on micro-computers using floppy disks, or even cassettes. Most small system BASICs start each new program CHAINed at its first line number, not having the option to start elsewhere.

The following 3 programs demonstrate how CHAINing can be accomplished on a TRS-80 Disk system. The word RUN is used instead of CHAIN. Note the new program's name is enclosed in quotes.

```
10 REM *MAIN* PROGRAM
20 PRINT
30 PRINT "THIS IS THE MAIN CONTROL PROGRAM."
40 INPUT"SHALL WE 'CHAIN' TO PROGRAM #1 OR #2
   (TYPE 1 OR 2)";I
```

```
50 PRINT "STAND BY FOR LOADING - - -"
60 ON I GOTO 70, 80
70 RUN "TEST1"
80 RUN "TEST2"
99 END


10 REM *TEST1* PROGRAM
20 PRINT "TEST PROGRAM NUMBER 1 IS NOW RUNNING"
30 FOR X=1 TO 9
40 PRINT "ONE",
50 NEXT X
60 PRINT
70 PRINT "WE WILL NOW CHAIN BACK TO THE MAIN PROGRAM---"
80 RUN "MAIN"
99 END


10 REM *TEST2* PROGRAM
20 PRINT "TEST PROGRAM NUMBER 2 IS NOW RUNNING"
30 FOR X=1 TO 9
40 PRINT "TWO",
50 NEXT X
60 PRINT
70 PRINT "WE WILL NOW CHAIN BACK TO THE MAIN PROGRAM---"
80 RUN "MAIN"
99 END
```

Type in each program and save it on Disk under the name given in each Line 10. Then RUN the MAIN program. Watch the screen and disk drive(s) CHAIN the programs together and execute them.

Variations In Usage

None other known.

Also See

```
CLOAD, CSAVE, COMMON, RUN
```

CHANGE is a statement used by the DEC-10 computer to convert strings of characters to their ASCII numbers, and numbers back to character strings.

CHANGE X$ TO X converts each character in string X$ to its ASCII number and stores them all in an array named X. The LENgth of the string, LEN(X$) is stored in array element X(0).

CHANGE X TO X$ converts values stored in array X into a character string X$. The number of values to be converted is found in X(0). Each value of X must be between 0 and 255.

Test Program #1

```
10 REM 'CHANGE X$ TO X' TEST
20 DIM X(6)
30 X$ = "SYSTEM"
40 CHANGE X$ TO X
50 PRINT "CHANGE HAS CONVERTED 'SYSTEM' TO"
60 FOR N=1 TO X(0)
70 PRINT X(N);
80 NEXT N
99 END
```

Sample Run

```
CHANGE HAS CONVERTED 'SYSTEM' TO
 83 89 83 84 69 77
```

Test Program #2

```
10 REM 'CHANGE X TO X$' TEST
20 DIM X(6)
30 READ X(0)
40 FOR I=1 TO X(0)
50 READ X(I)
60 NEXT I
70 CHANGE X TO X$
80 PRINT "CHANGE ";X$;" THE TEST"
90 DATA 6, 00, 65, 83, 83, 69, 68
99 END
```

Sample Run

```
CHANGE PASSED THE TEST
```

IF YOUR COMPUTER DOESN'T HAVE IT

CHANGE can be simulated by using LEN, ASC, MID$ and CHR$. In TEST PROGRAM #1 replace line 40 with:

```
40 X(Ø) = LEN(X$)
41 FOR I=1 TO X(Ø)
42 X(I) = ASC(MID$(X$,I,1))
43 NEXT I
```

In TEST PROGRAM #2 replace line 70 with:

```
70 X$ = ""
71 FOR I=1 TO X(Ø)
72 X$=X$ + CHR$(X(I))
73 NEXT I
```

Also See

LEN, ASC, MID$, CHR$, DIM and refer to the ASCII table in Appendix A.

The CHR$ function is used to retrieve the single character represented by the decimal ASCII number code enclosed in parentheses. For example: PRINT CHR$(75) prints the letter K.

CHR
CHAR
CHAR$
CHR⋈

The ASCII code can be represented by a number or variable within the ASCII code range (typically 0 – 127). Many computers have an extended ASCII code (up to 255) which includes special capabilities and graphics characters. Most computers set aside certain ASCII numbers for special "non-standard" purposes (typically, control a line printer, erase the screen, "put out the cat," etc.).

This program lets you test any ASCII code number and view the ASCII character, if it is printable.

Test Program

```
10 REM 'CHR$' TEST PROGRAM
20 PRINT "ENTER THE LOWEST ASCII CODE NUMBER";
30 INPUT L
40 PRINT "ENTER THE HIGHEST ASCII CODE NUMBER";
50 INPUT H
60 FOR X=L TO H
70 PRINT "ASCII CODE";X;"= ";
80 PRINT CHR$(X)
90 FOR Y=1 TO 150
100 NEXT Y
110 NEXT X
999 END
```

Sample Run *(checking only 4 numbers)*

```
ENTER THE LOWEST ASCII CODE NUMBER? 65
ENTER THE HIGHEST ASCII CODE NUMBER? 68
ASCII CODE 65 = A
ASCII CODE 66 = B
ASCII CODE 67 = C
ASCII CODE 68 = D
```

Try this program using your computer's full range of ASCII codes.

Alternate Spellings

Several different spellings are used for CHR$, e.g. CHR (SOL and SWTP 4K), CHAR$ (Micropolis BASIC), and CHAR (MAX-BASIC).

Variations In Usage

The Swedish ABC-80 uses CHR¤ to convert up to four ASCII numbers to their corresponding characters. (¤ is the Swedish currency symbol which stands for "string", replacing the $.)

CHAR(N1,N2), found in MAXBASIC requires two numbers. The first is the ASCII code and the second tells how many characters to generate. CHAR(73,1) is the equivalent of CHR$(73). CHAR(65,4) = AAAA. See STRING$ for more details.

Also See

ASC, STRING$, ASCII code in Appendix A

CINT is used to convert individual numbers or numeric variables to their integer value. Variables used in the CINT function return to their original precision if they are used again without the CINT function.

Numbers are always rounded down — that is, the whole number remains the same regardless of the value of numbers removed to the right of the decimal point. When a negative number is integered, the resultant number will be rounded off to the next smaller whole number.

For example, PRINT CINT(-4.65) will print the number -5.

Most computers do not allow numbers assigned to the CINT function to be smaller than −32768 or larger than +32767. The INT function is very similar but not restricted by such a narrow number range.

Test Program

```
10 REM 'CINT' TEST PROGRAM
20 DEFDBL X
30 X=12345.6789
40 PRINT "CINT CHANGES THE VALUE OF X FROM";X;"TO";
   CINT(X)
50 PRINT "AND BACK TO THE VALUE OF";X;"WHEN REMOVED"
99 END
```

Sample Run

```
CINT CHANGES THE VALUE OF X FROM 12345.6789 TO 12345
AND BACK TO THE VALUE OF 12345.6789 WHEN REMOVED
```

Variations In Usage

None known.

Also See

DEFINT, INT, DEFDBL, DEFSNG, CDBL, CSNG, !, #, %

CLR

CLEAR is used by a few computers to erase the resident program. Type:

```
10 REM CLEAR TEST PROGRAM
```

Then type CLEAR. . . then LIST. If no lines were listed, CLEAR passed this test and there's no need to try the remaining usages.

CLEAR is most commonly used to set all numeric variables to zero and erase all data that may be held by string variables.

Test Program #1

```
10 REM 'CLEAR' TEST PROGRAM
20 A=300
30 A$="TEST STRING"
40 PRINT "BEFORE THE 'CLEAR' COMMAND A=";A
50 PRINT "AND STRING VARIABLE A$ = ";A$
60 CLEAR
70 PRINT "AFTER THE 'CLEAR' COMMAND A=";A
80 PRINT "AND STRING VARIABLE A$=";A$
99 END
```

Sample Run

```
BEFORE THE 'CLEAR' COMMAND A=300
AND STRING VARIABLE A$=TEST STRING
AFTER THE 'CLEAR' COMMAND A=0
AND STRING VARIABLE A$=
```

CLEAR is used by some computers to specify the number of bytes to reserve in memory for strings. This feature lets the programmer conserve memory by specifying the actual amount of space needed for string storage.

For example, CLEAR 100 sets 100 bytes of memory aside for string storage.

It is common for interpreters with CLEAR capability to automatically reserve 50 bytes in memory for strings. Others reserve up to 200 bytes for this purpose. CLEAR ### allows this "default" reserve to be changed.

The amount of space remaining for string storage in memory can be checked by interpreters with the FRE(A$) function when used in a PRINT statement.

Test Program #2

```
10 REM 'CLEAR X' TEST PROGRAM
20 CLEAR 5
30 PRINT "ENTER FROM 1 TO 5 CHARACTERS";
40 INPUT A$
```

```
50 PRINT "STRING "A$;" USED ALL BUT";FRE(A$);"BYTES"
60 PRINT "OF STRING SPACE,"
70 GOTO 20
99 END
```

Sample Run *(using T and TEST)*

```
ENTER FROM 1 TO 5 CHARACTERS? T
STRING T USED ALL BUT 4 BYTES
OF STRING SPACE,
ENTER FROM 1 TO 5 CHARACTERS? TEST
STRING TEST USED ALL BUT 1 BYTES
OF STRING SPACE,
ENTER FROM 1 TO 5 CHARACTERS?
```

Some computers with CLEAR capability allow the CLEAR value to be specified by a variable. To test this feature, make these changes to the second Test Program;

```
20 A=5
25 CLEAR A
```

If the interpreter accepted this program change, the sample run should not change.

Alternate Spellings

The Apple II and PET both use CLR as an alternate spelling of CLEAR.

Variations In Usage

Some computers use CLEAR as a special statement to clear terminal input or output buffers. WANG computers use CLEAR as a command only. Used alone, CLEAR erases all program lines and variables from memory. It performs the same function as NEW or SCRATCH does in other computers. CLEAR P removes program lines but leaves variables alone. CLEAR P $n1$, $n2$ will remove program lines with line numbers between $n1$ and $n2$. If $n2$ is left out, it will erase all program lines from $n1$ on. CLEAR V removes only the variables from memory while CLEAR N removes only non-common variables.

In Microsoft BASIC 5.0 (BASIC-80), CLEAR does not reserve any string space but does provide an option to reserve space at top of memory. For example, CLEAR, 32000 sets all numeric variables to 0 and string variables to null while reserving memory beyond 32000 for machine language programs.

Also See

FRE(A$), COMMON, NEW, SCRATCH

Function

CLOG

The CLG(n) function is used by the Honeywell Series 60 BASIC to compute the value of the common (base 10) logarithm of any number (n) whose value is greater than 0.

Test Program

```
10 REM 'CLG' TEST PROGRAM
20 PRINT "ENTER A POSITIVE NUMBER"
30 INPUT X
40 L=CLG(X)
50 PRINT "THE COMMON LOG OF";X; "IS";L
30999 END
```

Sample Run *(using 100)*

```
ENTER A POSITIVE NUMBER? 100
THE COMMON LOG OF 100 IS 2
```

Alternate Spelling

CLOG is used by some computers instead of CLG.

IF YOUR COMPUTER DOESN'T HAVE IT

If your computer failed the TEST PROGRAM, try the TEST PROGRAMs in LOG10, and LOG. If they also fail, substitute the subroutine found under LOG. To make it compute the common logarithm (instead of the natural logarithm), make the following changes:

```
30150 REM * COMMON LOGARITHM SUBROUTINE * INPUT X,
      OUTPUT L
30197 L=L*.4342945
```

To use this subroutine with the TEST PROGRAM, change line 40 to:

```
40 GOSUB 30150
```

CONVERSION FACTORS

To convert a common log to a natural log, multiply the common log value times 2.302585.

For example, `X=CLG(N)*2.302585`

To convert a natural log to a common log, multiply the natural log value times .4342945.

Variations In Usage

None known.

Also See

`LOG10, LOG`

Function

CLK

CLK$ is used with PRINT statements in the DEC BASIC-PLUS-2 and the Texas Instruments 990 BASIC to indicate the time of day in hours (0 to 24), minutes, and seconds (hh:mm:ss). The computer automatically inserts a colon after the hour and minute values and prints the time as a string.

For example, PRINT CLK$ will print a time similar to 22:19:15, indicating the current time is 10:19 p.m. plus 15 seconds.

Test Program

```
10 REM 'CLK$' TEST PROGRAM
20 PRINT "THE CURRENT TIME IS ";
30 PRINT CLK$
40 PRINT "'CLK$' PASSED THE TEST IF A SIX DIGIT NUMBER
   IS PRINTED"
99 END
```

Sample Run *(typical)*

```
THE CURRENT TIME IS 10:28:45
'CLK$' PASSED THE TEST IF A SIX DIGIT NUMBER IS PRINTED
```

Alternate Spelling

CLK(*n*) is used by the Sperry Univac System/9 BASIC to indicate time (hhmmss). A numeric expression (enclosed in parentheses) following CLK is required, although it has no effect on the CLK function. Change line 30 of Test Program to 30 PRINT CLK(0) and run the program to see if your computer accepts CLK.

Variations In Usage

None known.

Also See

TIME, TIME$

CLOAD

CLOAD is a special command used by some interpreters (e.g. those with Microsoft BASIC) to load a program into the computer from a cassette tape.

Test Program

Enter this program into the computer from the keyboard, then store the program on cassette tape. (See CSAVE for details.)

```
10 REM 'CLOAD' TEST PROGRAM
20 PRINT "THIS PROGRAM TESTS THE CLOAD FEATURE"
99 END
```

Once the program is recorded on cassette tape, erase the computer memory with NEW, SCRATCH, or whatever is appropriate.

Rewind the tape, then set the recorder to the Play mode and type the CLOAD command.

The cassette recorder's motor is controlled by the computer which turns it on and off before and after the "load" cycle. The cassette should "play back" the program, LOADing it into the computer.

List the program to verify that the program held in the computer's memory is identical to that originally entered (see LIST). If all looks well, RUN the program.

Sample Run

```
THIS PROGRAM TESTS THE CLOAD FEATURE
```

CLOAD "program name" is used by some CLOAD-equipped computers to load only that program on the cassette that has a matching program name. A program name used to identify a specific program may contain more than one letter or number, but the computer *may* recognize only the first character.

Record the TEST PROGRAM onto the cassette using CSAVE"A" (see CSAVE), erase the computer memory, then load "A" back into the computer using CLOAD"A". List the program to check for possible errors.

CLOAD? "program name" is used by some CLOAD-equipped computers to compare a program stored in the computer's memory with a program stored on cassette under the program name indicated. The computer does a bit-by-bit comparison of the two and prints an error message if any difference is encountered. This allows you to compare the tape with the memory contents to verify that you executed a successful CSAVE, or CLOAD, before erasing either.

Check the TEST PROGRAM on cassette tape (stored with the program name "A") against the computer using the CLOAD?"A" command. If an error message is not printed, the two programs matched.

Add this line to the test program stored in the computer.

```
30 REM EXTRA LINE
```

Again check the "A" program on cassette tape using the command CLOAD?"A". An error message should be printed, indicating the computer found a difference between the program stored in the computer and the program stored on tape.

CLOAD* (array name) is used by a few CLOAD-using computers as a command to load an array stored on cassette tape (under the same array name). Example: CLOAD*A means "load array A".

CLOAD*(array name) can also be used as a program statement so array data can be loaded as a program is being executed.

Variations In Usage

None other known.

Also See

```
CSAVE, LIST, CHAIN, RECALL, APPEND
```

The CLRDOT statement is used by Sweden's ABC 80 as a graphics feature to "turn off" a graphics block on the display screen. The block to be "turned off" is specified by the L,C coordinates following the CLRDOT statement. L specifies the line (0 to 71 in graphics mode) and C specifies the column (2 to 79 in graphics mode).

For example, CLRDOT 9,15 causes the computer to turn off the block located in the tenth row and sixteenth column from the upper left corner. To turn on the graphics block see SETDOT.

Test Program

```
10 REM 'CLRDOT' TEST PROGRAM
20 PRINT CHR¤ (12)      'CLEARS SCREEN
30 PRINT "CLRDOT PASSED THE TEST IF A LINE APPEARS"
40 PRINT "AND THEN DISAPPEARS,"
50 FOR T=1 TO 2000 : NEXT T
60 PRINT CLR¤ (12)
70 FOR R=0 TO 23
80 PRINT CUR(R,0); CHR¤ (151);
90 NEXT R
100 R=5
110 FOR C=2 TO 35
120 SETDOT R,C
130 NEXT C
140 FOR T=1 TO 2000 : NEXT T
150 FOR C=2 TO 35
160 CLRDOT R,C
170 NEXT C
180 FOR T=1 TO 2000 : NEXT T
999 END
```

Sample Run

```
CLRDOT PASSED THE TEST IF A LINE APPEARS
AND THEN DISAPPEARS,
```
(A horizontal line should appear briefly near the top of the screen.)

Variations In Usage

None known.

Also See

RESET, SETDOT, SET, ¤

The CLS (clear screen) command is used to perform the same function as the CLEAR key on many keyboards. It erases the entire screen instantly without disturbing the program. CLS can also be used as a program statement to clear the screen before starting a graphics display or a new "page" of printed information.

Test Program

```
10 REM 'CLS' TEST PROGRAM
20 FOR X=1 TO 15
30 PRINT "THIS LINE SHOULD DISAPPEAR"
40 NEXT X
50 CLS
60 PRINT "IF THIS IS ALL THAT'S ON THE SCREEN"
70 PRINT "THE CLS STATEMENT PASSED THE TEST"
99 END
```

Sample Run

```
IF THIS IS ALL THAT'S ON THE SCREEN
THE CLS STATEMENT PASSED THE TEST
```

IF YOUR COMPUTER DOESN'T HAVE IT

Many video screens can be cleared or "erased" by using an ASCII character. Try this change to the test program:

```
50 PRINT CHR$(24)
```

If CHR$(24) fails (due to nonconformity of some manufacturer's use of ASCII numbers), try this program to search for an ASCII screen-clear:

Test Program

```
10 REM ASCII CLEAR SCREEN SEARCH
20 FOR X=0 TO 128
30 PRINT "ASCII CODE";X;
40 PRINT CHR$(X)
50 FOR Y=1 TO 200
60 NEXT Y
70 NEXT X
99 END
```

Variations In Usage

The TRS-80 COLOR COMPUTER uses CLS(*n*) to clear the screen and set the background color. The numbers 0 thru 8 below indicate which number turns on which color. If CLS is used without a number, the color used is the current background color.

0 = BLACK	3 = BLUE	6 = CYAN
1 = GREEN	4 = RED	7 = MAGENTA
2 = YELLOW	5 = BUFF	8 = ORANGE

Note that the CLS and CLEAR statements are completely different.

Also See

CHR$(X), ASCII table in Appendix A,

The CODE function is used by the Sinclair ZX80 to convert a character to its "numeric code". Sinclair does not use the ASCII code used by virtually all other computers.

For example, PRINT CODE("A") prints 38. PRINT CODE (A$) prints the code of the first character of the string stored in variable A$.

Test Program

```
10 REM 'CODE' TEST PROGRAM
20 PRINT "THE NUMERIC CODE FOR THE LETTER A IS";
30 PRINT CODE("A")
40 PRINT
50 PRINT "TYPE ANY LETTER, NUMBER OR CHARACTER";
60 INPUT A$
70 PRINT "THE NUMERIC CODE FOR ";A$" IS";CODE(A$)
99 END
```

Sample Run

```
THE NUMERIC CODE FOR THE LETTER A IS 38

TYPE ANY LETTER, NUMBER OR CHARACTER? *
THE NUMERIC CODE FOR * IS 20
```

Also See

ASC, CHR$

COLOR is used in the APPLE II BASIC as a special feature to specify a color to be displayed on the screen by the graphics statements PLOT, HLIN-AT and VLIN-AT. The same color is displayed each time a graphics statement is executed. To change colors, a new color must be specified by the COLOR statement.

The computer displays 16 different colors, and each is assigned a number (from 0 to 15). They are:

0	BLACK	8	BROWN
1	MAGENTA	9	ORANGE
2	DARK BLUE	10	GREY
3	PURPLE	11	PINK
4	DARK GREEN	12	GREEN
5	GREY	13	YELLOW
6	MEDIUM BLUE	14	AQUA
7	LIGHT BLUE	15	WHITE

An equal sign (=) must be placed between COLOR and the COLOR value. This value may be a number or a numeric variable.

For example, COLOR = 13 selects the color yellow for the next graphics statement. COLOR can be used as both a command and a program statement.

Test Program

```
10 REM 'COLOR' TEST PROGRAM
20 GR
30 FOR X=0 TO 15
40 COLOR = X
50 Y=X*2
60 HLIN 0,39 AT Y
70 NEXT X
99 END
```

Sample Run

If your computer accepted the TEST PROGRAM, each of the 16 colors should be displayed as a horizontal line across the screen.

Variations In Usage

See ATARI and TRS-80 Color Computer summaries.

Also See

GR, PLOT, HLIN-AT, VLIN-AT

Statement

COM

The COMMON statement is used in some computers to transfer values from one program to another. If each of two (or more) programs contains similar COMMON statements, when the second program is CHAINed to the first, the current values stored in the variables named in COMMON will be available to the second program. (See CHAIN.)

Example: If the first program contains the statement

```
10 COMMON A , B , C , I , J
```

and the second program contains the statement

```
30 COMMON X , Y , Z , T , V
```

then the final value of A becomes the initial value of X, the final value of B becomes the initial value of Y, etc.

Alternate Spelling

COM is used by some computers (e.g. WANG 2200) as a short form of COMMON

Test Program

Save this program on disk or tape under the name "TEST".

```
10 REM * TEST * PROGRAM
20 COMMON A
30 PRINT "THE 'TEST' PROGRAM RECEIVED A";A
40 A=A*2
50 CHAIN MAIN , 50
99 END
```

Now enter the following program into the computer and save it on the same tape following TEST, or on disk under the name "MAIN".

```
10 REM * MAIN * PROGRAM
20 COMMON A
30 A = 5
40 CHAIN TEST
50 PRINT "AND RETURNED A";A
99 END
```

Prepare your disk or tape to be read on program command, then RUN.

Sample Run

```
THE 'TEST' PROGRAM RECEIVED A 5
AND RETURNED A 10
```

Variations In Usage

The COM statement (on the WANG) also provides the ability to specify the length of string variables up to a maximum of 64 characters. (Its default length is 16 characters.)

For example, `COM A$(100)1, B$8` establishes a single character string array A$($n$) with 100 elements and the string variable B$ with a length of 8 characters.

Also See

`CHAIN, DIM`

Command

CON
CO
C.

The CONTinue command restarts program execution after it was "broken" due to a STOP statement, or use of a keyboard BREAK key. Unlike the RUN command, which causes execution to start at the program's beginning, CONT resumes execution at the line following the break and variables are **not** reset to zero.

CONT has no application as a program **statement** since it is only used when the program has STOPped.

Test Program

```
10 REM 'CONT' TEST PROGRAM
20 PRINT "ENTER THE 'CONT' COMMAND"
30 STOP
40 PRINT "THE CONT COMMAND PASSED THE TEST"
99 END
```

Sample Run

```
ENTER THE 'CONT' COMMAND
BREAK AT 30
CONT
THE CONT COMMAND PASSED THE TEST
```

Alternate Spellings

Several other abbreviations of CONTinue are used, among them are CON, CO and C. Try each with the Test Program to see which your computer accepts.

Variations In Usage

None known.

Also See

STOP, END, RUN

The COS(A) function computes the COSINE of the angle A, when that value is expressed **in Radians (not in degrees).** One radian = approximately 57 degrees.

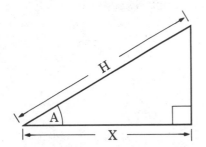

**COSD
COSG**

Cosine (COS) is defined as the ratio of the length of the side adjacent to the angle being investigated to the length of the hypotenuse, in a right triangle.

```
COS(A)=X/H
```

The opposite of COS is ARCCOS. ARCCOS (abbreviated ACS) finds the value of the angle when its COS, or ratio of sides (X/H) is known.

Test Program

```
10 REM 'COS' TEST PROGRAM
20 PRINT "ENTER AN ANGLE (EXPRESSED IN RADIANS)";
30 INPUT R
40 Y=COS(R)
50 PRINT "THE COSINE OF A";R;"RADIAN ANGLE IS";Y
30999 END
```

Sample Run *(for input of 1)*

```
ENTER AN ANGLE (EXPRESSED IN RADIANS)? 1
THE COSINE OF A 1 RADIAN ANGLE IS .540302
```

To convert values from degrees to radians, multiply the angle in degrees times .0174533.

For example: `R=COS(A*.0174533)`

To convert values from radians to degrees, multiply radians times 57.29578

Some computers accept the measure of the angle in either degrees or grads (100 grads = 90 degrees). These computers use the function COSD with degrees and COSG with grads. Substitute each of these functions in line 40 of TEST PROGRAM and run it. Using 1 in the sample run should produce .999848 with COSD and .999877 with COSG.

IF YOUR COMPUTER DOESN'T HAVE IT

If your interpreter does not have the COSine capability, the following subroutine can be substituted.

The subroutine program you'll find under SIN **must** be added to this one to make it work (saves space not to duplicate it here).

```
30000 GOTO 30999
30330 REM * COSINE SUBROUTINE * INPUT X IN RADIANS,
      OUTPUT Y
30332 REM ALSO USES C, D, W AND Z INTERNALLY
30334 X=X*57.29578
30336 W=ABS(X)/X
30338 D=X
30340 X=X+90
30342 GOSUB 30366
30344 X=D/57.29578
30346 IF Z<>-1 THEN 30352
30348 IF W<>1 THEN 30352
30350 Y=-Y
30352 RETURN
```

To use the subroutines with the TEST PROGRAM to find the COSine of an angle (expressed in Radians), make the following TEST PROGRAM changes:

```
35 X=R
40 GOSUB 30330
```

To find the COSine of an angle (expressed in Degrees), either delete line 30334, or change line 40 to:

```
40 GOSUB 30336
```

Variations In Usage

Some (rare) interpreters convert everything to degrees automatically.

Also See

```
SIN, ASN, ATN, TAN, ACS, COSH, SINH, TANH
```

COSH(N) is a function that calculates the hyperbolic cosine of a number. Hyperbolic functions express relationships based on a hyperbola similar to the way trigonometric

CSH

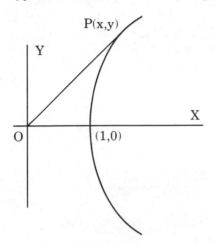

functions are identified on a circle. If, on the unit hyperbola (i.e. the graph of X*X − Y*Y = 1), a line is drawn from the origin to a point ,P, on the curve (see diagram), a region is formed with an area N/2. COSH(N) will give the value of the X coordinate of the point of intersection. [SINH(N) will give the value of Y.]

Unlike the trig functions, N does **not** name the measure of an angle and, therefore, is not in degrees or radians. N can be any real number, positive or negative but COSH(N) is always greater than or equal to 1.

Test Program

```
10 REM 'COSH' TEST PROGRAM
20 PRINT "ENTER A VALUE";
30 INPUT N
40 C=COSH(N)
50 PRINT "THE HYPERBOLIC COSINE OF";N;"IS";C
30999 END
```

Sample Run *(using the value 1)*

```
ENTER A VALUE? 1
THE HYPERBOLIC COSINE OF 1 IS 1.54308
```

IF YOUR COMPUTER DOESN'T HAVE IT

If your computer doesn't accept COSH, you can compute the value by substituting the EXP function, as follows:

```
40 C=.5 *(EXP(N)+EXP(-N))
```

If your computer doesn't have EXP function either, substitute the following subroutine, instead. The subroutine program found under EXP must also be included.

```
30000 GOTO 30999
30430 REM * COSH SUBROUTINE * INPUT N, OUTPUT C
30432 REM ALSO USES A, B, E, L AND X INTERNALLY
30434 X=N
30436 GOSUB 30200
30438 C=E
30440 X=-N
30442 GOSUB 30200
30444 C=.5*(C+E)
30446 RETURN
```

To use this subroutine, make the following change in TEST PROGRAM:

```
40 GOSUB 30430
```

Alternate Spelling

Harris BASIC-V uses CSH for the COSH function.

Variations In Usage

None known.

Also See

SINH, TANH, EXP

COUNT is a function in the ACORN ATOM computer that "counts" the number of characters printed since the last carriage return. COUNT is similar to POS (see POS for more information).

Test Program

```
10 REM 'COUNT' TEST PROGRAM
20 PRINT "THIS LINE HAS A CHARACTER COUNT OF";
30 K = COUNT
40 PRINT K+3
99 END
```

Sample Run

```
THIS LINE HAS A CHARACTER COUNT OF 37
```

Also See

POS

Command

CSAVE is used by some computers (e.g. those with a Microsoft interpreter) to record programs from computer memory onto cassette tape.

Test Program

```
10 REM 'CSAVE' TEST PROGRAM
20 PRINT "THIS PROGRAM TESTS THE
   CSAVE FEATURE"
99 END
```

Set up the cassette recorder for Recording and type the command CSAVE. The computer should control the operation of the cassette recorder by turning the motor on and off at the beginning and end of the record cycle.

Once the program is recorded on cassette tape, type NEW (or whatever is required) to clear the program from memory. Load the program from tape back into the computer (see CLOAD). List the program to verify that the program held in the computer's memory is identical to that originally entered (see LIST).

Sample Run

```
THIS PROGRAM TESTS THE CSAVE FEATURE
```

CSAVE (program name) is used by some computers using CSAVE to assign a specific name to the program being recorded on cassette tape. The file name may contain one or more letters, numbers, or other selected ASCII symbols, but only the first character *may* be recognized by the computer. The program name identifies the program for later retrieval via the CLOAD (program name) command.

Record the TEST PROGRAM on cassette tape using the command CSAVE"A", erase the memory, then load the program back into the computer using the CLOAD"A" command.

List the program to check for possible errors.

Variations In Usage

CSAVE* can be used in Microsoft BASIC 5.0 to save the values of a numeric array on tape.

Also See

```
CLOAD, LIST, STORE
```

CSNG is used to change numbers or numeric variables which are previously defined as being of "double-precision" back to regular "single-precision". Variables listed in the CSNG function return to their original double-precision status if they are used again without the CSNG function.

Single-precision variables are capable of storing numbers containing no more than 7 digits (only 6 digits are printed). Double-precision means being accurate to 17 digits. If CSNG is used with a double-precision number containing more than 6 digits, that number is "rounded-off" to six significant places.

Test Program

```
10 REM 'CSNG' TEST PROGRAM
20 DEFDBL X
30 X=1234567890123456
40 PRINT "CSNG CHANGES THE VALUE OF X FROM";X;
   "TO";CSNG(X)
50 PRINT "AND BACK TO THE VALUE OF";X;"WHEN REMOVED"
99 END
```

Sample Run

```
CSNG CHANGES THE VALUE OF X FROM 1234567890123456 TO
   1.23457E+15
AND BACK TO THE VALUE OF 1234567890123456 WHEN REMOVED
```

Variations In Usage

None known.

Also See

DEFSNG, DEFDBL, DEFINT, CDBL, !, #, %, CINT

CUR is a function used with a PRINT statement by Sweden's ABC-80 computer. It positions the next print character at a desired location L,C. PRINT CUR(L,C) produces results similar to PRINT AT (64*L+C) or PRINT @ (64*L+C).

Test Program

```
10 REM 'CUR' PROGRAM
20 PRINT CHR¤ (12) 'CLEARS SCREEN ON ABC 80
30 PRINT CUR(12,16); "MIDDLE"
40 PRINT "CUR PASSED IF MIDDLE IS IN THE CENTER"
99 END
```

Sample Run

```
                MIDDLE
    CUR PASSED IF MIDDLE IS IN THE CENTER
```

Also See

PRINT AT, @, LOCATE

D is used to indicate "double precision" in numbers expressed in "exponential" or "standard scientific notation".

For example, 1.23456789D+20.

Numbers expressed in single precision are written in exponential notation using the letter "E".

For example, 1.234E+20

Test Program

```
10 REM 'D' DOUBLE PRECISION EXPONENT TEST PROGRAM
20 A#=1234567890123456789
30 PRINT "EXPONENTIAL NOTATION 'D' PASSED THE TEST IF"
40 PRINT A#; "CONTAINS THE LETTER 'D'"
99 END
```

Sample Run

```
EXPONENTIAL NOTATION 'D' PASSED THE TEST IF
 1.234567890123457D+18 CONTAINS THE LETTER 'D'
```

Variations In Usage

The letter "D", like all other letters of the alphabet, is used by all computers to indicate a numeric variable.

Also See

```
E, #, !, DEFDBL, DEFSNG
```

Statement

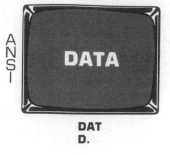

ANSI

DATA

DAT
D.

A DATA statement contains data to be read by a READ statement. The items in the DATA statement must be separated by commas and may include both positive and negative numbers.

Test Program #1

```
10 REM 'DATA' TEST PROGRAM
20 DATA 20,-10,,5
30 READ A,B,C
40 D=A+B+C
50 PRINT "D =";D
60 PRINT "DATA PASSED THE TEST IF D
   = 10.5"
99 END
```

Sample Run

```
D = 10.5
DATA PASSED THE TEST IF D = 10.5
```

Most computers allow strings in a DATA statement. Some require that the strings always be enclosed in quotes, while others require quotes only when the string is preceded by, encloses, or is followed by a blank, comma or colon.

Test Program #2

```
10 REM 'DATA' TEST PROGRAM USING STRINGS
20 DATA "LINE NUMBER",20,"PASSED"
30 READ A$,A,B$
40 PRINT "DATA STATEMENT IN ";A$;A;B$;" THE TEST"
99 END
```

Sample Run

```
DATA STATEMENT IN LINE NUMBER 20 PASSED THE TEST
```

Remove the quotation marks from the String Variables in line 20 and run again to see if they are needed in your interpreter.

DATA statements may be placed at any location in a program.

Alternate Spellings

DAT (by PDP-8E) and D. (Tiny BASIC) are used as abbreviations for DATA.

Variations In Usage

None known.

Also See

READ, RESTORE

Statement

ANSI

The DEF statement allows the user to DEFine (create) new functions (most computers have some built in functions) which can then be used the same as any intrinsic (built in) function.

For example, DEF FNA(R) = R*R*3.14159. The expression R*R*3.14159 (the formula to find the area of a circle, normally written πr^2) is DEFined in this example as the function FNA. FN (an abbreviation for the word FuNction) is used in DEF statements followed by any legal numeric variable. "A" is used in this example to identify function FNA as the Area of a circle, but any variable could have been used. Once a function is defined, it usually cannot be redefined in the same program.

The variable enclosed in parentheses [(R) above] must match the variable used in the statement to the right of the equal sign. These are commonly referred to as "dummy" variables.

The operation stored in the FN (variable) function by the DEF statement can be used to manipulate any number or numeric variable.

For example,

```
10 X=2
20 DEF FNA(N)=3*N-1
30 PRINT FNA(X)
```

The FN function in this example is named "A" (FNA), and is assigned the equation 3*N-1 in line 20. The numeric variable (X) following FNA is substituted for the "dummy variable" (N) in the DEF statement each time FNA is executed.

Test Program #1

```
10 REM 'DEF' TEST PROGRAM
20 PRINT "ENTER THE RADIUS OF A CIRCLE (IN INCHES)";
30 INPUT R
40 DEF FNC(X)=2*3.14159*X
50 PRINT "THE CIRCUMFERENCE OF A CIRCLE"
60 PRINT "WITH A RADIUS OF";R;"INCHES IS";FNC(R);
   "INCHES"
99 END
```

Sample Run *(using 4)*

```
ENTER THE RADIUS OF A CIRCLE (IN INCHES)? 4
THE CIRCUMFERENCE OF A CIRCLE
WITH A RADIUS OF 4 INCHES IS 25.1327 INCHES
```

Some computers allow more than one variable in the DEFined expression. Each of these variables must be listed after the FN(variable) function.

Test Program #2

```
10 REM 'DEF' MULTIPLE VARIABLE TEST PROGRAM
20 DEF FNA(X,Y)=(X+Y)/2
30 PRINT "ENTER ANY TWO NUMBERS";
40 INPUT X,Y
50 A=FNA(X,Y)
60 PRINT "THE AVERAGE OF";X;"AND";Y;"IS";A
999 END
```

Sample Run *(using 20 and 40)*

```
ENTER ANY TWO NUMBERS? 20,40
THE AVERAGE OF 20 AND 40 IS 30
```

Some computers allow the same function to be DEFined in more than one line. In the following TEST PROGRAM the function FNA is DEFined as X*2 if the value of variable X is less than 10, or as X/2 if the value of X is greater than or equal to 10.

Test Program #3

```
10 REM 'DEF' REQUIRING MORE THAN ONE LINE
20 PRINT "ENTER A VALUE FOR X THAT IS GREATER
   OR LESS THAN 10";
30 INPUT X
40 DEF FNA(X)
50 FNA=X*2
60 IF X <10 THEN 80
70 FNA=X/2
80 FNEND
90 PRINT "THE VALUE OF THE FUNCTION IS";FNA(X)
999 END
```

Sample Run *(using 12)*

```
ENTER A VALUE FOR X THAT IS GREATER OR LESS THAN 10? 12
THE VALUE OF THE FUNCTION IS 6
```

The FNEND statement in the last TEST PROGRAM tells the computer to stop defining function FNA. Multiple line DEF statements must always end with the FNEND statement, and the computer does not allow branching into or out of multiple line DEF statements. For more information see FNEND.

IF YOUR COMPUTER DOESN'T HAVE IT

If your computer does not have the DEF capability, substitute FN with a subroutine containing the same equation.

For example, the DEF statement in TEST PROGRAM #2 can be replaced with the following subroutine:

```
100 A=(X+Y)/2
110 RETURN
```

and these TEST PROGRAM CHANGES:

Delete line 20 and add

```
50 GOSUB 100
70 GOTO 999
```

"Dummy" variables cannot be used with GOSUB, so the actual variables in the subroutine will have to be given values before each call.

Some BASICs allow string functions to be defined by the DEF statement. For example, 10 DEF FNL$(A$)=LEFT$(A$,1) returns the first character of a string (handy for checking keyboard input).

Variations In Usage

None other known.

Also See

FN, FNEND, GOSUB, RETURN

DEFDBL is used to DEFine (declare) a variable or variables as being accurate to "DouBLe-precision". Double-precision variables are capable of storing numbers accurate to 17 digits (only 16 digits are printed). Single-precision variables are typically accurate to 6 digits.

Caution: DEFDBL should only be used where single-precision accuracy is not adequate, since double-precision variables require more memory space and their manipulation requires more time. In most computers the DEFDBL line must be executed before the variable listed in the DEFDBL statement is assigned a numeric value.

Test Program #1

```
10 REM 'DEFDBL' TEST PROGRAM
20 A=1.234567890123456
30 PRINT "DEFDBL IN LINE 50 CHANGED THE VALUE OF
   VARIABLE 'A'"
40 PRINT "FROM";A;"TO";
50 DEFDBL A
60 A=1.234567890123456
70 PRINT A
99 END
```

Sample Run

```
DEFDBL IN LINE 50 CHANGED THE VALUE OF VARIABLE 'A'
FROM 1.23457 TO 1.234567890123456
```

Most computers with DEFDBL capability also allow designation of more than one variable as "double-precision" by a single DEFDBL statement. For example, `DEFDBL A,F,M` defines the variables A, F and M as having double-precision, and `DEFDBL A-M` defines all variables that begin with letters A *thru* M as being double-precision.

Test Program #2

```
10 REM 'DEFDBL' (WITH MULTIPLE VARIABLES) TEST PROGRAM
20 DEFDBL A,G,I-N
30 A=1/3
40 G=2/3
50 L=1/9
60 M=1.2345678901234567D+38
70 N=-1.2345678901234567D+38
80 PRINT "DEFDBL PASSED THE TEST IF THE FOLLOWING"
90 PRINT "NUMBERS CONTAIN MORE THAN 7 DIGITS:"
100 PRINT A;G;L;M;N
999 END
```

Sample Run

```
DEFDBL PASSED THE TEST IF THE FOLLOWING
NUMBERS CONTAIN MORE THAN 7 DIGITS:
   .3333333333333333  .6666666666666667  .1111111111111111
  1.234567890123457D+38 -1.234567890123457D+38
```

The "D" before " +38" is the same as an "E" in exponential notation, but signifies that the number is "double-precision accurate".

Some computers may not print the first three values as shown in the SAMPLE RUN due to the calculation being done in single precision. This problem can be eliminated in computers that have a Double Precision Declarative sign (e.g. the # sign). Place the sign after each fraction in lines 30, 40 and 50 as follows to produce the correct results.

```
30  A=1/3#
40  G=2/3#
50  L=1/9#
```

Variations In Usage

None known.

Also See

DEFSNG, DEFINT, #, %, !, CDBL, CSNG, CINT, D and E

DEFINT is used to DEFine (declare) that the variables listed by the DEFINT statement are INTegers. Variables defined as integers store the integer (whole number) value of assigned numbers. This is especially useful in large programs since less memory is required to store integer values than non-integers.

A potential disadvantage of using the DEFINT statement is the inability of many interpreters to process numeric values larger than that allowed by the interpreter's INT function (typically −32767 to +32767).

The DEFINT line must be executed by the computer before a variable listed in the DEFINT statement is assigned a numeric value.

Test Program #1

```
10 REM 'DEFINT' TEST PROGRAM
20 DEFINT A
30 A=12.68
40 B=12.68
50 IF A=12 THEN 70
60 GOTO 80
70 IF B=12.68 THEN 100
80 PRINT "DEFINT FAILED THE TEST LINE 20"
90 GOTO 999
100 PRINT "THE DEFINT STATEMENT PASSED THE TEST
     IN LINE 20 BY"
110 PRINT "CHANGING THE VALUE OF VARIABLE A FROM";B;
     "TO";A
999 END
```

Sample Run

```
THE DEFINT STATEMENT PASSED THE TEST IN LINE 20 BY
CHANGING THE VALUE OF VARIABLE A FROM 12.68 TO 12
```

Most computers with DEFINT capability also allow assignment of multiple variables (separated by comma) in a single DEFINT statement. For example, DEFINT A,F,M defines the variables A, F and M as integers. DEFINT A-M defines all variables that begin with letters A *thru* M as integers.

Test Program #2

```
10 REM 'DEFINT' (WITH MULTIPLE VARIABLES) TEST PROGRAM
20 DEFINT A,G,L-N
30 A=6.25
40 B=21.42
50 G=-6.19
60 L=4.001
70 M=32000.999
80 N=14.8
90 PRINT "IF THE NUMBERS";A;G;L;M;N;" ARE INTEGERS,"
100 PRINT "AND THE NUMBER";B;"IS A DECIMAL, THEN DEFINT"
110 PRINT "PASSED THE MULTIPLE VARIABLE TEST IN LINE 20."
999 END
```

Sample Run

```
IF THE NUMBERS 6 -7 4 32000 14 ARE INTEGERS,
AND THE NUMBER 21.42 IS A DECIMAL, THEN DEFINT
PASSED THE MULTIPLE VARIABLE TEST IN LINE 20.
```

If the interpreter has a double-precision declarative character (e.g. the # sign in Microsoft BASIC) and/or a single precision declarative character (e.g. the ! sign in Microsoft BASIC), and one of these characters is assigned to a variable that is listed in the DEFINT statement, the variable is treated as double precision (or single precision) because Declarative Characters over-ride the DEFINT statement. For more details see #, ! and % operators.

Test Program #3

```
10 REM 'DEFINT' TEST PROGRAM
20 REM USES DOUBLE-PRECISION TYPE DECLARATION
   CHARACTER'#'
30 DEFINT A,B
40 A=9.123456789012345
50 B#=9.123456789012345
60 IF A=B# THEN 110
70 PRINT "A =";A
80 PRINT "B# =";B#
90 PRINT "THE TEST PASSED, SHOWING # OVER-RIDING DEFINT"
100 GOTO 999
110 PRINT "THE # CHARACTER OVER-RIDE FEATURE FAILED
   THE TEST"
999 END
```

Sample Run

```
A = 9
B# = 9.123456789012345
THE TEST PASSED, SHOWING # OVER-RIDING DEFINT
```

Variations In Usage

None known.

Also See

INT, #, DEFSNG, DEFDBL, CINT, CSNG, CDBL, % and !

DEFSNG is used to DEFine (declare) specified variables as being of "SiNGle precision". Single-precision variables are capable of storing numbers containing no more than 7 digits (only 6 digits are printed). Double precision means having 16-digit precision.

Since most interpreters automatically treat variables as having single precision, the DEFSNG statement is used in programs to redefine variables as having only single precision after one or more were defined as double precision by a previous DEFDBL or as integer by a DEFINT statement.

In most computers the DEFSNG line must be executed before the variable listed in the DEFSNG statement is assigned a numeric value. Line 20 below declares both X and Y to be maintained with double precision.

Test Program #1

```
10 REM 'DEFSNG' TEST PROGRAM
20 DEFDBL X,Y
30 X=1.234567890123456
40 Y=X
50 PRINT "DOUBLE PRECISION VALUE OF Y=";Y
60 DEFSNG Y
70 Y=X
80 PRINT "SINGLE PRECISION VALUE OF Y=";Y
99 END
```

Sample Run

```
DOUBLE PRECISION VALUE OF Y= 1.234567890123456
SINGLE PRECISION VALUE OF Y= 1.23457
```

Most computers with DEFSNG capability also allow assignment of multiple variables (separated by comma) in a single DEFSNG statement. For example, DEFSNG A,F,M defines the variables A, F and M as single precision, and DEFSNG A-M defines all variables that begin with the letters A *thru* M as single precision.

Test Program #2

```
10 REM 'DEFSNG' (WITH MULTIPLE VARIABLES) TEST PROGRAM
20 DEFDBL A,G,L-N
30 GOSUB 200
40 PRINT "THE DOUBLE PRECISION VALUES OF A,G,L,M AND N
     ARE"
50 PRINT A;G;L;M;N
60 DEFSNG A,G,L-N
70 GOSUB 200
80 PRINT "THE SINGLE PRECISION VALUES OF A,G,L,M AND N
     ARE"
90 PRINT A;G;L;M;N
100 GOTO 999
200 REM SUBROUTINE
210 A=1234.567890
220 G=A/10
230 L=G/10
240 M=L/10
250 N=M/10
260 RETURN
999 END
```

Sample Run

```
THE DOUBLE PRECISION VALUES OF A,G,L,M AND N ARE
  1234.56789 123.456789 12.3456789 1.23456789 .123456789
THE SINGLE PRECISION VALUES OF A,G,L,M AND N ARE
  1234.57 123.457 12.3457 1.23457 .123457
```

If the interpreter has a double-precision declarative character (e.g. the #
sign in Microsoft BASIC) and/or an integer declarative character (e.g. the %
sign in Microsoft BASIC), and one of these characters is assigned to a
variable that is listed in the DEFSNG statement, the variable is treated as
double precision (or integer) because Declarative Characters over-ride the
DEFSNG statement. For more details see #, ! and % operators.

Test Program #3

```
10 REM 'DEFSNG' TEST PROGRAM
20 REM USES DOUBLE PRECISION DECLARATION CHARACTER '#'
30 DEFSNG A,B
40 A=1.234567890123456
50 B#=1.234567890123456
60 IF A=B# THEN 110
70 PRINT "A =";A
80 PRINT "B# =";B#
90 PRINT "THE TEST PASSED WITH # OVER-RIDING DEFSNG"
100 GOTO 999
110 PRINT "THE # CHARACTER OVER-RIDE FEATURE FAILED THE
      TEST"
999 END
```

Sample Run

```
A = 1.23457
B# = 1.234567890123456
THE TEST PASSED WITH # OVER-RIDING DEFSNG
```

Variations In Usage

None known.

Also See

DEFINT, #, DEFDBL, !, CSNG, CDBL, CINT, %

The DEFSTR statement is used to specify designated variables as string variables. A variable listed in the DEFSTR statement is treated the same as if it was defined as a string variable by the $ (string) sign.

It is important in large programs to specify only those variables that need string storage, since string variables require more memory space than numeric variables.

The DEFSTR line must be executed before the defined variable is assigned a string notation.

Test Program #1

```
10 REM 'DEFSTR' TEST PROGRAM
20 A=25
30 PRINT "NUMERIC VARIABLE A =";A
40 DEFSTR A
50 A="TEST STRING"
60 PRINT "STRING VARIABLE A = ";A
99 END
```

Sample Run

```
NUMERIC VARIABLE A = 25
STRING VARIABLE A = TEST STRING
```

Most computers with DEFSTR capability also allow assignment of multiple variables (separated by comma) by a single DEFSTR statement. For example, DEFSTR A,F,M defines the variables A, F, and M as string variables. DEFSTR A-M defines all variables that begin with the letters A *thru* M as string variables.

Test Program #2

```
10 REM DEFSTR (WITH MULTIPLE VARIABLES) TEST PROGRAM
20 DEFSTR A,G,L-N
30 A="DEFSTR "
40 G="PASSED THE "
50 L="MULTIPLE VARIABLE "
60 M="TEST "
70 N="IN LINE 20."
80 PRINT A;G;L;M;N
99 END
```

Sample Run

```
DEFSTR PASSED THE MULTIPLE VARIABLE TEST IN LINE 20.
```

Some interpreters require that space be reserved in memory for the assigned strings by use of a DIM or CLEAR statement.

Interpreters with declarative characters (e.g. %, #, or !) take precedence over the DEFSTR function when added to variables listed in the DEFSTR statement. This feature can be tested by making these changes to the second TEST PROGRAM.

```
70 N="IN LINE"
80 PRINT A;G;L;M;N;
85 A!=20
90 PRINT A!
```

The single-precision declarative character (!) added to lines 85 and 90 should over-ride the DEFSTR statement in line 20 and print the sample run.

Variations In Usage

None known.

Also See

DEFDBL, DEFINT, DEFSNG, DIM, CLEAR, $, D (exponential notation), E (exponential notation), % (integer operator), # (double precision) and ! (single precision).

DEG is used by a few computers (e.g. the Cromemco 16K Extended BASIC) as a command which causes the computer to execute trigonometric functions in **degrees** (rather than in radians). One degree = approximately .02 radians.

DEGREE

Test Program #1

```
10 REM 'DEG COMMAND' TEST PROGRAM
20 A=SIN(1.4)
30 PRINT "THE SINE OF 1.4 RADIANS IS";A
99 END
```

Sample Run

As shown above, the computer will execute the program and compute the sine of an angle of 1.4 radians.

```
THE SINE OF 1.4 RADIANS IS .98545
```

Type the command DEG. Then RUN. The computer will output the sine of the angle measuring 1.4 DEGrees.

```
THE SINE OF 1.4 RADIANS IS.024432
```

To change the computer back to the radian mode, type RAD or SCR. (SCR will also SCRatch the entire program.)

IF YOUR COMPUTER DOESN'T HAVE IT

If your computer does not have the DEG **command**, it can be simulated in the program by multiplying degree values times .0174533. To use this conversion in the first TEST PROGRAM, make this program change:

```
20 A=SIN(1.4*.0174533)
```

Variations In Usage

DEG converts angle measures from degree, minute, second form to degree and decimal fraction form on the TRS-80 Pocket computer.

Example: By entering DEG 33.4025
DEG converts a measure of 33° 40' 25" to 33.6736 degrees.

DMS can be used on the Pocket computer to convert back from decimal degrees to Degree-Minute-Second form.

Example: By entering DMS 33.6736
DMS converts a measure of 33.6736 degrees to 33° 40' 25".

A few computer (e.g. those using MAX BASIC) have DEG(n) as an intrinsic function to convert a value (n) expressed in **radians** to **degrees**.

Test Program #2

```
10 REM 'DEG FUNCTION' TEST PROGRAM
20 PRINT "ENTER AN ANGLE (EXPRESSED IN RADIANS)";
30 INPUT A
40 B=DEG(A)
50 PRINT "THE RADIAN ANGLE OF";A;"IS EQUAL TO";B;"DEGREES"
99 END
```

Sample Run *(using 1.4)*

```
ENTER AN ANGLE (EXPRESSED IN RADIANS)? 1.4
THE RADIAN ANGLE OF 1.4 IS EQUAL TO 80.2141 DEGREES
```

Alternate Spelling

Some computers (e.g. Sharp/TRS-80 Pocket) use DEGREE as the statement that sets the computer in degree mode for trig calculations.

IF YOUR COMPUTER DOESN'T HAVE IT

If your computer does not have the DEG **function**, it can be simulated by multiplying the radian values times .57.29578. To use this conversion in the second TEST PROGRAM, make this program change:

```
40 B=A*57.29578
```

Also See

```
SIN, COS, TAN, ATN, RAD, ASN, ACS
```

The DELETE command is used to "erase" specified program lines from the computer's memory.

DEL

Test Program

```
10 REM 'DELETE' TEST PROGRAM
20 PRINT "LINE 20"
30 PRINT "LINE 30"
40 PRINT "LINE 40"
50 PRINT "LINE 50"
60 PRINT "LINE 60"
70 PRINT "LINE 70 - END OF DELETE TEST"
99 END
```

RUN the program to ensure that all lines are properly entered.

Sample Run

```
LINE 20
LINE 30
LINE 40
LINE 50
LINE 60
LINE 70 - END OF DELETE TEST
```

A single program line can be eliminated from the computer's memory using the command DELETE(line number). To test this feature, try the command DELETE 50 and run the program. This command should have eliminated the printing of "LINE 50". Check by LISTing and RUNning.

More than one program line can be eliminated from memory by some computers using the command DELETE(line#-line#). All line numbers within the range specified by this command are eliminated. To test this feature, try the command DELETE 30-40, then RUN the program. Lines 30 and 40 should be gone. Some computers require that the first and/or last line numbers actually exist. Others erase all numbers in the range even if the numbers specified at each end are not in use.

DELETE-(line number) is used by some computers to eliminate all line numbers from the first line number in the program to the line number specified in the DELETE command. To test this feature, try the command DELETE -60 and run the program. All lines should be eliminated except line 70 and 99.

Some computers with the DELETE feature allow eliminating of groups of line numbers plus individual line numbers by use of commas.

For example, DELETE 20,40-50,90 eliminates lines 20, 40, 50 and 90 from the program. To test for this feature, re-enter the test program and try the command DELETE 20, 40-60. LIST the program to verify that all lines except 10, 30, 70 and 99 have been eliminated.

A few computers use DELETE(line number)- to eliminate all line numbers starting from the line number specified in the DELETE command to the end. To test for this feature, try the command `DELETE 30-`. LIST the program to verify that only line 10 remains.

Alternate Spelling

Some computers (e.g. DEC-10 and Apple) use DEL as the DELETE command. DEL on the DEC-10 responds as described above.

The Apple version of DEL uses commas where DELETE uses hyphens. To DELete lines 20 thru 50, type `DEL 20,50`. DELeting a single line requires `DEL 30,30` (or simply typing the line number and pressing RETURN).

IF YOUR COMPUTER DOESN'T HAVE IT

If your computer does not have the DELETE command, the same thing can be accomplished by typing each line number individually, followed by pressing the ENTER or RETURN key. To eliminate all line numbers in one operation, use the NEW or SCRATCH command.

Also See

`NEW, LIST, SCRATCH`

DET is the determinant function which returns the single numeric value associated with a square matrix (i.e. a two dimensional array having the same number of rows as columns). If D=DET(A) where A is a 2x2 array, then D=A(1,1)*A(2,2)-A(1,2)*A(2,1). If A were a 3x3 array, the determinant would then be formed by 6 products. The determinant of a 4x4 matrix is made up of sums and differences of 24 products.

Test Program #1

```
10 REM * DET * TEST PROGRAM
20 DIM A(3,3)
30 FOR I=1 TO 3
40  FOR J=1 TO 3
50   READ A(I,J)
60  NEXT J
70 NEXT I
80 D=DET(A)
90 PRINT "THE DETERMINANT OF ARRAY A IS ";D
100 DATA 1,1,1, 1,2,3, 1,4,9
30999 END
```

Sample Run

```
THE DETERMINANT OF ARRAY A IS 2
```

Some interpreters calculate DET only if MAT INV has first been used on the array. (See MAT INV for information.) Once the inverse of the matrix is calculated with MAT B=INV(A), DET reports the determinant value of matrix A. If DET=0, then matrix A has no inverse and the values of array B are invalid.

Test Program #2

```
10 REM * DET WITH MAT INV * TEST PROGRAM
20 DIM A(3,3), B(3,3)
30 FOR I=1 TO 3
40  FOR J=1 TO 3
50   READ A(I,J)
60  NEXT J
70 NEXT I
80 MAT B=INV(A)
90 PRINT "THE DETERMINANT OF MATRIX A IS ";DET
100 DATA 1,1,1 1,2,3, 1,4,9
30999 END
```

Sample Run

```
      THE DETERMINANT OF MATRIX A IS 2
```

IF YOUR COMPUTER DOESN'T HAVE IT

If your computer doesn't allow either form of the DET function, substitute
the following subroutine:

```
30000 GOTO 30999
30940 REM * DET SUBROUTINE * INPUT N, A( , ), OUTPUT D
30942 REM ALSO USES I, J, K, L AND R INTERNALLY
30944 REM >> VALUES OF ARRAY A ARE ALTERED BY THIS
      ROUTINE <<
30946 D=1
30948 FOR K=2 TO N
30950  L=K-1
30952  IF A(L,L)<>0 THEN 30976
30954  FOR I=K TO N
30956   IF A(I,L)<>0 THEN 30964
30958  NEXT I
30960  D=0
30962  GOTO 30996
30964  FOR J=1 TO N
30966   R=A(J,L)
30968   A(J,L)=A(J,I)
30970   A(J,I)=R
30972   D=-D
30974  NEXT J
30976  FOR I=K TO N
30978   R=A(I,L)/A(L,L)
30980   FOR J=K TO N
30982    A(I,J)=A(I,J)-R*A(L,J)
30984   NEXT J
30986  NEXT I
30988 NEXT K
30990 FOR L=1 TO N
30992  D=D*A(L,L)
30994 NEXT L
30996 RETURN
```

To use this subroutine with TEST PROGRAM #1, make these changes:

```
75 N=3
80 GOSUB 30940
```

Variations In Usage

None known.

Also See

```
MAT INV, DIM
```

DIGITS

The DIGITS statement is used in TSC Extended BASIC to specify the maximum number of digits to be printed by a PRINT statement. For example, 20 DIGITS 8,2 might be used in a program where all the printed values represent dollars and cents. The first number specifies the **total** number of digits to be printed and the second the number of places to the right of the decimal. The second number must not be greater than the total number of digits to be printed.

If the actual value is too large to be printed in the number of places allowed, the value is printed in exponential form. The fractional part of the number is rounded to the desired number of digits where necessary and the right-most digits are not displayed.

Test Program

```
10 REM DIGITS TEST PROGRAM
20 DIGITS 6,4
30 X = 0.1234567
40 PRINT X
50 PRINT "DIGITS PASSED THE TEST IF 0.1235 WAS PRINTED"
99 END
```

Sample Run

```
0.1235
DIGITS PASSED THE TEST IF 0.1235 WAS PRINTED
```

PERCOM Super BASIC uses the DIGITS statement to specify only the number of digits to be printed after the decimal point. For example, 20 DIGITS = 4 limits all printed values to four decimal places.

IF YOUR COMPUTER DOESN'T HAVE IT

If DIGITS isn't available on your computer, try the PRECISION statement in line 20.

The maximum number of digits after the decimal point can also be controlled by deleting line 20 and replacing line 40 with:

```
40 PRINT USING "##.####";X
```

If PRINT USING isn't available either, don't despair! Substitute

```
40 PRINT INT(X*10000 + .5)/10000
```

Variations In Usage

None known.

Also See

PRECISION, PRINT USING, IMAGE, FMT, INT

The DIMension statement is used to establish the number of elements allowed in a numeric or string array.

An array DIMension is established by placing the array variable after the DIM statement, followed by the array size enclosed in parentheses.

For example, DIM A(20) allows array variable A to use the 21 array elements from A(0) to A(20). [Some computers start with array element A(1), while a few computers (e.g. those conforming to ANSI BASIC) can define the lowest array element as either 0 or 1 by using the BASE statement. For more information see BASE.]

When the DIM statement is executed, the computer sets the values stored in each designated array element to zero.

Test Program #1

```
10 REM 'DIM' NUMERIC ARRAY TEST PROGRAM
20 DIM A(10)
30 PRINT "THESE NUMBERS ARE STORED IN AND PRINTED"
40 PRINT "FROM A SINGLE DIMENSION NUMERIC ARRAY."
50 FOR X=1 TO 10
60 A(X)=X
70 PRINT A(X);
80 NEXT X
99 END
```

Sample Run

```
THESE NUMBERS ARE STORED IN AND PRINTED
FROM A SINGLE DIMENSION NUMERIC ARRAY.
 1   2   3   4   5   6   7   8   9   10
```

To check your interpreter's ability to use array elements starting at 0, make this change in the TEST PROGRAM:

```
50 FOR X=0 TO 10
```

If your interpreter accepted the array element A(0), a Sample Run should print numbers from 0 to 10.

Most computers allow each array to use elements from 0 (or 1) to 10 without the need for DIMensioning. Delete line 20 from the Test Program to test for this capability.

If it works, make this change in line 50:

```
50 FOR X=1 TO 15
```

and RUN. Since a few computers (e.g. TRS-80 Level I) do not require **any** dimensioning, their array size is automatically limited only by the amount of unused memory. TRS-80 Level I allows only one array, named A(n). Most computers allow the full range of Alphabetic variables, and many allow arrays to have Alpha/Numeric array names [e.g. A3(n)].

Assuming that line 50 change above caused a crash, make this change to line 20:

```
20 DIM A(15)
```

and RUN

Sample Run

```
THESE NUMBERS ARE STORED IN AND PRINTED
FROM A SINGLE DIMENSION NUMERIC ARRAY.
  1   2   3   4   5   6   7   8   9   10   11   12   13   14   15
```

This next program tests the computer's ability to DIMension **string** arrays. Some computers (e.g. Hewlett-Packard) require dimensioning of all strings, including string arrays, with no string space set aside without DIM.

Test Program #2

```
10 REM 'DIM' STRING ARRAY TEST PROGRAM
20 DIM A$(4)
30 FOR X=1 TO 4
40 READ A$(X)
50 NEXT X
60 PRINT "THE 'DIM' STATEMENT PASSED THE ";
70 FOR X=1 TO 4
80 PRINT A$(X);
90 NEXT X
100 DATA T,E,S,T
999 END
```

Sample Run

```
THE 'DIM' STATEMENT PASSED THE TEST
```

DIM is also used in some computers to set the maximum element size for numeric and string arrays which contain two dimensions (or more).

For example, `DIM A(20,25)` establishes the maximum size of the first dimension at 20, and the second at 25.

Most computers with two and three dimension array capability automatically reserve space for 10 elements in each dimension. Many smaller computers (e.g. Microsoft interpreter variations) reserve element space for only the first and second dimension.

Test Program #3

```
10 REM 'DIM' TWO DIMENSION ARRAY TEST PROGRAM
20 DIM A(3,4)
30 PRINT "THESE NUMBERS ARE STORED IN AND PRINTED"
40 PRINT "FROM A TWO DIMENSION NUMERIC ARRAY."
50 FOR I=1 TO 3
60 FOR J=1 TO 4
70 A(I,J)=I
80 NEXT J
90 NEXT I
100 FOR I=1 TO 3
110 FOR J=1 TO 4
120 PRINT A(I,J),
130 NEXT J
140 PRINT
150 NEXT I
999 END
```

Sample Run

```
THESE NUMBERS ARE STORED IN AND PRINTED
FROM A TWO DIMENSION NUMERIC ARRAY.
 1              1              1              1
 2              2              2              2
 3              3              3              3
```

Test Program #4

This program tests the computer's ability to DIMension three dimension numeric array variables.

```
10 REM 'DIM' THREE DIMENSION ARRAY TEST PROGRAM
20 DIM A(3,4,2)
30 PRINT "THESE NUMBERS ARE STORED IN AND PRINTED"
40 PRINT "FROM A THREE DIMENSION NUMERIC ARRAY."
50 FOR K=1 TO 2
60 FOR I=1 TO 3
70 FOR J=1 TO 4
80 A(I,J,K)=I
90 NEXT J
100 NEXT I
110 NEXT K
120 FOR K=1 TO 2
130 FOR I=1 TO 3
140 FOR J=1 TO 4
150 PRINT A(I,J,K),
160 NEXT J
170 NEXT I
180 PRINT
190 NEXT K
999 END
```

Sample Run

```
THESE NUMBERS ARE STORED IN AND PRINTED
FROM A THREE DIMENSION NUMERIC ARRAY.
1               1               1               1
2               2               2               2
3               3               3               3

1               1               1               1
2               2               2               2
3               3               3               3
```

IF YOUR COMPUTER DOESN'T HAVE IT

If your computer doesn't allow multidimensional arrays, simulating them with a single dimension is not difficult. To use a two-dimensional array such as A(3,4), DIMension the array as A(12) and replace each reference to A(I,J) with A((I-1)*4+J). If the zero subscripts will be used, the array will be DIMensioned as A(19), i.e. (3+1)*(4+1)-1 = 19. Then use A(I*4+J) in place of A(I,J).

Similarly for three dimensions, to declare array A(3,4,2), use DIM A(24) [or DIM A(59) if using zero as a subscript] and replace A(I,J,K) with A(((I-1)*4+(J-1))*2+K) [or with A((I*4+J)*2+K) if using the zero subscripts].

Generally:

For an MxN array:
 without zero subscript   DIM A(M*N) and use A((I-1)*N+J)
 with zero subscript   DIM A((M+1)*(N+1)-1) and use A(I*N+J)

For LxMxN array:
 without zero subscript   DIM A(L*M*N) and use A(((I-1)*M+(J-1))*N+K)

 with zero subscript   DIM A((L+1)*(M+1)*(N+1)-1) and use A((I*M+J)*N+K)

Variations In Usage

None other known.

Also See

CLEAR, MAT INPUT, MAT PRINT, MAT READ

The DOT function is used by Sweden's ABC-80 computer to indicate whether or not a specific graphics block on the video screen is "turned on". The graphics block is specified by the L,C coordinates following the DOT function, where L determines the line (0 to 71 in graphics mode) and C determines the column (2 to 79 in graphics mode).

For example, IF DOT (9,15) THEN 950 causes the computer to branch to line 950 if the block located in the tenth row and sixteenth column from the upper left corner is "on".

To turn on the graphics block see SETDOT.

Test Program

```
10 REM 'DOT' TEST PROGRAM
20 PRINT CHRX (12)      'CLEARS SCREEN
30 R=5
40 PRINT CUR(R,0);CHRX (151);   'SETS GRAPHICS MODE
50 FOR C=1 TO 35
60 SETDOT R,C
70 NEXT C
80 PRINT
90 IF DOT (5,12) THEN 120
100 PRINT "THE BLOCK IS OFF"
110 GOTO 130
120 PRINT "THE BLOCK IS ON"
130 FOR T=1 TO 2000 : NEXT T
140 PRINT CHRX (12)
999 END
```

Sample Run

```
THE BLOCK IS ON
```

Variations In Usage

None known.

Also See

```
POINT, SETDOT, CLRDOT, X
```

DRAWTO

DRAW is used by several computers (e.g. Apple II) to draw a pre-defined shape (numbered N) starting at location X,Y.

Example: `DRAW N AT X,Y`

Another version, `DRAW X,Y` is used on the Sinclair ZX80 to draw a line from a current position (H,K) to a new position (X + H, Y + K).

The Atari computer uses a line drawing statement `DRAWTO X,Y` that draws a line from the current position to position (X,Y).

Some computers use PLOT in the same way these computers use DRAW. See PLOT for more information.

Also See

`PLOT, XDRAW`

DSP is used in the APPLE II BASIC as an analytical tool to display a specific variable and its value each time the variable is assigned a value. The variable's associated line number is also displayed preceded by a # sign. More than one DSP statement is allowed in a program.

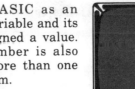

For example:

```
10 DSP X
20 DSP Y
```

instructs the computer to display (print) variables X and Y, and their values, along with the line numbers each time they are assigned or reassigned a value.

Test Program

```
10 REM 'DSP' TEST PROGRAM
20 DSP A
30 DSP B
40 A=5
50 B=10
60 C=A*B
70 A=A+C
80 PRINT "THE DSP STATEMENT PASSED THE TEST"
99 END
```

Sample Run

```
#40 A=5
#50 B=10
#70 A=55
THE DSP STATEMENT PASSED THE TEST
```

IF YOUR COMPUTER DOESN'T HAVE IT

This very handy troubleshooting feature can be duplicated by adding a temporary test line at each point where the variable being traced is changed. For example,

```
10 REM DSP SIMULATION
40 A=5
41 PRINT "#40 A=";A
50 B=10
51 PRINT "#50 B=";B
60 C=A*B
70 A=A+C
71 PRINT "#70 A=";A
80 PRINT "END OF THE DSP SIMULATION"
99 END
```

Variations In Usage

None known.

Also See

TRON, TRACE

E is used to indicate "exponential notation", or "standard scientific notation".

For example, 1.23E+12 means 123 followed by 10 zeros.

Numbers expressed in double precision are written in exponential notation using the letter "D".

For example, 1.23456789D+20

Test Program

```
10 REM 'E' SINGLE PRECISION EXPONENT TEST PROGRAM
20 A=123456789
30 PRINT "EXPONENTIAL NOTATION 'E' PASSED THE TEST IF"
40 PRINT A;"CONTAINS THE LETTER 'E'"
99 END
```

Sample Run

```
EXPONENTIAL NOTATION 'E' PASSED THE TEST IF
 1.23457E+08 CONTAINS THE LETTER 'E'
```

Variations In Usage

The letter "E", like all other letters of the alphabet, is used by all computers to indicate a numeric variable.

Also See

D, !, #, DEFSNG, DEFDBL, CSNG, CDBL

EDIT

EDIT is a special command used by some computers (e.g. those using Microsoft BASIC) which allows editing of the program line specified by the EDIT command. It is similar to the RUN and LIST commands in that if no number follows it, the first program line is automatically implied---in some computers.

Test Program

```
10 REM 'EDIT' TEST PROGRAM
20 PRINT "CAN THIS PROGRAM BE
   MODIFIED"
30 PRINT "BY THE EDIT COMMAND?"
99 END
```

After loading this program, type EDIT 20 to determine if the computer has the EDIT feature. The computer should print the number 20 followed possibly by a cursor. This indicates the computer is in the EDIT mode and is ready to modify line 20.

The EDIT command may call up your editor, but you'll have to check the machine's manual to see how to perform the editing and get back into BASIC. Sometimes it's as easy as hitting the carriage return. Other times (especially on large multi-language time-sharing machines) it takes a whole series of commands to get in and out of the "editor".

Variations In Usage

There are many versions of text, character and line editors. Each speaks its own "language," and it is not BASIC. *The BASIC Handbook* will therefore not cover Editor languages.

ELSE is used to execute an alternate statement when the condition of an IF-THEN statement is not met. For example, IF X=3 THEN 100 ELSE STOP instructs the computer to branch to line 100 if X equals 3, but STOP if X does not equal 3.

Test Program

```
10 REM 'ELSE' TEST PROGRAM
20 X=1
30 IF X < 5 THEN 60 ELSE GOTO 90
40 PRINT "ELSE FAILED THE TEST"
50 GOTO 99
60 PRINT X;
70 X=X+1
80 GOTO 30
90 PRINT "'ELSE' PASSED THE TEST"
99 END
```

Sample Run

```
1  2  3  4  'ELSE' PASSED THE TEST
```

IF YOUR COMPUTER DOESN'T HAVE IT

If your computer does not have the ELSE statement, it can be simulated in the test program by changing line 30 to

```
30 IF X < 5 THEN 60
```

and adding the following new line.

```
35 GOTO 90
```

Variations In Usage

None known.

Also See

```
IF-THEN, GOTO
```

Statement

A N S I

E.

The END statement is used to terminate execution of the program. Many computers require it to be placed at the highest line number in the program, while others accept it at any point.

The END statement is optional with many computers (mostly micros).

Test Program

```
10 REM 'END' TEST PROGRAM
20 PRINT "THE FIRST END STATEMENT FOLLOWS"
30 END
40 PRINT "THE SECOND END STATEMENT FOLLOWS"
99 END
```

Sample Run

```
THE FIRST END STATEMENT FOLLOWS
```

If your computer does not pass this test and will not allow an END statement at line 30, delete line 30 and run the program again.

Then delete line 99 to see if your computer accepts END as an **optional** statement.

Alternate Spelling

E. is used by TRS-80 Level I and other computers with Tiny BASIC as an abbreviation for END.

Also See

STOP (for the many problems encountered when using END and STOP in the same program).

EQ is used in a few computers (e.g. the T.I. 990) as an optional word for the equal sign when used as a relational operator. (See Line 30.) It cannot be used to assign a value to a variable. That's why Line 20 uses an = sign.

For more information see =.

Test Program

```
10 REM 'EQ (EQUAL)' TEST PROGRAM
20 A=10
30 IF A EQ 10 THEN 60
40 PRINT "THE EQ OPERATOR FAILED THE TEST"
50 GOTO 99
60 PRINT "THE EQ OPERATOR PASSED THE TEST"
99 END
```

Sample Run

```
THE EQ OPERATOR PASSED THE TEST
```

Variations In Usage

None known.

Also See

=, <>, IF-THEN, GE, GT, LE, LT, NE, <, >, <= and >=

ERASE is a command used to delete a program from memory. It is the equivalent of NEW or SCRATCH used by other computers. To test ERASE on your computer, enter a short program, such as

```
10 REM THIS IS A SHORT PROGRAM
99 END
```

Type LIST to see that the program is there.

Type ERASE, then type LIST again. If ERASE did the job, the program should be gone.

Some interpreters (e.g. BASIC-80) use ERASE as a statement to remove an array from a program and release the storage space it used. By using ERASE within a program, an array can be redimensioned while the program is RUNning, a procedure prohibited by most interpreters and compilers.

Some computers allow redimensioning of arrays without this statement, but most give an error message if the same array name appears in two DIM statements.

Test Program

```
10 REM 'ERASE' TEST PROGRAM
20 DIM A(15)
30 FOR I=1 TO 15
40 A(I) =I
50 NEXT I
60 ERASE A
70 PRINT "ERASE PASSED THE TEST IF 0 =";A(1)
80 DIM A(5,5)
90 A(5,5)=2
100 PRINT "ERASE PASSED";A(5,5);" TESTS."
999 END
```

Sample Run

```
ERASE PASSED THE TEST IF 0 = 0
ERASE PASSED 2 TESTS.
```

Also See

NEW, SCRATCH, DIM, LIST

The ERL function is used with the ON-ERROR statement to identify the last line number in which an error has occurred.

ERRL

The ERL function initializes at the numeric line number value of 65535 (the maximum two-byte value). When an error occurs, ERL changes to the line number in which the error occurred. The line number contained in the ERL function changes each time an error occurs in a different line.

By using ERL in "error-trapping" routines, it is possible to identify the "errored" line and take appropriate action.

Test Program

```
10 REM 'ERL' TEST PROGRAM
20 ON ERROR GOTO 100
30 PRINT "ENTER THE NUMBER 10, 20, THEN 30";
40 INPUT N
50 A=10/(N-10)
60 A=10/(N-20)
70 A=10/(N-30)
80 PRINT "THE NUMBER ";N;"DID NOT CAUSE AN ERROR"
90 GOTO 30
100 PRINT "AN ERROR HAS JUST OCCURRED IN LINE"; ERL
110 RESUME 30
999 END
```

Sample Run

```
ENTER THE NUMBER 10, 20, THEN 30? 10
AN ERROR HAS JUST OCCURRED IN LINE 50
ENTER THE NUMBER 10, 20, THEN 30? 20
AN ERROR HAS JUST OCCURRED IN LINE 60
ENTER THE NUMBER 10, 20, THEN 30? 30
AN ERROR HAS JUST OCCURRED IN LINE 70
ENTER THE NUMBER 10, 20, THEN 30?
```

Alternate Spelling

Hewlett-Packard's 35, 45, and 85 computers use ERRL.

Variations In Usage

None known.

Also See

ERROR, ON-ERROR-GOTO, RESUME

Function

ERRN

ERR is used in some computers (e.g. those with Microsoft BASIC) to identify the error code of the last error which occurred in a program. The error code contained in the ERR function changes each time a different error occurs. By using ERR in "error-trapping" routines, it is possible to identify the type of error which occurred and take appropriate action. Refer to the computer's manual for a listing of its particular error codes.

Test Program

```
10 REM 'ERR' TEST PROGRAM
20 DIM A(5)
30 CLEAR
40 ON ERROR GOTO 100
50 PRINT "ENTER A SAMPLE NUMBER";
60 INPUT N
70 A(N)=10/N
80 PRINT "THE NUMBER";N;"DID NOT CAUSE AN ERROR"
90 GOTO 50
100 IF ERR = 9 THEN 130
110 IF ERR = 11 THEN 160
120 GOTO 180
130 PRINT "THE NUMBER";N;"IS TOO LARGE"
140 PRINT "USE A NUMBER BETWEEN 1 AND 5"
150 RESUME 30
160 PRINT "THE SMALLEST NUMBER ALLOWED IS 1"
170 RESUME 30
180 PRINT "THE NUMBER";N;"CAUSED AN ERROR CODE OF";ERR
999 END
```

Sample Run *(Typical)*

```
ENTER A SAMPLE NUMBER? 12
THE NUMBER 12 IS TOO LARGE
USE A NUMBER BETWEEN 1 AND 5
ENTER A SAMPLE NUMBER? 0
THE SMALLEST NUMBER ALLOWED IS 1
THE NUMBER 1 DID NOT CAUSE AN ERROR
ENTER A SAMPLE NUMBER?
```

Alternate Spelling

Hewlett-Packard's 35, 45, and 85 computers use ERRN.

Variations In Usage

The TRS-80 Level II BASIC stores a value in the ERR function that does not equal the actual error code. To convert the value stored in the ERR function to the actual error code, divide the ERR value by 2 and add 1.

For example, `PRINT ERR/2+1`

Also See

`ERL, ON-ERROR, RESUME, DIM, CLEAR`

ERROR

ERROR ## is used to intentionally cause the computer to report an ERROR. The nature of the error is specified by an error code in the ERROR statement. The ERROR statement is commonly used in programs to execute error trapping routines, or to print a specified error message.

Test Program #1 *(for a Microsoft Interpreter)*

```
10 INPUT N
20 IF N > 32000 THEN ERROR 7
99 END
```

When a value greater than 32000 is assigned to variable N, the condition of the IF-THEN statement in line 20 is met and the computer generates the ERROR message.

```
OM ERROR IN 20
```

(out of memory in line 20), even though the computer is not actually out of memory.

Variables cannot be used as ERROR codes. Each code must be specified by an actual integer error code number. If the specified error code is not recognized by the computer's interpreter, then ERROR message "UNPRINTABLE ERROR" is printed by most computers.

ERROR can also be entered as a command to test specific error codes. See your computer's manual for a listing of its error messages.

Test Program #2

```
10 REM 'ERROR' TEST PROGRAM
20 PRINT "ERROR PASSED THE TEST IF ERROR MESSAGE 'OS' OR"
30 PRINT "'OUT OF STRING SPACE' IS PRINTED,"
40 ERROR 14
99 END
```

Sample Run *(typical)*

```
ERROR PASSED THE TEST IF ERROR MESSAGE 'OS' OR
'OUT OF STRING SPACE' IS PRINTED,
?OS ERROR IN 40
```

Variations In Usage

None known.

Also See

```
ON-ERROR-GOTO, RESUME, ERR, ERL
```

EXAM(*n*) is used by some computers (e.g. the Digital Group MAXI-BASIC, the North Star BASIC, and the Processor Technology 8K BASIC) to read the contents of specified addresses in the computer's memory.

For example, X=EXAM(200) assigns the value stored in memory address 200 to variable X.

The EXAM function gives us the contents of that memory address as a decimal between 0 and 255 (the range of values that can be held in an 8 bit memory byte). EXAM can be used with the FILL statement to read what FILL has stored in memory. (Some computers use POKE or STUFF.) The highest numbered address that can be EXAMined depends of course on the computer's memory size.

Check your computer's manual before executing this TEST PROGRAM to determine that memory addresses 18368 to 18380 are reserved as "free" memory. This avoids FILLing data into memory addresses reserved for other computer operations. If addresses 18368 to 18380 are not reserved as free memory in your computer, select a group of 12 adjacent memory addresses and change lines 20 and 60 in the TEST PROGRAM accordingly.

Test Program

```
10 REM 'EXAM' TEST PROGRAM
20 FOR X=18368 TO 18380
30 READ Y
40 FILL X,Y
50 NEXT X
60 FOR X=18368 TO 18380
70 Y=EXAM(X)
80 PRINT CHR$(Y);
90 NEXT X
100 DATA 84,69,83,84,128,67,79,77,80,76,69,84,69
999 END
```

Sample Run

```
TEST COMPLETE
```

Variations In Usage

None known.

Also See

```
FILL, POKE, PEEK, USR, SYSTEM, STUFF, FETCH
```

Statement

EXCHANGE is a statement available in a few BASICs (e.g. TDL BASIC) that switches the values of two variables or array elements. For example, EXCHANGE A,B results in the original value of A being stored in B and the former value of B being stored in A. EXCHANGE is very useful for arranging values of an array in ascending or descending order.

Test Program

```
10 REM 'EXCHANGE' TEST PROGRAM
20 PRINT "ENTER TWO VALUES (SEPARATED BY COMMAS)"
30 INPUT A,B
40 IF A<=B THEN 60
50 EXCHANGE A,B
60 PRINT A;" IS LESS THAN OR EQUAL TO ";B
70 GOTO 20
99 END
```

Sample Run

```
ENTER TWO VALUES (SEPARATED BY COMMAS)
? 3,7
3 IS LESS THAN OR EQUAL TO 7
ENTER TWO VALUES (SEPARATED BY COMMAS)
? 9,1
1 IS LESS THAN OR EQUAL TO 9
ENTER TWO VALUES (SEPARATED BY COMMAS)
?
```

MAXBASIC uses a double equal sign (= =) to exchange the contents of two variables of the same type. For example, 50 A == B is equivalent to line 50 of the TEST PROGRAM.

IF YOUR COMPUTER DOESN'T HAVE IT

If EXCHANGE doesn't work with your computer, try SWAP in line 50. If neither is available, the values can be exchanged by replacing line 50 with:

```
48 T=A
50 A=B
52 B=T
```

Also See

SWAP

EXIT is a statement used by some BASICs (e.g. North Star BASIC) to EXIT from a FOR-NEXT loop before that loop has completed the specified number of cycles. EXIT transfers program control to the line number designated and cancels the FOR-NEXT loop. The value of the loop counter at that time continues available for use in the rest of the program.

Test Program

```
10 REM 'EXIT' TEST PROGRAM
20 PRINT "ENTER A WORD - TYPE 'DONE' TO QUIT"
30 FOR I=1 TO 500
40 INPUT A$
50 IF A$="DONE" THEN EXIT 100
60 PRINT "ANOTHER";
70 NEXT I
80 PRINT "'EXIT' FAILED THE TEST."
90 GOTO 999
100 PRINT "'EXIT' PASSED THE TEST. 'DONE' WAS WORD
    NUMBER", I
999 END
```

Sample Run *(typical)*

```
ENTER A WORD - TYPE 'DONE' TO QUIT
?START
ANOTHER ?CHECK
ANOTHER ?EXIT
ANOTHER ?HERE
ANOTHER ?DONE
'EXIT' PASSED THE TEST. 'DONE' WAS WORD NUMBER 5
```

IF YOUR COMPUTER DOESN'T HAVE IT

GOTO can replace EXIT in most cases. Some computers will not know which loop is active if another FOR I= etc. follows the loop just EXITed in this way. In those computers, replace line 50 with:

```
50 IF A$<>"DONE" THEN 60
52 J = I   'J STORES THE CURRENT VALUE OF THE LOOP
    COUNTER
54 I = 999 'SET I TO A VALUE ABOVE THE LIMIT OF THE
    LOOP
56 GOTO 70
```

and add lines 75 and 95

```
75 IF I=999 THEN 95
95 I=J
```

These lines let the loop terminate "normally" before going on to the rest of the program.

Also See

FOR, NEXT, GOTO

The EXP(*n*) function computes the natural logarithm's base value e (2.718282...) raised to the power of (*n*).

This is just the opposite of what happens when the LOG function is used.

For example, A = EXP (3) is the same as A = 2.718282 * 2.718282 * 2.718282.

The value (*n*) can be written as a number or a numeric variable.

Test Program

```
10 REM 'EXP' TEST PROGRAM
20 N=4.60517
30 E=EXP(N)
40 PRINT "IF THE NATURAL EXPONENTIAL OF";N;"IS";E
50 PRINT "THEN THE EXP FUNCTION PASSED THE TEST."
30999 END
```

Sample Run

```
IF THE NATURAL EXPONENTIAL OF 4.60517 IS 100
THEN THE EXP FUNCTION PASSED THE TEST.
```

IF YOUR COMPUTER DOESN'T HAVE IT

If your interpreter did not accept the EXP function, substitute the following subroutine for EXP:

```
30000 GOTO 30999
30200 REM * EXPONENTIAL SUBROUTINE * INPUT X, OUTPUT E
30202 REM ALSO USES A, B AND L INTERNALLY
30204 L=INT (1.4427*X)+1
30206 IF ABS(L)<127 THEN 30218
30208 IF X<=0 THEN 30214
30210 PRINTX; "IS OUT OF RANGE"
30212 STOP
30214 E=0
30216 RETURN
30218 E=.693147*L-X
30220 B=X
30222 A=1.32988E-3-1.41316E-4*E
30224 A=((A*E-8.30136E-3)*E+4.16574E-2)*E
30226 E=(((A-.166665)*E+.5)*E-1)*E+1
30228 A=2
30230 IF L>0 THEN 30238
30232 A=.5
30234 L=-L
30236 IF L=0 THEN 30244
```

```
30238 FOR X=1 TO L
30240 E=A*E
30242 NEXT X
30244 X=B
30246 RETURN
```

To use this subroutine with the TEST PROGRAM, make the following program changes:

```
25 X=N
30 GOSUB 30204
```

Also See

```
LOG, LOG10, CLG
```

FETCH(*n*) is used in the Digital Group Opus 1 and Opus 2 BASIC to read the contents of addresses in the computer's memory.

For example, X=FETCH(3000) assigns the decimal value stored in memory address 3000 to the variable X.

That value will be a number between 0 and 255 (the range of values that can be held in an 8 bit memory byte). The highest numbered address that can be FETCHed depends of course on the computer's memory size.

FETCH can be used with the STUFF statement to check what STUFF has stored in memory. (Some computers use POKE or FILL instead.)

Check your computer's manual before executing this TEST PROGRAM to determine that memory addresses 18368 to 18377 are reserved as free memory. This avoids STUFFing data into memory reserved for special purposes. If addresses 18368 to 18377 are not reserved as free memory in your computer, then select a group of 10 free consecutive memory addresses and change lines 30 and 70 in the TEST PROGRAM accordingly.

Test Program

```
10 REM 'FETCH' TEST PROGRAM
20 Y=1
30 FOR X=18368 TO 18377
40 STUFF X,Y
50 Y=Y+1
60 NEXT X
70 FOR X=18368 TO 18377
80 Y=FETCH(X)
90 PRINT Y;
100 NEXT X
110 PRINT
120 PRINT "'FETCH' PASSED THE TEST IF #1 THRU #10
    ARE PRINTED"
999 END
```

Sample Run

```
1  2  3  4  5  6  7  8  9  10
'FETCH' PASSED THE TEST IF #1 THRU #10 ARE PRINTED
```

Variations In Usage

None known.

Also See

STUFF, POKE, PEEK, FILL, USR, SYSTEM, EXAM

FILL is used by a few interpreters (e.g. the NORTH STAR BASIC and the Digital Group MAXI-BASIC) to assign a specified byte in the computer's memory an integer value between 0 and 255 (the maximum 8 bit value).

For example, FILL 3000,15 "fills-in" memory address 3000 with the decimal number 15.

The EXAM function can be used to inspect what FILL has placed into memory. (Some computers use PEEK or FETCH instead.)

Computers vary in the amount of available memory and memory addresses that can be FILLed without erasing memory dedicated to other purposes. Check your computer's manual before running this TEST PROGRAM to determine that memory addresses 18368 to 18380 are noncritical memory locations.

Test Program

```
10 REM 'FILL' TEST PROGRAM
20 FOR X=18368 TO 18380
30 READ Y
40 FILL X,Y
50 NEXT X
60 FOR X=18368 TO 18380
70 Y=EXAM(X)
80 PRINT CHR$(Y);
90 NEXT X
100 DATA 84,69,83,84,128,67,79,77,80,76,69,84,69
999 END
```

Sample Run

```
TEST COMPLETE
```

Variations In Usage

None known.

Also See

POKE, STUFF, EXAM, PEEK, FETCH, USR, SYSTEM

Function

The FIX function is used to remove all numbers to the right of the decimal point. Its operation is similar to the INT function except FIX does not round negative numbers down.

Example:
```
10 PRINT FIX(3.6)
20 PRINT FIX(-3.6)
```

prints the numbers 3 and -3. While

```
10 PRINT INT(3.6)
20 PRINT INT(-3.6)
```

prints the numbers 3 and -4.

FIX is capable of handling any number, large or small, within the limitations of the computer's interpreter.

Test Program

```
10 REM 'FIX' TEST PROGRAM
20 N=-12.3456
30 A=FIX(N)
40 PRINT "FIX PASSED THE TEST IF ";N;"IS CHANGED TO ";A
99 END
```

Sample Run

```
FIX PASSED THE TEST IF -12.3456 IS CHANGED TO -12
```

IF YOUR COMPUTER DOESN'T HAVE IT

If your interpreter does not have the FIX function capability, but has the ABS, INT and SGN functions, then line 30 in the TEST PROGRAM can be replaced with:

```
30 A=SGN(N)*INT(ABS(N))
```

Variations In Usage

None known.

Also See

```
INT, ABS, SGN
```

FLASH is used by the APPLE II as either a command or a statement to put the screen in its FLASHing mode. In this mode, all output from the computer is displayed alternately as white characters on black background and then as black characters on white background.

To restore the display to its non-flashing, normal mode, type NORMAL.

Test Program

```
10 REM 'FLASH' TEST PROGRAM
20 FLASH
30 PRINT "THIS IS A FLASHY MESSAGE."
99 END
```

To run this program, clear the screen and type RUN.

Sample Run

THIS IS A FLASHY MESSAGE. (The screen should be flashing)

Variations In Usage

None known.

Also See

NORMAL, INVERSE

FLOW is a command used by Micropolis BASIC to activate a feature which prints program line numbers on the screen as each line is executed by the computer. It is used as a program trouble-shooting aid and is turned off by the word NOFLOW.

FLOW may be used within a program in conjunction with NOFLOW to trace only a desired section of the program.

Test Program

```
10 REM 'FLOW' TEST PROGRAM
20 PRINT "'FLOW' TRACES EACH LINE"
30 FLOW
40 GOTO 90
50 PRINT "UNTIL TURNED OFF BY"
60 NOFLOW
70 PRINT "THE 'NOFLOW' STATEMENT"
80 GOTO 110
90 PRINT "THAT FOLLOWS THE 'FLOW' STATEMENT"
100 GOTO 50
110 PRINT "AS ILLUSTRATED BY THIS LINE"
999 END
```

Sample Run

```
'FLOW' TRACES EACH LINE
<40> <90> THAT FOLLOWS THE 'FLOW' STATEMENT
<100> <50> UNTIL TURNED OFF BY
<60> THE 'NOFLOW' STATEMENT
AS ILLUSTRATED BY THIS LINE
```

Variations In Usage

None known.

Also See

NOFLOW, TRACE, TRACE ON, TRON

The FMT function is used in some BASICs (e.g. Micropolis BASIC) to format the output of a PRINT statement. It bears a vague resemblance to PRINT USING, and is somewhat similar to formatting as used in the FORTRAN computer language.

FMT

FMT expresses the format of the numeric that is to be printed in a string expression. The string expression must be enclosed in quotes.

The following are valid characters for the string expression:

9   Each 9 determines the position of one digit in the output field. If a 5-digit number is to be printed, five 9's can be used in the string expression ("99999"). If a number has fewer digits than are specified by FMT, the left most positions are printed as zeros.

Z   Z can be used in place of 9 as above. Leading zeros are suppressed (replaced by blanks) if Z is used.

V   V aligns the decimal points. It doesn't cause a decimal point to be printed, however, and does not allocate an additional print position.

$ If $ is used to the left of Z or 9, a $ is printed in front of the number. Two or more $ give a "floating" $ result, i.e., the $ is printed in the position immediately to the left of the first digit of the number.

*   An * is printed wherever a leading zero might occur. If both * and $ are used the $ should be placed to the left of * (just the opposite of PRINT USING).

.(period) A period is printed only if a period is present in the string expression.

,(comma) Commas may be used to indicate inclusion of commas in the printed value. Commas that would occur ahead of the first digit are not printed.

Any character string that can't be interpreted as one of the above will be printed as text. Therefore, labeled values can be formatted with the FMT function.

If the field is too small to handle the numeric value, question marks (?) are printed at every position in the field, including any text positions.

FMT always truncates (i.e. chops) trailing digits for which no provision has been made by the formatting expression.

Test Program

```
10 REM 'FMT' TEST PROGRAM
20 PRINT FMT(2401,"999999")
99 END
```

Sample Run

```
002401
```

Other examples:

Statement	Result

```
20 PRINT FMT(-2401,"999999")                                    0-2401
20 PRINT FMT(2401,"ZZZZ99")                                       2401
20 PRINT FMT(123.456,"ZZZZV99")                                  12345
20 PRINT FMT(123.456,"ZZZZV.99")                                123.45
20 PRINT FMT(12345,"Z,ZZZ,ZZZ")                                 12,345
20 PRINT FMT(1000000,"THIS BOOK IS WORTH $$$,$$$,$$$")
                            THIS BOOK IS WORTH $1,000,000
20 PRINT FMT(123,"*****99")                                    ****123
```

Variations In Usage

FMT is used as a statement (Honeywell) to format a print line similar to an IMAGE statement. The PRINT statement that uses this format line must contain the line number of FMT as the first item following the word PRINT.

For example:

```
180 PRINT, 190, X, T
190 FMT F6.2, X6, E12.5
```

The F6.2, X6 and E12.5 tell the computer how and where to print the values of X and T.

F   indicates that the value is to be printed with a decimal point. The first number (6) tells the width of the field (i.e. the maximum number of characters to be printed including sign, if any, and the decimal point) and the second (2) tells the number of digits to be included to the right of the decimal.

E   signals exponential form (Example: $1.385E+05$). The first number again is the width of the field but the second number states the number of significant digits to be printed (whole number and fraction combined).

Xn says skip the number of places indicated by the number n. In our example, six spaces will appear in the print line separating the values of X and T.

IF YOUR COMPUTER DOESN'T HAVE IT

If your computer doesn't have FMT in either form, you should try PRINT USING. The PRINT USING equivalent of "ZZZZV.99" is "####.##". E12.5 can be changed to "##.#####^^^^", etc.

Also See

```
PRINT USING, IMAGE
```

Function

FN is a function that allows a "user-defined" process to be used as if it were a built-in function. The user-defined function is named by a letter following FN and accompanied by one or more values enclosed in parentheses, such as FNA(X,N).

The DEF statement defines the process that will be executed when FN is used later.

For example:

```
10 DEF FNA(X)=1/X
20 PRINT FNA(N)
```

The FN function in this example is named "A"(FNA), and is defined in line 10 as the function 1/X. FNA is used here to compute the reciprocal of any numerical expression (except one having a value of zero, of course).

The numeric variable (N) following FNA is substituted for the "dummy variable" (X in this example) in the DEF statement each time FNA is executed. Any valid numeric variable or expression can be used in place of N.

Test Program

```
10 REM 'FN' TEST PROGRAM
20 DEF FNX(A) = (A-32)*.5555555
30 PRINT "ENTER A TEMPERATURE IN FAHRENHEIT DEGREES";
40 INPUT F
50 C = FNX(F)
60 PRINT F;"DEGREES FAHRENHEIT =";C;"DEGREES CELSIUS."
99 END
```

Sample Run *(using 70)*

```
ENTER A TEMPERATURE IN FAHRENHEIT DEGREES? 70
 70 DEGREES FAHRENHEIT = 21.1111 DEGREES CELSIUS.
```

Variations In Usage

Some BASICs (e.g. DEC BASIC-PLUS) allow FN to be defined as a function acting on strings.

Example: `DEF FNP$(A$,N) = RIGHT$(STRING$(N," ")+A$,N)`

can be used to "pad" a string of characters with leading blanks to cause it to have length N.

IF YOUR COMPUTER DOESN'T HAVE IT

If your computer doesn't allow you to define functions this way, you will have to write the desired function in each program line where it is needed.

Also See

DEF , FNEND

Statement

The FNEND statement is used in computers which have the capability of DEFining and reDEFining a function at different points throughout a program. It ENDs the function's DEFining process.

Each DEF statement which is spread out over more than one line must end with a FNEND statement, and the computer cannot branch out of or into these DEF statements before the FNEND statement is executed.

Test Program

```
10 REM 'FNEND' TEST PROGRAM
20 PRINT "ENTER A VALUE FOR X THAT IS
   GREATER OR LESS THAN 10";
30 INPUT X
40 DEF FNA(X)
50 FNA=X*2
60 IF X<10 THEN 80
70 FNA=X/2
80 FNEND
90 PRINT "THE NEW VALUE FOR X IS";FNA(X)
999 END
```

Sample Run *(using 6)*

```
ENTER A VALUE FOR X THAT IS GREATER OR LESS THAN 10? 6
THE NEW VALUE FOR X IS 12
```

Variations In Usage

None known.

Also See

DEF, FN

The FOR statement is part of a FOR-TO-NEXT statement and is used to assign numbers to numeric variables within the range specified by FOR-TO.

FOR

A N S I

F.

The first number immediately following the FOR is incremented by 1 each time its corresponding NEXT statement is executed. When the number following TO is exceeded, program execution continues at the line following the corresponding NEXT statement.

Test Program

```
10 REM 'FOR' TEST PROGRAM
20 FOR X=1 TO 5
30 PRINT X;
40 NEXT X
50 PRINT "THE 'FOR' STATEMENT PASSED THE TEST"
99 END
```

Sample Run

```
 1  2  3  4  5 THE 'FOR' STATEMENT PASSED THE TEST
```

Some computers use the STEP statement to increment FOR-TO-NEXT by a value other than one, and to allow decrementing (changing numbers in descending order).

For more information see STEP.

Alternate Spelling

Some computers (e.g. ACORN and TRS-80 Level I) allow F. to be used in place of FOR.

IF YOUR COMPUTER DOESN'T HAVE IT

If your computer doesn't accept the FOR statement, you can use a counting loop to replace it. Replace lines 20 and 40 with

```
20 X=1
35 X=X+1
40 IF X<=5 THEN 30
```

Variations In Usage

Some computers (e.g. DEC BASIC-PLUS-2), under specific conditions allow a FOR-TO with the NEXT only implied, not actually written.

Example:

```
10 PRINT X,SQR(X) FOR X=1 TO 12
```

prints a table of values for the numbers 1 to 12 and their square roots.

Also See

```
NEXT, STEP
```

The FRAC function is used by some BASICs (e.g. Micropolis BASIC) to isolate the fractional part of a number along with its proper sign. For example, 30 F = FRAC(-12.345) gives F the value -0.345.

Test Program

```
10 REM 'FRAC' TEST PROGRAM
20 N = -12.5
30 F = FRAC(N)
40 PRINT "FRAC PASSED THE TEST IF -0.5 ="; F
99 END
```

Sample Run

```
FRAC PASSED THE TEST IF -0.5 = -0.5
```

IF YOUR COMPUTER DOESN'T HAVE IT

If FRAC didn't pass the test, replace line 30 with

```
30 F = N - SGN(N)*INT(ABS(N))
```

and RUN the Test Program again.

Also See

```
INT, FIX
```

Function

FREE

The FRE(string) function is used to report the numer of bytes of total string space allocated but unused in the computer's memory. Any character (enclosed in quotes) or string variable can be used with the FRE function. The B$ in line 50 below is completely arbitrary.

Most computers with FRE capability automatically reserve 50 bytes of string space when the computer is turned on.

Test Program #1

```
10 REM 'FRE(STRING)' TEST PROGRAM
20 PRINT "ENTER ANY COMBINATION OF LETTERS AND NUMBERS";
30 INPUT A$
40 PRINT "THE AMOUNT OF UNUSED STRING SPACE=";
50 PRINT FRE(B$)
99 END
```

Sample Run *(Typical, using COMPUTER)*

```
ENTER ANY COMBINATION OF LETTERS AND NUMBERS? COMPUTER
THE AMOUNT OF UNUSED STRING SPACE = 42
```

Try various combinations of letters and numbers in the test program to demonstrate the action of the FRE function.

Some computers use numbers or numeric variables in the FRE function to report the **total** amount of memory remaining (not just that part reserved for strings), similar to the MEM statement.

Test Program #2

```
10 REM 'FRE(MEMORY)' TEST PROGRAM
20 PRINT FRE(N);"BYTES OF MEMORY REMAIN."
99 END
```

Sample Run

```
13504 BYTES OF MEMORY REMAIN.
```

The amount of memory remaining will depend on the memory size of your computer.

Typing NEW usually resets all String (and Numeric) variables back to null (and zero), so the full memory is again available.

Alternate Spelling

A number of BASICs, among them North Star, Processor Technology and Digital Group MAXI-BASIC, use FREE(0) to report the total amount of memory remaining. Try FREE(0) in line 20 of Test Program #2 to see if your computer accepts it.

Variations In Usage

None known.

Also See

MEM, CLEAR, $, NEW

Operator

GE

GE is used in some computers (e.g. the TI 990) as an abbreviation for the "greater than or equal to" sign ($>=$).

For more information see $>=$.

Test Program

```
10 REM 'GE' (GREATER THAN OR EQUAL TO) TEST PROGRAM
20 IF 20 GE 10 THEN 50
30 PRINT "THE GE OPERATOR FAILED THE TEST IN LINE 20"
40 GOTO 99
50 IF 20 GE 20 THEN 80
60 PRINT "THE GE OPERATOR FAILED THE TEST IN LINE 50"
70 GOTO 99
80 PRINT "THE GE OPERATOR PASSED THE TEST"
99 END
```

Sample Run

```
THE GE OPERATOR PASSED THE TEST
```

Variations In Usage

None known.

Also See

```
>= , IF-THEN
```

GET is a statement used by some computers (e.g. PET and APPLE II) to accept a single character from the keyboard without displaying it on the screen and without waiting for the RETURN key to be pressed. Its use is similar to INKEY$.

With a numeric variable such as GET A, GET accepts only numeric input. A string variable (e.g. GET A$) will accept input from any key except the STOP key.

The GET statement in the APPLE II causes program execution to pause until a key is pressed. In the PET, GET scans the keyboard. If it finds no key pressed, it stores a null character and proceeds to the rest of the program. (See INKEY$ for more information.)

Test Program

```
10 REM 'GET' TEST PROGRAM
20 PRINT "TYPE IN ANY CHARACTER"
30 GET A$
40 IF A$="" THEN 30
50 PRINT "YOU JUST PRESSED THE ";A$;" KEY,"
60 PRINT "PRESS ";A$;" AGAIN TO CONTINUE,"
70 GET B$
80 IF B$=A$ THEN 20
90 GOTO 70
99 END
```

Sample Run (using X)

```
TYPE IN ANY CHARACTER
YOU JUST PRESSED THE X KEY,
PRESS X AGAIN TO CONTINUE,
```

Variations In Usage

Many computers (e.g. DEC PDP-11) use GET# to read a record from disk or tape.

Example: GET #2, REC%

READs information stored in record number REC% from file #2.

A few BASICs (e.g. NEC's N-BASIC, TRS-80 Extended Color BASIC, and Microsoft Level III BASIC) provide a GET@ which stores information displayed in a section on the screen. The X,Y locations of opposite corners of the boundary rectangle must be specified, plus the name of the array which will store it.

Example:

```
GET@(10,8)-(25,14),A%
```

saves, in array A%, characters and graphics symbols in columns 10 thru 25 on lines 8 thru 14. The information can be put back on the screen with a similar PUT@ statement.

GET is used by Hewlett-Packard BASICs to LOAD a program or data file from disk or tape. From example:

```
GET "PROG"
```

erases any program in memory and LOADs in PROG.

GET can also be used to APPEND a program segment to the end of an existing program by specifying the first number to be assigned to the program being loaded.

```
GET "SUB1", 500
```

will renumber program SUB1 as it is loaded into memory, starting with line 500. All lines of the existing program with line numbers smaller than 500 will be retained and will have the SUB1 program lines attached at the end.

IF YOUR COMPUTER DOESN'T HAVE IT

If your computer wasn't able to run the Test Program, it may use another word to accept a character from the keyboard. Try the Test Program using one of the following words in lines 30 and 70: INKEY$, KEY$, INCH, INCHAR, KEYIN.

Also See

```
INKEY$, KEY$, PUT, APPEND, #
```

GO is used as part of GO TO and GO SUB statements. GO usually has meaning only when combined with another BASIC word. Most computers don't care if there is a space after the GO, converting automatically to GOTO or GOSUB. Others (e.g. TRS-80 Level I) do not allow the space.

This program uses GO in the GO TO statement. For more information see GOTO.

Test Program #1

```
10 REM 'GO' TEST PROGRAM
20 PRINT "THE GO STATEMENT";
30 GO TO 60
40 PRINT "FAILED THE TEST"
50 GOTO 99
60 PRINT "PASSED THE TEST."
99 END
```

Sample Run

```
THE GO STATEMENT PASSED THE TEST.
```

This program uses GO in the GO SUB statement. For more information see GOSUB.

Test Program #2

```
10 REM 'GO' (USED WITH SUB) TEST PROGRAM
20 GO SUB 100
30 PRINT "PASSED THE TEST WHEN USED WITH SUB."
40 GO TO 999
100 REM SUBROUTINE
110 PRINT "THE GO STATEMENT";
120 RETURN
999 END
```

Sample Run

```
THE GO STATEMENT PASSED THE TEST WHEN USED WITH SUB.
```

Variations In Usage

GO is used by DATAPOINT as a short form of GOTO as a statement and as a direct command. As a command, GO n restarts the program at line n.

Also See

```
GOTO, GOSUB, IF-GOTO, ON-GOTO, GOTO-OF, ON-
GOSUB, GOSUB-OF, CONT
```

Statement

GOS.

GOSUB is used to branch out of a program's "mainstream" to a Subroutine. The GOSUB statement must be followed by a line number to indicate the first line of the subroutine to be executed.

A RETURN statement must be used at the end of a subroutine's execution to return control from the subroutine to the main program.

Test Program

```
10 REM 'GOSUB' TEST PROGRAM
20 GOSUB 100
30 PRINT "PASSED THE TEST AT LINE 20"
40 GOTO 999
100 REM SUBROUTINE
110 PRINT "THE GOSUB STATEMENT ";
120 RETURN
999 END
```

Sample Run

```
THE GOSUB STATEMENT PASSED THE TEST AT LINE 20
```

Some computers (e.g. Sinclair ZX-80 and the ACORN ATOM) allow variable expressions in the GOSUB statement. On such computers GOSUB N and even GOSUB N*10+100 are acceptable statements. N must be given a suitable value during the execution of the program. If N is a small integer, GOSUB N*10 gives a result similar to ON N GOSUB 10, 20, 30,... Insert these lines into the Test Program to test for this feature:

```
15 N=100
20 GOSUB N
```

and RUN the program.

Alternate Spelling

GOS. is used in various Tiny BASIC's as an abbreviation for GOSUB.

Variations In Usage

None known.

Also See

```
RETURN, ON-GOSUB, IF-GOSUB
```

146

GOSUB-OF is a multiple subroutine branching scheme similar to ON-GOSUB used by H-P and Tektronix computers.

For example, GOSUB X OF 1000,2000 causes the computer to branch to the subroutine at 1000 if X has a value of 1, and to 2000 if the value of X is 2.

Test Program

```
10 REM 'GOSUB-OF' TEST PROGRAM
20 PRINT "ENTER THE NUMBER 1, 2, OR 3";
30 INPUT X
40 PRINT "THE GOSUB-OF STATEMENT ";
50 GOSUB X OF 100, 200, 300
60 GOTO 20
100 REM SUBROUTINE #1
110 PRINT "BRANCHED TO SUBROUTINE #1"
120 RETURN
200 REM SUBROUTINE #2
210 PRINT "BRANCHED TO SUBROUTINE #2"
220 RETURN
300 REM SUBROUTINE #3
310 PRINT "BRANCHED TO SUBROUTINE #3"
320 RETURN
999 END
```

Sample Run

```
ENTER THE NUMBER 1, 2, OR 3? 1
THE GOSUB-OF STATEMENT BRANCHED TO SUBROUTINE #1
ENTER THE NUMBER 1, 2, OR 3? 2
THE GOSUB-OF STATEMENT BRANCHED TO SUBROUTINE #2
ENTER THE NUMBER 1, 2, OR 3? 3
THE GOSUB-OF STATEMENT BRANCHED TO SUBROUTINE #3
ENTER THE NUMBER 1, 2, OR 3?
```

Variations In Usage

None known.

Also See

ON-GOSUB, GOTO-OF, ON-GOTO

Statement

ANSI

GO TO
GOT
G.

The GOTO statement causes program execution to "jump" to a specified line number. Many computers also accept this statement as two words; GO TO.

Test Program

```
10 REM 'GOTO' STATEMENT TEST PROGRAM
20 PRINT "THE GOTO STATEMENT ";
30 GOTO 60
40 PRINT "FAILED,"
50 STOP
60 PRINT "HAS PASSED THE TEST,"
99 END
```

Sample Run

```
THE GOTO STATEMENT HAS PASSED THE TEST,
```

Some computers (e.g. Sinclair ZX-80, the ACORN ATOM and those using Micropolis BASIC) allow variable expressions in the GOTO statement. On those computers, statements such as GOTO N and even GOTO N*10 + 100 are acceptable. N must be given a suitable value during the execution of the program so that an existing line number is referenced. If N is a small integer, GOTO N*10 gives a result similar to ON N GOTO 10, 20, 30, . . . Insert the following lines into the Test Program to test this feature:

```
25 N=60
30 GOTO N
```

and RUN the program.

Variations In Usage

GOTO is often used in conjunction with other key words.

Alternate Spellings

Try GOT and G. in line 30 of the test program to see if your computer accepts these abbreviations.

Also See

```
IF-GOTO, ON-GOTO, and GOTO-OF
```

GOTO-OF is used by some computers (e.g. Hewlett Packard and Tektronix) as a multiple branching tool which incorporates a number of IF-THEN tests into a single statement.

For example, GOTO X OF 100,200,300 instructs the computer to branch to lines 100, 200 or 300 if the integer value of X is 1, 2 or 3 respectively. If INT X is less than 1 or more than 3, the tests in this example all fail and execution defaults to the next program line. The INT value of X cannot exceed the number of possible branches in the statement.

Most computers accept both GO TO (two words) and GOTO (one word) while a few (e.g. the VARIAN 620) accept *only* the two words GO TO.

Test Program

```
10 REM 'GOTO-OF' TEST PROGRAM
20 X=2
30 GOTO X OF 40,60
40 PRINT "'GOTO-OF' FAILED THE TEST"
50 GOTO 99
60 PRINT "'GOTO-OF' PASSED THE TEST"
99 END
```

Sample Run

```
'GOTO-OF' PASSED THE TEST
```

Variations In Usage

None known.

Also See

```
ON-GOTO, ON-GOSUB, IF-THEN, INT, GOSUB-OF
```

GR is used in the APPLE II BASIC as both a command and a program statement to change the computer's operation from the TEXT mode to the GRaphics mode. GR must be executed before using the special graphics statements PLOT, HLIN-AT and VLIN-AT.

GR can also be used to clear the screen before starting a new graphics display. Each time GR is executed, the computer erases the entire screen.

Test Program

```
10 REM 'GR' TEST PROGRAM
20 GR
30 COLOR=6
40 HLIN 0,39 AT 20
50 END
```

Sample Run

If the computer accepted the GR statement, a blue horizontal line should appear across the screen.

Variations In Usage

None known.

Also See

```
TEXT, COLOR, HLIN-AT, VLIN-AT, PLOT, CLS
```

GT is used in some computers (e.g. the TI 990) as an alternate word for the "greater-than" sign (>).

For more information see >.

Test Program

```
10 REM 'GT (GREATER THAN)' TEST
   PROGRAM
20 IF 10 GT 5 THEN 50
30 PRINT "THE GT OPERATOR FAILED
   THE TEST"
40 GOTO 99
50 PRINT "THE GT OPERATOR PASSED THE TEST"
99 END
```

Sample Run

```
THE GT OPERATOR PASSED THE TEST
```

Variations In Usage

None known.

Also See

>, IF-THEN, >=, <, <=, =, <>, EQ, GE, LE, LT, NE

GRAD is used in a few computers (e.g. Sharp/TRS-80 Pocket Computer and Tektronix 4050 Series) to make them calculate in GRADs instead of radians. (100 grads = 90 degrees) Most computers are in the radian mode when powered up, but some also have the capability of calculating trigonometric functions in degrees and a few can use grads.

Test Program

```
10 REM 'GRAD' TEST PROGRAM
20 R = SIN(40)
30 PRINT "THE SINE OF 40 RADIANS IS";R
40 GRAD
50 G = SIN(40)
60 PRINT "THE SINE OF 40 GRADS IS";G
99 END
```

Sample Run

```
THE SINE OF 40 RADIANS IS 0.745113
THE SINE OF 40 GRADS IS 0.587785
```

Also See

RAD, DEG, ACS, ASN, ATN, COS, SIN, TAN

HLIN-AT is used in APPLE II BASIC as a special feature to display a **H**orizontal **LIN**e **AT** a specified row on the screen.

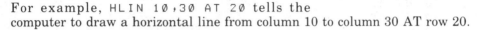

The horizontal line length is determined by two numbers following the HLIN statement. These numbers indicate the bounds between which the line will extend. The line may extend any length between columns 0 to 39.

The number following AT represents the row number which the line must occupy. This number may range from 0 to 39.

For example, HLIN 10,30 AT 20 tells the computer to draw a horizontal line from column 10 to column 30 AT row 20.

The **GR**aphics statement must be executed before the computer can accept the HLIN-AT statement (see GR). The line's color is determined by the COLOR statement (see COLOR).

Test Program

```
10 REM 'HLIN-AT' TEST PROGRAM
20 GR
30 Y=0
40 FOR X=0 TO 39
50 COLOR = Y
60 HLIN 0,39 AT X
70 Y=Y+1
80 IF Y < 16 THEN 100
90 Y=0
100 NEXT X
999 END
```

Sample Run

If the computer accepted the HLIN-AT statement, the screen should be filled with 39 horizontal lines of various colors.

APF BASIC does not use AT in its HLIN statement. A comma is used instead. The shape and color to be used are declared in the SHAPE and COLOR statements prior to using HLIN.

Variations In Usage

None known.

Also See

GR, COLOR, PLOT, VLIN-AT, TEXT

HOME is a command used to clear the screen and position the cursor in the upper left corner. It is similar to CLS found on other computers.

HOME can also be included as a program statement to clear the screen before the program creates a graphics display.

Test Program

```
10 REM 'HOME' TEST PROGRAM
20 FOR I=1 TO 12
30 PRINT "THIS NEEDS TO BE ERASED"
40 NEXT I
50 HOME
60 PRINT "HOME PASSED IF THIS IS ALL THAT IS DISPLAYED"
99 END
```

Sample Run

```
HOME PASSED IF THIS IS ALL THAT IS DISPLAYED
```

Also See

CLS

A
N
S
I

The IF statement is part of the conditional branching statements IF-THEN, IF-GOTO, IF-GOSUB, IF-LET, etc., and is used to indicate the variable to be tested by one of the relational operators (see $=$, $<$, $>$, $<=$, $>=$, $<>$).

For example: IF X=3 THEN 100 the computer branches or "jumps" to line 100 **IF** X equals 3. If the condition is not met (i.e. X ≠ 3), the test "falls through" and program execution continues on the next line.

These conditional IF-THEN tests must be placed **last** on multiple statement lines because the computer either branches to the indicated line number (if the test is true), or falls through to the next **numbered** line (if the test is false).

For example: 30 IF X=3 THEN 100:PRINT "X=3". The PRINT statement can never be executed.

Test Program

```
10 REM 'IF' TEST PROGRAM
20 X=10
30 IF X=10 THEN 60
40 PRINT "'IF' FAILED THE TEST"
50 GOTO 99
60 PRINT "'IF' PASSED THE TEST"
99 END
```

Sample Run

```
'IF' PASSED THE TEST
```

To further check the computer's IF capability, see the TEST PROGRAMS under IF-GOTO and IF-LET.

Variations In Usage

A few BASICs (e.g. DEC BASIC-PLUS-2) use IF as a modifier of most other statements.

For example: X=Y IF X<Y

The assignment statement X = Y will be executed only if the current value of X is smaller than the value of Y.

Also See

IF-THEN, IF-GOTO, IF-LET, ELSE

Statement

IF-G.
IF-GOT

IF-GOTO is a conditional branching statement using one of the relational operators (see =, <, >, <=, >=, <>).

When the condition of the IF-GOTO statement is met, the computer executes the branching statement GOTO.

For example, IF X=3 GOTO 100 tells the computer to branch or "jump" to line 100 if X equals 3. If the condition is not met (i.e. X ≠ 3), the test "falls through" and the program execution continues on the next line.

Test Program

```
10 REM 'IF-GOTO' TEST PROGRAM
20 X=30
30 IF X=30 GOTO 60
40 PRINT "THE IF-GOTO STATEMENT FAILED THE TEST"
50 GOTO 99
60 PRINT "THE IF-GOTO STATEMENT PASSED THE TEST"
99 END
```

Sample Run

```
THE IF-GOTO STATEMENT PASSED THE TEST
```

Alternate Spellings

Some computers allow IF-GOT (e.g. PDP-8E) or IF-G. (e.g. TRS-80 Level I) to be used as short forms of IF-GOTO.

Variations In Usage

Some interpreters allow the statement THEN to be used in place of GOTO. See IF-THEN.

Also See

GOTO, GOSUB, ELSE, IF-THEN, IF

The IF-LET statement is a conditional LET statement using one of the relational operators (see =, <, >, <=, >=, <>).

When the condition of the IF-LET statement is met, the computer assigns a value to the variable following LET.

Test Program

```
10 REM 'IF-LET' TEST PROGRAM
20 X=30
30 IF X>20 LET X=10
40 PRINT "X =";X
50 PRINT " 'IF-LET' PASSED THE TEST IF THE VALUE OF
   X IS 10"
99 END
```

Sample Run

```
X = 10
'IF-LET' PASSED THE TEST IF THE VALUE OF X IS 10
```

Variations In Usage

Computers are not uniform in their use of the LET statement. Most allow LET to be omitted while others allow the THEN statement in place of LET.

Most computers that allow IF-LET will allow almost any executable statement such as PRINT, READ, INPUT, GOSUB, another IF, etc.

Example:

Change 30 IF X>20 IF X<40 X=10

Also See

IF-THEN, LET, IF

157

Statement

ANSI

IF-THEN

IF-THE
IF-T.

The IF-THEN statement is a conditional branching statement using one of the relational operators (see $=$, $<$, $>$, $<=$, $>=$, $<>$).

When the condition of the IF-THEN statement is met, the computer executes the branching statement number following THEN. For example, IF X=3 THEN 100 tells the computer to branch or "jump" to line 100 if X equals 3. If the condition is not met (i.e. $X \neq 3$), the test "falls through" and program execution continues on the next line.

Test Program #1

```
10 REM 'IF-THEN' TEST PROGRAM
20 X=30
30 IF X=30 THEN 60
40 PRINT "THE IF-THEN STATEMENT FAILED THE TEST"
50 GOTO 99
60 PRINT "THE IF-THEN STATEMENT PASSED THE TEST IN
   LINE 30"
99 END
```

Sample Run

```
THE IF-THEN STATEMENT PASSED THE TEST IN LINE 30
```

Some computers allow math operations to be performed when the IF-THEN statement is satisfied. For example, IF A=3 THEN X=2*(A + 6)/3 calculates for the value of X if the variable A is equal to 3. If not, the test fails and execution proceeds to the next line.

To test this feature in your computer, add the following program lines:

```
70 IF X=30 THEN X=X+90
80 PRINT "X=";X
90 PRINT"IF-THEN PASSED THE TEST IN LINE 70 IF X=120"
```

Sample Run

```
THE IF-THEN STATEMENT PASSED THE TEST IN LINE 30
X=120
IF-THEN PASSED THE TEST IN LINE 70 IF X=120
```

Some interpreters allow any of the operating statements to be performed when the IF-THEN condition is met. For example, IF X=3 THEN END will stop program execution when the value of X equals 3.

Add the following line to the test program to check this capability:

```
100 IF X=120 THEN PRINT "IF-THEN PASSED THE TEST IN
    LINE 100"
```

Sample Run

```
THE IF-THEN STATEMENT PASSED THE TEST IN LINE 30
X=120
IF-THEN PASSED THE TEST IN LINE 70 IF X=120
IF-THEN PASSED THE TEST IN LINE 100
```

Computers are not uniform in their use of the THEN statement. Many allow THEN to be omitted when IF is followed directly by a math operator, operating statement, or branching statement.

Test Program #2

This program tests for three variations which imply (but do not use) THEN.

```
10 REM TEST PROGRAM WITH IMPLIED 'THEN' IN LINES 30,
   60 AND 999
20 X=30
30 IF X=30 GOTO 60
40 PRINT "LINE 30 FAILED THE TEST"
50 GOTO 999
60 IF X=30 GOSUB 100
70 GOTO 999
100 REM SUBROUTINE
110 PRINT "LINES 30 AND 60 PASSED THE TEST. DOES LINE
    999?"
120 RETURN
999 IF X=30 END
```

Sample Run

```
LINES 30 AND 60 PASSED THE TEST. DOES LINE 999?
```

Great caution must be used with interpreters which allow use of multiple statement lines. The "falling thru" of an IF-THEN test is to the **next line**, not the next statement on the same line. For this reason, IF-THEN tests are usually not followed by other statements on the same line. It's bad programming style.

For example: IF X=5 THEN X=X+Y:PRINT X. On most computers, the PRINT statement is not executed if the value of X does not equal 5.

Some computers accept a statement such as 50 IF X THEN 120. Such computers will transfer program control to line 120 when X contains a non-zero value and will execute the line following line 50 when X = 0.

Test Program #3

```
10 REM 'IF X THEN' TEST PROGRAM
20 PRINT "TYPE IN A NUMBER"
30 INPUT X
40 IF X THEN 70
50 PRINT "YOUR NUMBER WAS ZERO THAT TIME."
60 GOTO 20
70 PRINT "YOU ENTERED A NON-ZERO VALUE OF";X
80 GOTO 20
99 END
```

Sample Run

```
TYPE IN A NUMBER ? 4
YOU ENTERED A NON-ZERO VALUE OF 4
TYPE IN A NUMBER ? 0
YOUR NUMBER WAS ZERO THAT TIME.
TYPE IN A NUMBER ?
```

Alternate Spellings

Some computers allow IF-THE (e.g. PDP-8E) or IF-T. (e.g. TRS-80 Level I) to be used as short forms of IF-THEN.

Also See

```
IF, IF-GOTO, IF-LET, ELSE, GOTO, GOSUB, STOP, END
```

The IMAGE statement is used by some computers (e.g. Hewlett-Packard) to specify the print format to accompany a PRINT USING statement. For example:

```
110 IMAGE 6A, 2D, ":", 2D, ":", 2D
    .
    .
190 PRINT USING 110, "TIME: ", H, M, S
```

results in something like

```
TIME: 12:55:31
```

The format characters that can be used in an HP IMAGE statement are:

A   used once for each letter to be printed (a number may preceed A, e.g. 6A, to indicate the number of characters to be printed)

D   used once for each digit to be printed (a number may also preceed D)

E   used to indicate exponential format (example: 12345.67 printed with format D.4DE would be 1.2346E+04)

S   used to indicate a + or − sign is to be printed

X   used once for each blank to be printed (a number may also preceed X)

.(period)   used to indicate where a decimal point should be printed (3D.2D)

,(comma)   and / (slash) are used as format separators. The / also generates a new line.

()   used to repeat a group of format descriptions (example: 2(5D.2D, 3X, 4D) is the same as 5D.2D, 3X, 4D, 5D.2D, 3X, 4D)

+   suppresses the line feed at the end of the print line causing the next PRINT statement to print at the beginning of same line

−   suppresses the carriage return causing the next PRINT statement to print in the next position but one line down

suppresses both the carriage return and the line feed causing the next PRINT statement to print where the current line ends

String constants in quotes may be used anywhere in the IMAGE line.

Variations In Usage

None known.

Also See

FMT, :, PRINT USING

The INDEX tells us the starting position of the first character in a string which is part of a larger string. Position is counted from the left. For example:

```
INDEX("ABADABA","DAB") = 4
```

If it turns out that the small string is **not** part of the larger string, INDEX = 0.

Index is similar to INSTR as used on other computers.

Test Program

```
10 REM 'INDEX' TEST PROGRAM
20 A$ = "KEYBOARD"
30 B$ = "OAR"
40 K = INDEX(A$,B$)
50 IF K<>5 THEN 110
60 B$ = "ORE"
70 K = INDEX(A$,B$)
80 IF K<>0 THEN 110
90 PRINT "'INDEX' PASSED THE TEST"
100 GOTO 30999
110 PRINT "'INDEX' FAILED THE TEST"
30999 END
```

Sample Run

```
'INDEX' PASSED THE TEST
```

IF YOUR COMPUTER DOESN'T HAVE IT

If the Test Program failed try INSTR or POS in place of INDEX. If neither work on your computer, use the subroutine listed under INSTR (saves space not to duplicate it here).

To use the subroutine with this Test Program, make these program changes:

```
35 N = 1
40 GOSUB 30060
70 GOSUB 30060
```

Variations In Usage

None known.

Also See

```
INSTR, POS
```

Function

The INKEY$ function is used to read a character from the keyboard each time INKEY$ is executed. Unlike the INPUT statement, INKEY$ does not halt execution waiting for the ENTER key to be pressed. The computer just keeps "circling" until it receives a message from the keyboard. Until a key on the keyboard is pressed, INKEY$ simply reads an "empty" string (ASCII code of 0).

Since INKEY$ doesn't wait for you to enter a character from the keyboard and "ENTER", it usually is placed in a program loop to repeatedly scan the keyboard looking for a pressed key.

For example:

```
10 IF INKEY$="X" GOTO 100
20 GOTO 10
100 PRINT "YOU HIT 'X', DIDN'T YOU?"
110 GOTO 10
```

The INKEY$ function repeatedly looks for the letter X at the keyboard to meet the condition of the IF-THEN statement. When the letter X is entered, the condition of the IF-THEN statement is met and the computer branches to line 100.

Test Program

```
10 REM 'INKEY$' TEST PROGRAM
20 CLS
30 PRINT "PRESS ANY KEY ON THE KEYBOARD"
40 A$=INKEY$
50 IF A$="" GOTO 40
60 PRINT "YOU HAVE JUST PRESSED THE ";A$;" KEY"
70 PRINT: PRINT "PRESS THE ";A$;" KEY AGAIN TO START
   OVER"
80 IF INKEY$=A$ GOTO 20
90 GOTO 80
99 END
```

Sample Run *(using R)*

```
PRESS ANY KEY ON THE KEYBOARD
YOU HAVE JUST PRESSED THE R KEY

PRESS THE R KEY AGAIN TO START OVER
```

Variations In Usage

None known.

Also See

INPUT, IF-THEN, INPUT$, GET

Statement

INP stands for "INput from a Port".

The INP statement is used to read the decimal value of a byte of information at a specified computer port. The byte value can be any positive integer from 0 to 255.

For example: `PRINT INP(X)` prints the decimal value of the byte at port X.

INP is a useful tool to monitor ports for a specific condition, such as an input request from a remote peripheral device. Other applications might include reading temperatures from remote sensors on a solar hot water heating system, etc.

Test Program

```
10 REM 'INP' TEST PROGRAM
20 FOR X=0 TO 255
30 PRINT "THE DECIMAL VALUE OF THE BYTE AT PORT#";
40 PRINT X;"IS";INP(X)
50 NEXT X
99 END
```

Sample Run *(typical)*

```
THE DECIMAL VALUE OF THE BYTE AT PORT# 0 IS 255
                        .
                        .
                        .
THE DECIMAL VALUE OF THE BYTE AT PORT# 255 IS 127
```

Variation In Usage

INP is also used in versions of the PDP-8 as an abbreviation for the INPUT statement.

For more information see INPUT.

Also See

`OUT, PEEK, POKE, INPUT, PIN`

The INPUT statement allows the user to assign data to variables from the keyboard. When the computer executes an INPUT statement, it prints a question mark indicating it is waiting for you to assign a value to a variable. It will continue to wait until the ENTER (or RETURN) key is pressed.

INPUT

ANSI

IN.
I.

Test Program #1

```
10 REM 'INPUT' STATEMENT TEST PROGRAM
20 PRINT "ASSIGN A VALUE TO THE VARIABLE X"
30 INPUT X
40 PRINT "THE VALUE OF X IS";X
99 END
```

Sample Run *(using 10)*

```
ASSIGN A VALUE TO THE VARIABLE X
? 10
THE VALUE OF X IS 10
```

Alternate Spellings

Most Tiny BASICs as well as the ACORN computer allow IN. as an abbreviation for INPUT. TRS-80 Level I will also accept I., and some versions of the PDP-8 allow INP.

Variations In Usage

An increasingly common variation found in microcomputer interpreters allows INPUT to serve in both PRINT and INPUT capacities (thus conserving space).

Test Program #2

```
10 REM 'INPUT/PRINT' STATEMENT TEST PROGRAM
20 INPUT "ASSIGN A VALUE TO THE VARIABLE 'X'"; X
30 PRINT "THE VALUE OF X IS";X
99 END
```

Sample Run *(using 10)*

```
ASSIGN A VALUE TO THE VARIABLE 'X' ? 10
THE VALUE OF X IS 10
```

Note that no PRINT statement preceded the INPUT statement. Both functions were combined in line 20.

Also See

INPUT1, INKEY$, INP, INPUT$, PIN, LINEINPUT, INPUTLINE

INPUTLINE is similar to INPUT. It is used in TSC Extended BASIC and in PRIME BASIC/VM to accept an entire LINE of input and assigns it to a single string variable. INPUTLINE prompts the user (with a !) the same as INPUT. The string it "inputs" may include commas, colons and other special characters without the need for enclosing them in quotes.

INPUTLINE is similar to LINEINPUT. (See LINEINPUT for more information.)

Test Program

```
10 REM INPUTLINE TEST PROGRAM
20 PRINT "TYPE YOUR NAME - LAST, FIRST";
30 INPUTLINE N$
40 PRINT "HELLO, ";N$;", I'M COMPUTER, MICRO,"
99 END
```

Sample Run

```
TYPE YOUR NAME - LAST, FIRST ! DOE, JOHN
HELLO, DOE, JOHN, I'M COMPUTER, MICRO,
```

Also See

```
LINEINPUT, INPUT
```

Function

INPUT$(*n*) is a Microsoft BASIC function used to read a specified number of characters from the keyboard without displaying them on the screen. The ENTER or RETURN key does not have to be pressed after the last character is entered, but the correct number of characters must be typed before the program will proceed.

Example: Z$ = INPUT$(5) causes the program to pause while the user enters five characters.

Test Program

```
10 REM INPUT$() TEST PROGRAM
20 PRINT "TYPE IN ANY COMBINATION OF 3 CHARACTERS."
30 A$ = INPUT$(3)
40 PRINT "YOU JUST TYPED ";A$
99 END
```

Sample Run *(Typical)*

```
TYPE IN ANY COMBINATION OF 3 CHARACTERS.
YOU JUST TYPED QWE
```

Variations In Usage

None known.

Also See

INKEY$, KEY$, GET, INPUT

The INPUT1 statement is used by a few computers (e.g. North Star and Digital Group with Maxi-BASIC) in a manner similar to the INPUT statement, but INPUT1 stops the carriage return and line feed after the INPUT data has been assigned to a variable.

For more information see INPUT.

Test Program

```
10 REM 'INPUT1' TEST PROGRAM
20 PRINT "ENTER A VALUE FOR THE VARIABLE X"
30 INPUT1 X
40 PRINT " VARIABLE X=";X
50 PRINT "INPUT1 PASSED THE TEST IF THE WORDS
   VARIABLE X =";  X
60 PRINT "ARE PRINTED ON THE SAME LINE AS THE ? SIGN"
99 END
```

Sample Run *(using 10)*

```
ENTER A VALUE FOR THE VARIABLE X
? 10 VARIABLE X = 10
INPUT1 PASSED THE TEST IF THE WORDS VARIABLE X = 10
ARE PRINTED ON THE SAME LINE AS THE ? SIGN
```

Variations In Usage

None known.

Also See

INPUT, INP, INPUTLINE, LINEINPUT, PIN

Function

INSTR(N,A$,B$) is a string function that locates the starting position of the first occurrence of string B$ within string A$. If B$ is not found in A$, INSTR = 0. N is optional and is used to start the search at the Nth character of A$. See POS for more information.

Test Program #1

```
10 REM 'INSTR' TEST PROGRAM
20 A$ = "PROGRAM"
30 B$ = "RAM"
40 K = INSTR(A$,B$)
50 IF K<>5 THEN 110
60 B$ = "ROM"
70 K = INSTR(A$,B$)
80 IF K<>0 THEN 110
90 PRINT "'INSTR(A$,B$)' PASSED THE TEST"
100 GOTO 30999
110 PRINT "'INSTR(A$,B$)' FAILED THE TEST"
30999 END
```

Sample Run

```
'INSTR(A$,B$)' PASSED THE TEST
```

Test Program #2

```
10 REM 'INSTR(N,A$,B$)' TEST PROGRAM
20 A$ = "COMPUSOFT"
30 B$ = "O"
40 K = INSTR(4,A$,B$)
50 IF K=7 THEN 80
60 PRINT "'INSTR(N,A$,B$)' FAILED THE TEST"
70 GOTO 30999
80 PRINT "'INSTR(N,A$,B$)' PASSED THE TEST"
30999 END
```

Sample Run

```
'INSTR(N,A$,B$)' PASSED THE TEST
```

IF YOUR COMPUTER DOESN'T HAVE IT

If both tests failed, try the POS and INDEX functions. If your computer uses the MID$ and LEN functions this subroutine can be used.

```
30000 GOTO 30999
30060 REM * INSTR SUBROUTINE * INPUT N, A$, B$, OUTPUT K
30062 REM ALSO USES L INTERNALLY
30064 L = LEN(B$)
30066 FOR K=N TO LEN(A$)-L+1
30068 IF B$=MID$(A$,K,L) THEN 30074
30070 NEXT K
30072 K=0
30074 RETURN
```

To use this subroutine with Test Program #1 make these changes:

```
35 N = 1
40 GOSUB 30060
70 GOSUB 30060
```

For Test Program #2 make these changes:

```
35 N = 4
40 GOSUB 30060
```

Also See

```
POS, INDEX, MID$, LEN
```

Function

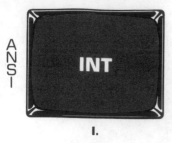

ANSI

I.

The INTeger function is used to round numbers off to their integer (whole number) value. In BASIC *numbers are always rounded down.* The whole number remains the same regardless of the value of the numbers removed from the right of the decimal point; except, when a negative number is integered, the resultant number is rounded off to the next smaller whole number. For example, INT (−4.65) becomes −5.

There are limits to the size of the number that some computers will process with the INT function. Some microcomputers will not accept a number smaller than −32768 or larger than +32767.

Test Program

```
10 REM 'INT' TEST PROGRAM
20 READ X
30 PRINT "THE INTEGER VALUE OF"; X;
40 X = INT(X)
50 PRINT "IS"; X
60 IF X=999 THEN 999
70 GOTO 20
80 DATA 3.33,2.864,.35,-3.15,32766.853,-32766.853,999.99
999 END
```

Sample Run

```
THE INTEGER VALUE OF 3.33 IS 3
THE INTEGER VALUE OF 2.864 IS 2
THE INTEGER VALUE OF .35 IS 0
THE INTEGER VALUE OF -3.15 IS -4
THE INTEGER VALUE OF 32766.853 IS 32766
THE INTEGER VALUE OF -32766.853 IS -32767
THE INTEGER VALUE OF 999.99 IS 999
```

Alternate Spelling

I. is used by most Tiny BASICs as an abbreviation for INT.

Variations In Usage

None, other than the limitation indicated.

Also See

```
CINT, %, FIX
```

INVERSE is used by the APPLE II as either a command or a statement to display its screen output in INVERSE mode. In this mode, output from the computer is displayed as black characters on a white background. To restore the display to its normal mode, type NORMAL.

Test Program

```
10 REM INVERSE TEST PROGRAM
20 PRINT "THIS DEMONSTRATES ";
30 INVERSE
40 PRINT "INVERSE PRINTING."
99 END
```

To run this program, clear the screen and type RUN.

Sample Run

THIS DEMONSTRATES INVERSE PRINTING.

Variations In Usage

None known.

Also See

NORMAL, FLASH

Function

KEY

The KEY$ function is used in APF Imagination Machine BASIC to input a character without displaying it on the screen. KEY$(*n*) accepts one of only three different values for *n*.

KEY$(0) reads the keyboard, KEY$(1) reads the right hand game control and KEY$(2) reads the left hand game control.

For example, A$ = KEY$(0) scans the keyboard looking for any key that is pressed. If no key is pressed, A$ = "" (null), otherwise A$ "reads" the character that is typed. KEY$(0) is equivalent to INKEY$. (See INKEY$ for more information.)

Test Program #1

```
10 REM KEY$(0) TEST PROGRAM
20 CALL 17046 'CLEARS THE SCREEN IN APF BASIC
30 PRINT "TYPE ANY CHARACTER"
40 A$ = KEY$(0)
50 IF A$="" THEN 40
60 PRINT "YOU JUST TYPED A ";A$
70 PRINT "TO REPEAT, TYPE ";A$;" AGAIN."
80 IF KEY(0)=A$ THEN 20
90 GOTO 80
99 END
```

Sample Run *(using #)*

```
TYPE ANY CHARACTER
YOU JUST TYPED A #
TO REPEAT, TYPE # AGAIN.
```

R$ = KEY$(1) checks the right hand game control. If no key is pressed, R$ = "". If one of the numeric keys 0-9 is pressed, R$ becomes that numeric character.

When the CL button is pressed, a "?" is stored in R$. R$ = KEY$(1) will set R$ to "!" when the EN or FIRE buttons are pressed.

Finally, R$ receives N, S, E or W to indicate which way the directional knob has been pushed. L$ = KEY$(2) reads the left hand game control in similar fashion.

Test Program #2

```
10 REM KEY$(1 & 2) TEST PROGRAM
20 R$ = KEY$(1)
30 IF R$="" THEN 20
40 L$ = KEY$(2)
50 IF L$="" THEN 40
60 PRINT "THE RIGHT HAND CONTROL GENERATED ";R$
70 PRINT "THE LEFT HAND CONTROL GENERATED ";L$
99 END
```

Sample Run *(typical)*

```
THE RIGHT HAND CONTROL GENERATED !
THE LEFT HAND CONTROL GENERATED N
```

Alternate Spelling

KEY is used by Texas Instruments' TI 99/4 in a CALL statement (i.e. CALL KEY) to do the same thing as KEY$(0).

Also See

```
INKEY$, PDL, GET, INPUT
```

Operator

LE is used in some computers (e.g. the TI 990) as an alternate word for the "less than or equal to" sign (< =).

For more information see < =.

Test Program

```
10 REM 'LE (LESS THAN OR EQUAL TO)' TEST PROGRAM
20 IF 10 LE 20 THEN 50
30 PRINT "THE LE OPERATOR FAILED THE TEST IN LINE 20"
40 GOTO 99
50 IF 20 LE 20 THEN 80
60 PRINT "THE LE OPERATOR FAILED THE TEST IN LINE 50"
70 GOTO 99
80 PRINT "THE LE OPERATOR PASSED THE TEST"
99 END
```

Sample Run

```
THE LE OPERATOR PASSED THE TEST
```

Variations In Usage

None known.

Also See

<=, <, >=, >, =, <>, EQ, GE, GT, LT, NE, IF-THEN

LEFT

The LEFT$(*string,n*) function is used to extract a specific number (*n*) of string characters starting from the left-most character in the string.

For example, PRINT LEFT$("RUNNING",3) prints the letters RUN, which are the left 3 characters in the string RUNNING.

The string must be enclosed in quotes or listed as a string variable. The number of characters (*n*) can be expressed as a variable, number or arithmetic operation. A comma must separate the string from the number.

If the value of (*n*) is a decimal, the computer automatically finds its integer value.

Test Program

```
10 REM 'LEFT$' TEST PROGRAM
20 A$="THEATER"
30 B$=LEFT$("TESTING",4)
40 PRINT LEFT$(A$ ,3);"'LEFT$' FUNCTION PASSED THE";B$
99 END
```

Sample Run

```
THE 'LEFT$' FUNCTION PASSED THE TEST
```

Alternate Spelling

Some BASICs (e.g. MAX BASIC and DEC BASIC-PLUS) use the LEFT(string,n) instead.

Variations In Usage

None known.

Also See

```
PRINT, RIGHT$, MID$, CHR$, SPACE$, STR$, STRING$,
INKEY$, INSTR, POS, SEG$, DEFSTR
```

Function

L.

The LEN function is used to measure the LENgth of strings by counting the number of characters enclosed in quotes or assigned to string variables.

For example, `10 PRINT LEN("TEST")` should print 4, the number of letters in the word "TEST".

Test Program

```
10 REM 'LEN' TEST PROGRAM
20 PRINT "TYPE ANY COMBINATION OF LETTERS AND NUMBERS"
30 INPUT A$
40 PRINT "YOU ENTERED ";A$" WHICH CONTAINS";
50 PRINT LEN(A$); "CHARACTERS"
99 END
```

Sample Run *(using ABC123)*

```
TYPE ANY COMBINATION OF LETTERS AND NUMBERS
? ABC123
YOU ENTERED ABC123 WHICH CONTAINS 6 CHARACTERS
```

Alternate Spelling

The British ACORN ATOM computer allows L. as an abbreviation for LEN.

Variations In Usage

None known.

Also See

ASC, FRE, LEFT$, MID$, RIGHT$, STR$, VAL, SEG$

The LET statement is used to assign values to variables (e.g. LET X=20). LET is required by a few computers, but is optional on most. When not required, it is sometimes used as a method of "flagging" variables that are being assigned new values or where special identification is desired.

Test Program

```
10 REM 'LET' TEST PROGRAM
20 LET X=20
30 PRINT "THE LET STATEMENT PASSED THE TEST IN LINE";X
99 END
```

Sample Run

```
THE LET STATEMENT PASSED THE TEST IN LINE 20
```

To determine if LET is required by your computer, delete LET from line 20 and try again.

Variations in Usage

None known.

The LIN(*n*) statement (used in the Hewlett-Packard 2000 BASIC and the Digital Group Opus 1 and Opus 2 BASIC) causes the computer to skip a specified number (*n*) of lines on a printer or CRT before printing the next line.

Test Program

```
10 REM 'LIN' TEST PROGRAM
20 PRINT "THE LIN STATEMENT PASSED THE TEST"
30 LIN(5)
40 PRINT "IF 5 LINES ARE SKIPPED BEFORE THIS LINE IS
   PRINTED"
99 END
```

Sample Run

```
THE LIN STATEMENT PASSED THE TEST




IF 5 LINES ARE SKIPPED BEFORE THIS LINE IS PRINTED
```

Some computers use LIN as a function in a PRINT statement. If the test program didn't work, try it with

```
30 PRINT LIN(5)
```

IF YOUR COMPUTER DOESN'T HAVE IT

If your computer does not have LIN(*n*), it can be easily simulated by substituting (*n*) number of PRINT statements for LIN (*n*).

For example, substitute the following for line 30 in the TEST PROGRAM:

```
28 FOR X=1 TO 5
30 PRINT
32 NEXT X
```

Since each PRINT statement triggers a line-feed, these lines will cause the computer to perform the same operation as LIN(5).

Variations In Usage

None known.

Also See

PRINT, VTAB

LINPUT

LINEINPUT is similar to INPUT. It accepts an entire LINE of input up to a maximum of 254 characters and assigns it to a single string variable.

No prompt symbol (such as a question mark) is given by LINEINPUT. The string it "inputs" may include commas, colons and other special characters without the need for enclosing them in quotes. Any character except a carriage return will be accepted.

Test Program

```
10 REM LINEINPUT TEST PROGRAM
20 PRINT "TYPE YOUR NAME - LAST, FIRST";
30 LINEINPUT N$
40 PRINT "HELLO, ";N$;". I'M -80, TRS."
99 END
```

Sample Run

```
TYPE YOUR NAME - LAST, FIRST DOE, JOHN
HELLO, DOE, JOHN. I'M -80, TRS.
```

LINEINPUT is able to print its own prompt message. Delete line 20 and change line 30 to

```
30 LINEINPUT "TYPE YOUR NAME - LAST, FIRST ";N$
```

The results should be the same as before.

Alternate Spelling

Some computers allow the shortened form, LINPUT, in place of LINEINPUT.

Also See

```
INPUTLINE, INPUT
```

The LIST command is used to display each program line in the numerical order in which it appears in the program. Some computers (or terminals) will scroll through the entire program list unless stopped by a specified key function. (Control C, Control S, SHIFT @, etc.) Others will stop after displaying the first 12, 16, 24 or more lines, then advance one or more additional lines each time the up-arrow, down-arrow or other appropriate key is pressed.

LIS
LI
L.

The LIST command can also be used in conjunction with a line number to specify a starting point other than at the beginning. Many computers will also accept a start and finish line number. For example, LIST10-40 or LIST 10-40 will list only those program lines with numbers from 10 to 40.

Test Program

```
10 REM 'LIST' COMMAND TEST PROGRAM
20 REM THIS COMMAND
30 REM WILL DISPLAY EACH LINE
40 REM AS HELD BY THE COMPUTER
50 PRINT "LIST TEST COMPLETE"
99 END
```

Sample Run

Type in LIST20-30 and your computer should print:

```
20 REM THIS COMMAND
30 REM WILL DISPLAY EACH LINE
```

If your computer will not accept the line number limitations, try entering LIST20.

Line 20 should be printed. If this test fails, try entering LIST without line numbers.

Some computers will display line 20 and all lines following when LIST 20 is entered. If your computer does then use LIST 20-20 or LIST 20,20 to list line 20 alone.

Try the following list commands:

```
LIST-
LIST30-
LIST-30
```

If your computer accepted these LIST commands, LIST- should have listed the entire program, LIST 30- the program starting with line 30, and LIST-30 the program starting with the first line and ending with line 30. If these commands failed, try using commas (,) in place of hyphens (-).

LIST is accepted by some computers as a program statement. To test this on your computer, add the following line to the Test Program:

```
60 LIST
```

If LIST is accepted as a program statement then it will print:

```
LIST TEST COMPLETE
10 REM 'LIST' COMMAND TEST PROGRAM
20 REM THIS COMMAND
30 REM WILL DISPLAY EACH LINE
40 REM AS HELD BY THE COMPUTER
50 PRINT "LIST TEST COMPLETE"
60 LIST
99 END
```

Alternate Spellings

Several abbreviations are in use, including LIS (PDP-8E), LI (Texas Instruments 990) and L. (Tiny BASIC.).

Also See

```
LLIST
```

LLIST is used by Microsoft BASIC to list the program currently in memory on a printer, instead of a screen. LLIST is most often used as a command, but may also be used as a statement within a program.

All the options available to LIST will work with LLIST. Since the listing is being produced on paper and not the video screen, it will not stop after 12, 16 or 24 lines (like LIST may do), but will continue to the end of the program or until BREAK, RESET, Control C, etc. is pressed.

CAUTION: A printer **must** be connected to the computer and ready to operate before you type the LLIST command. Otherwise the computer may get "hung". The TRS-80 Model III is an example of a computer which can be "unhung" by pressing the BREAK or similar key.

Test Program

```
10 REM LLIST COMMAND TEST PROGRAM
20 REM THE LLIST COMMAND
30 REM WILL PRINT THIS PROGRAM
40 REM ON THE PRINTER
99 END
```

Sample Run

Typing LLIST should produce the listing above at your printer. Typing LLIST 20-30 should print

```
20 REM THE LLIST COMMAND
30 REM WILL PRINT THIS PROGRAM
```

Typing LLIST-20 should list only the first two lines, and LLIST 40- should list only the last two lines.

To see if LLIST can be used as a program statement, add

```
50 LLIST
```

to the Test Program and type RUN. If LLIST is accepted it should print:

```
10 REM LLIST COMMAND TEST PROGRAM
20 REM THE LLIST COMMAND
30 REM WILL PRINT THIS PROGRAM
40 REM ON THE PRINTER
50 LLIST
99 END
```

Also See

LIST, LPRINT

The LOAD command is used to load a program into the computer from cassette tape or disk.

Test Program

Enter this program into the computer from the keyboard, then store it on cassette tape. (See SAVE for details.)

```
10 REM 'LOAD' TEST PROGRAM
20 PRINT "THIS PROGRAM TESTS THE LOAD FEATURE"
99 END
```

Once the program is recorded on cassette tape, erase the computer memory with NEW, SCRATCH or whatever is appropriate.

Rewind the tape, then set the recorder to the Play mode and type the LOAD command.

The cassette recorder's motor is controlled by the computer which turns it on and off before and after the LOAD cycle. The cassette should "play back" the program, LOADing it into the computer.

List the program to verify that the program held in the computer's memory is identical to that originally entered (see LIST). If all looks well, RUN the program.

If it is desired, the program can be given a name when it is SAVEd. Other programs will then be ignored and the specified one will be LOADed when found. Example: LOAD"TEST".

Sample Run

```
THIS PROGRAM TESTS THE LOAD FEATURE
```

Variations In Usage

LOAD "*filename*" is commonly used to LOAD in a program previously saved on Disk. A filename is required.

Also See

```
CLOAD, SAVE, CSAVE, LIST, NEW
```

Function

ANSI

LOGE
LN

The LOG(*n*) function computes the **natural** logarithm of any number (*n*) whose value is greater than 0. For common (base 10) logs see LOG10 or CLG.

Test Program

```
10 REM 'LOG' TEST PROGRAM
20 PRINT "ENTER A POSITIVE NUMBER";
30 INPUT N
40 L=LOG(N)
50 PRINT "THE NATURAL LOG OF";N;"IS";L
30999 END
```

Sample Run (using 100)

```
ENTER A POSITIVE NUMBER? 100
THE NATURAL LOG OF 100 IS 4.60517
```

Alternate Spellings

Some BASICs use LN (e.g. Micropolis BASIC), some use LOGE, while a few (e.g. DEC-10) use all three forms of the natural logarithm.

IF YOUR COMPUTER HAS NONE OF THEM

If they all fail, substitute the following subroutine:

```
30000 GOTO 30999
30150 REM * NATURAL LOGARITHM SUBROUTINE * INPUT X,
      OUTPUT L
30152 REM USES A, B, C, D AND E INTERNALLY
30154 IF X>0 THEN 30160
30156 PRINT "LOG UNDEFINED AT";X
30158 STOP
30160 A=1
30162 B=2
30164 C=.5
30166 D=X
30168 E=0
30170 IF X<A THEN 30178
30172 X=C*X
30174 E=E+A
30176 GOTO 30170
30178 IF X>=C THEN 30186
30180 X=B*X
30182 E=E-A
30184 GOTO 30178
30186 X=(X-.707107)/(X+.707107)
30188 L=X*X
30190 L=(((.598979*L+.961471)*L+2.88539)*X+E-.5)*.693147
30192 IF L>1E-6 THEN 30196
```

```
30194 L=0
30196 X=D
30198 RETURN
```

To use this subroutine in the TEST PROGRAM, make these program additions:

```
35 X=N
40 GOSUB 30150
```

CONVERSION FACTORS

To convert natural log to common log, multiply the natural log times .4342945. For example, X=LOG(N)* .4342945. To convert common log to natural log, multiply the common log times 2.302585.

Variations In Usage

A few computers (e.g. IMSAI 4K) use LOG to compute the COMMON LOG, **not** the NATURAL LOG (but this is a rare exception).

Also See

LOG10, CLG

Function

LOG10

LGT

The LOG10(*n*) function computes the value of the common (base 10) logarithm of any number (*n*) whose value is greater than 0.

Test Program

```
10 REM 'LOG10' TEST PROGRAM
20 PRINT "ENTER A POSITIVE NUMBER";
30 INPUT N
40 L=LOG10(N)
50 PRINT "THE COMMON LOG OF";N;"IS";L
30999 END
```

Sample Run *(for 100)*

```
ENTER A POSITIVE NUMBER? 100
THE COMMON LOG OF 100 IS 2
```

Alternate Spellings

Several other words are used by various BASICs. LGT is used by some (e.g. Tektronix 4050 series BASIC and MAX BASIC). CLG and CLOG are used by others.

IF YOUR COMPUTER DOESN'T HAVE IT

If your computer failed the TEST PROGRAM, try the TEST PROGRAM found under LOG. If LOG works, the common log can be computed from LOG by adding

```
40 L=LOG(N)*.4342945
```

If LOG's TEST PROGRAM also failed, substitute the subroutine found under LOG, making the following changes:

```
30150 REM * COMMON LOGARITHM SUBROUTINE * INPUT X,
      OUTPUT L
30197 L=L*.4342945
```

and these TEST PROGRAM changes:

```
35 X=N
40 GOSUB 30150
```

CONVERSION FACTORS

To convert a common log to a natural log, multiply the common log value times 2.302585.

For example: `X=LOG10(N)*2.302585`

To convert a natural log to a common log, multiply the natural log value times .4342945.

Also See

CLG, LOG

LPRINT is used by Microsoft BASIC to send a
PRINT statement to a printer instead of the
screen. LPRINT may be used as either a direct
command or a program statement.

All of the options available to the PRINT
statement are available to LPRINT with the
exception of @. Included are TAB, zone printing
with commas, close printing with semicolons and
LPRINT USING. See PRINT and PRINT USING
for more information.

Caution: a printer **must** be hooked up to the computer and be ready to
operate before RUNning a program using LPRINT. If not, the computer
may get "hung" and the program will be lost. Later versions of Microsoft
BASIC (e.g. TRS-80 Model III) allow escape from this "hang up" by simply
pressing the BREAK key.

Test Program

```
10 REM LPRINT TEST PROGRAM
20 LPRINT "YOU HAVE ONE FINE PRINTER HERE!"
30 LPRINT
40 A = 30
50 LPRINT TAB(A); A; A+4; A+8
60 LPRINT "JUST MEASURING THE LENGTH OF A LINE."
70 LPRINT 1,2,3
80 LPRINT " AND CHECKING ZONE PRINTING."
90 LPRINT "IT ALL LOOKS GOOD TO ME."
100 LPRINT USING "I'LL GIVE YOU $#.## FOR IT.",8/3
999 END
```

Sample Run

```
YOU HAVE ONE FINE PRINTER HERE!
                              30   34   38
JUST MEASURING THE LENGTH OF A LINE.
 1              2              3
AND CHECKING ZONE PRINTING.
IT ALL LOOKS GOOD TO ME.
I'LL GIVE YOU $2.67 FOR IT.
```

Also See

```
PRINT, PRINT USING, TAB, ,(comma),.;(semicolon), LLIST
```

LT is used in some computers (e.g. the TI 990) as an alternate word for the "less-than" sign (<).

For more information see <.

Test Program

```
10 REM 'LT(LESS-THAN)' TEST PROGRAM
20 IF 5 LT 10 THEN 50
30 PRINT "THE LT OPERATOR FAILED THE TEST"
40 GOTO 99
50 PRINT "THE LT OPERATOR PASSED THE TEST"
99 END
```

Sample Run

```
THE LT OPERATOR PASSED THE TEST
```

Variations In Usage

None known.

Also See

<, <=, >, >=, =, <>, EQ, GE, GT, LE, NE, IF-THEN

Command

MAN is used in APPLE II BASIC to allow MANual insertion of program line numbers.

If the computer is in the AUTOmatic line numbering mode, control X must be typed before the computer can accept the MAN command.

Test Procedure

To test the computer's MANual feature, place the computer in the AUTOmatic line numbering mode by typing the command AUTO and pressing the RETURN key. If line number 10 is printed, the computer successfully went into the AUTOmatic mode. Now type control X and the command MAN. Enter a few test program lines to verify that the computer passed the MANual command test.

Variations In Usage

None known.

Also See

AUTO

MAT CON is used by some computers to set the value of each element in an array to some CONstant--- typically the number 1.

CON may be used to redimension the array as well, provided the number of cells in the redimensioned array is less than or equal to the number of cells originally reserved by the DIM statement.

For example, if array A is declared a 3x5 array, then MAT A=CON stores fifteen 1's in 3 rows (with 5 in each row), while MAT A=CON(2,6) stores twelve 1's in 2 rows (with 6 1's in each row.)

Test Program #1

```
10 REM * MAT CON * TEST PROGRAM
20 DIM A(3,5)
30 MAT A=CON
40 FOR I=1 TO 3
50   FOR J=1 TO 5
60     PRINT A(I,J);
70   NEXT J
80   PRINT
90 NEXT I
100 PRINT "'MAT CON' PASSED THE TEST IF A"
110 PRINT "3X5 ARRAY OF ONES WAS PRINTED."
999 END
```

Sample Run

```
 1 1 1 1 1
 1 1 1 1 1
 1 1 1 1 1
'MAT CON' PASSED THE TEST IF A
3X5 ARRAY OF ONES WAS PRINTED.
```

Test Program #2

```
10 REM * MAT CON * REDIMENSION TEST PROGRAM
20 DIM A(3,5)
30 MAT A=CON(2,6)
40 FOR I=1 TO 2
50   FOR J=1 TO 6
60     PRINT A(I,J);
70   NEXT J
80   PRINT
90 NEXT I
100 PRINT "'MAT CON' PASSED THE REDIMENSION TEST IF A"
110 PRINT "2X6 ARRAY OF ONES WAS PRINTED"
999 END
```

Sample Run

```
1 1 1 1 1 1
1 1 1 1 1 1
'MAT CON' PASSED THE REDIMENSION TEST IF A
2X6 ARRAY OF ONES WAS PRINTED
```

IF YOUR COMPUTER DOESN'T HAVE IT

If your computer doesn't allow MAT CON, Line 30 can be replaced with FOR-NEXT loops.

```
22 FOR I=1 TO 3
26  FOR J=1 TO 5
30   A(I,J)=1
34  NEXT J
38 NEXT I
```

Also See

MAT ZER, MAT IDN, DIM, FOR, NEXT

MAT IDN is used on a square matrix (2 dimensional array whose dimensions are both the same) to form the identity matrix, a matrix with 1's on the main diagonal and 0's everywhere else.

For example, if matrix A is declared a 4x4 array then MAT A=IDN generates the following matrix:

```
1 0 0 0
0 1 0 0
0 0 1 0
0 0 0 1
```

Test Program #1

```
10 REM 'MAT IDN' TEST PROGRAM
20 DIM A(4,4)
30 MAT A= IDN
40 FOR I=1 TO 4
50  FOR J=1 TO 4
60    PRINT A(I,J);
70  NEXT I
80  PRINT
90 NEXT J
100 PRINT "'MAT IDN' PASSED THE TEST IF A 4X4 IDENTITY"
110 PRINT "MATRIX WAS PRINTED"
999 END
```

Sample Run

```
1 0 0 0
0 1 0 0
0 0 1 0
0 0 0 1
'MAT IDN' PASSED THE TEST IF A 4X4 IDENTITY
MATRIX WAS PRINTED
```

IDN may be used to redimension a matrix as well, provided that the number of cells in the redimensioned matrix is less than or equal to the number of cells originally reserved by the DIM statement.

Example: If A is a 2x5 array, MAT A=IDN(3,3) redimensions it as a 3x3 identity matrix.

Test Program #2

```
10 REM 'MAT IDN' REDIMENSION TEST PROGRAM
20 DIM A(2,5)
30 MAT A=IDN(3,3)
40 FOR I=1 TO 3
50  FOR J=1 TO 3
60   PRINT A(I,J);
70  NEXT J
80  PRINT
90 NEXT I
100 PRINT "'MAT IDN' PASSED THE REDIMENSION TEST IF A
    3X3 IDENTITY"
110 PRINT "MATRIX WAS PRINTED"
999 END
```

Sample Run

```
1 0 0
0 1 0
0 0 1
'MAT IDN' PASSED THE REDIMENSION TEST IF A 3X3 IDENTITY
MATRIX WAS PRINTED
```

IF YOUR COMPUTER DOESN'T HAVE IT

If your computer failed the IDN test, use the following procedure.

```
26 FOR I=1 TO 4
28  FOR J=1 TO 4
30   A(I,J)=0
32  NEXT J
34  A(I,I)=1
36 NEXT I
```

Also See

The other MAT statements, DIM, FOR, NEXT

MAT INPUT is used to assign values to each element in an array via the keyboard. A DIM statement establishes the number of array elements that may be assigned values.

For example:

```
10 DIM A(5)
20 MAT INPUT A
```

The DIM statement allows variable A to use array elements named A(0) to A(5). (For more information see DIM.) MAT INPUT assigns values for cells A(1) to A(5).

When the MAT INPUT statement is executed, the computer prints a ? indicating it is ready to receive a value for the first element in the array. If all elements are to be filled in one pass, a comma must be typed after each value before the RETURN or ENTER key is pressed. If each element in the array did not receive a value before the RETURN or ENTER key is pressed, the computer prints a double question mark (??) indicating more values are needed. As with an ordinary INPUT statement, values can be entered one at a time each followed by the RETURN.

The MAT INPUT statement assigns values to each vertical column in the first row of two-dimensional-array variables before assigning values to the following horizontal row.

For example,

```
10 DIM A(2,3)
20 MAT INPUT A
```

The computer assigns values to array variable elements A(1,1), A(1,2), and A(1,3) before A(2,1), A(2,2), and A(2,3).

Most MAT INPUT handling computers allow the array size to be established with the MAT INPUT statement if not more than 10 array elements are used. [e.g. MAT INPUT A(2,3).] If an array requires more than 10 elements, it must be DIMensioned.

For example:

```
10 DIM B(20,20)
20 MAT INPUT A(3,5)
30 MAT INPUT B(15,11)
```

Test Program

```
10 REM 'MAT INPUT' TEST PROGRAM
20 DIM A(3,4)
30 PRINT "ENTER 12 NUMBERS (SEPARATED BY COMMAS)"
40 MAT INPUT A
50 FOR I=1 TO 3
60  FOR J=1 TO 4
70   PRINT A(I,J);
80  NEXT J
90  PRINT
100 NEXT I
110 PRINT "THE MAT INPUT STATEMENT PASSED THE TEST"
120 PRINT "IF THE INPUT VALUES ARE PRINTED IN A"
130 PRINT "MATRIX HAVING THREE ROWS OF FOUR COLUMNS."
999 END
```

Sample Run *(typical)*

```
ENTER 12 NUMBERS (SEPARATED BY COMMAS)
?1,2,3,4,5,6,7,8,9,10,11,12
 1  2  3  4
 5  6  7  8
 9 10 11 12
THE MAT INPUT STATEMENT PASSED THE TEST
IF THE INPUT VALUES ARE PRINTED IN A
MATRIX HAVING THREE ROWS OF FOUR COLUMNS.
```

IF YOUR COMPUTER DOESN'T HAVE IT

If your computer does not have the MAT INPUT capability, it can be replaced by FOR-NEXT and INPUT statements. Substitute the following lines in the TEST PROGRAM:

```
33 FOR I=1 TO 3
36  FOR J=1 TO 4
40   INPUT A(I,J)
43  NEXT J
46 NEXT I
```

This substitution differs slightly from the MAT INPUT statement in that it **does** require the RETURN or ENTER key to be pressed after each value is typed.

Variations In Usage

None known.

Also See

```
MAT PRINT, MAT READ, FOR, INPUT, DIM, NUM
```

MAT INV is used on a square matrix (2 dimensional array whose dimensions are both the same) to form a matrix that is the inverse of the starting one.

Not all square matrices have inverses. If A is a matrix that has an inverse, when MAT B=INV(A) is executed, B is a matrix which, when multiplied times A, results in the identity matrix. (See MAT IDN.)

Some computers calculate the determinant (see DET) of the matrix along with the inverse. DET can then be tested to see if a true inverse exists. If DET = 0, the matrix has no inverse, and the values in B are invalid.

Test Program

```
10 REM * MAT INV * TEST PROGRAM
20 DIM A(3,3), B(3,3)
30 FOR I=1 TO 3
40   FOR J=1 TO 3
50     READ A(I,J)
60   NEXT J
70 NEXT I
80 MAT B=INV(A)
90 FOR I=1 TO 3
100   FOR J=1 TO 3
110     PRINT B(I,J);
120   NEXT J
130   PRINT
140 NEXT I
150 PRINT "'MAT INV' PASSED THE TEST IF 3 -.5 -.5"
160 PRINT "                              -1  0  1"
170 PRINT "                              -1  .5 -.5 WAS
    PRINTED"
180 DATA 1,1,1,  3,4,5,  1,2,1
30999 END
```

Sample Run

```
 3 -.5 -.5
-1  0  1
-1  .5 -.5
'MAT INV' PASSED THE TEST IF 3 -.5 -.5
                             -1  0  1
                             -1  .5 -.5 WAS PRINTED
```

IF YOUR COMPUTER DOESN'T HAVE IT

If MAT INV is not available on your computer, substitute the following subroutine.

```
30000 GOTO 30999
30850 REM * MAT INV SUBROUTINE * INPUT N, A( , )   OUTPUT B( , )
30852 REM   ALSO USES I, J, K, P AND R INTERNALLY
30853 REM DIMENSION ARRAY J HERE IF N>10
30854 FOR I=1 TO N
30856  FOR J=1 TO N
30858   B(I,J)=A(I,J)
30860  NEXT J
30862 NEXT I
30864 M=N-1
30866 FOR K=1 TO N
30867  J(K)=0
30868  P=B(K,1)
30870  IF P<>0 THEN 30894
30872  FOR I=K+1 TO N
30873   J(K)=I
30874   IF B(I,1)=0 THEN 30888
30876   FOR J=1 TO N
30878    R=B(K,J)
30880    B(K,J)=B(I,J)
30882    B(I,J)=R
30884   NEXT J
30886   GOTO 30868
30888  NEXT I
30890  PRINT"*** NO INVERSE EXISTS ***"
30892  GOTO 30999
30894  FOR J=1 TO M
30896   B(K,J)=B(K,J+1)/P
30898  NEXT J
30900  B(K,N)=1/P
30902  FOR I=1 TO N
30904   IF I=K THEN 30916
30906   R=B(I,1)
30908   FOR J=1 TO M
30910    B(I,J)=B(I,J+1)-R*B(K,J)
30912   NEXT J
30914   B(I,N)=-R*B(K,N)
30916  NEXT I
30918 NEXT K
30920 FOR K=M TO 1 STEP -1
30922  J=J(K)
30924  IF J=0 THEN 30936
30926  FOR I=1 TO N
30928   R=B(I,K)
30930   B(I,K)=B(I,J)
30932   B(I,J)=R
30934  NEXT I
30936 NEXT K
30938 RETURN
30999 END
```

To use this subroutine with the TEST PROGRAM, make the following changes to the TEST PROGRAM:

```
75 N=3
80 GOSUB 30850
```

Also See

```
MAT IDN, MAT *, DET, FOR , NEXT, DIM, MAT READ,
MAT PRINT
```

MAT PRINT is used to print the values stored in specified array elements. The number of elements printed is determined by the DIMensioned value assigned to the array. For more DIMensioning information see DIM.

For example,

```
10 DIM A(3)
20 MAT PRINT A
```

prints the three values assigned to the "A" array, A(1) thru A(3).

Test Program #1

```
10 REM 'MAT PRINT' TEST PROGRAM
20 DIM A(5)
30 FOR X=1 TO 5
40 A(X)=X
50 NEXT X
60 MAT PRINT A
70 PRINT "END OF MAT PRINT TEST"
99 END
```

Sample Run

```
1
2
3
4
5
END OF MAT PRINT TEST
```

Most computers with MAT PRINT capability allow a comma following the MAT PRINT statement, to print the array values in pre-established horizontal zones. (See Comma.) To test this feature in the TEST PROGRAM, change line 60 to:

```
60 MAT PRINT A,
```

and RUN.

Sample Run *(80 Column screen)*

```
1              2              3              4              5
 END OF MAT PRINT TEST
```

A semicolon (;) following the MAT PRINT statement may be used to print the array values in a horizontal line in packed format (i.e. with only one or two spaces separating them). (See Semicolon.) To test this feature, change line 60 to:

```
60 MAT PRINT A;
```

and RUN.

Sample Run

```
1  2  3  4  5
 END OF MAT PRINT TEST
```

The MAT PRINT statement can print the contents of arrays having more than one dimension. The number of elements in the first dimension specifies the number of rows to be printed while the number of elements in the second column determines the number of columns.

For example:

```
DIM A(2,3)
MAT PRINT A
```

The DIM statement establishes the A variable as being capable of storing values in a two dimensioned array which is printed by the MAT PRINT statement as a matrix having 2 rows and 3 columns.

The printing of more than one array can be ordered in one MAT PRINT statement by inserting a comma or semicolon between each array specified. The results are shown by the following TEST PROGRAM.

Test Program #2

```
10 REM 'MAT PRINT' WITH MULTIPLE ARRAY VARIABLES TEST
   PROGRAM
20 DIM A(3),B(3,5)
30  FOR I=1 TO 3
40   FOR J=1 TO 5
50    B(I,J)=J
60   NEXT J
70  A(I)=1
80  NEXT I
90 MAT PRINT A;B,
100 PRINT "END OF MAT PRINT TEST"
999 END
```

Sample Run

```
1   2   3
1               2           3           4           5
1               2           3           4           5
1               2           3           4           5
   END OF MAT PRINT TEST
```

A few computers will allow formatted printing of arrays with MAT PRINT USING. See PRINT USING for more information.

IF YOUR COMPUTER DOESN'T HAVE IT

If your computer does not have the MAT PRINT capability, it can be simulated with FOR-NEXT and PRINT statements. Substitute the following lines in TEST PROGRAM #2:

```
81    FOR X=1 TO 3
82       PRINT A(X);
84    NEXT X
86 PRINT
88    FOR I=1 TO 3
90       FOR J=1 TO 5
92          PRINT B(I,J),
94       NEXT J
95       PRINT
96    NEXT I
98 PRINT
```

Also See

```
MAT INPUT, MAT READ, ,(comma), ;(semicolon), FOR, PRINT, .DIM,
PRINT USING
```

Statement

MAT READ is used to read values from a DATA statement and assign them to an array. The DIM statement establishes the array size.

For example,

```
10 DIM A(5)
20 MAT READ A
```

The DIM statement allows variable A to use 6 array elements named A(0) to A(5). For more information see DIM. MAT READ fills cells A(1) thru A(5).

The MAT READ statement assigns values to each column in the first row of two dimensional-array variables before assigning values to the following row.

For example:

```
10 DIM A(2,3)
20 MAT READ A
```

The computer reads six values from the DATA statement and assigns them to array variables elements A(1,1), A(1,2), and A(1,3) before A(2,1), A(2,2), and A(2,3).

Test Program

```
10 REM 'MAT READ' TEST PROGRAM
20 DIM A(3,4)
30 MAT READ A
40 FOR I=1 TO 3
50  FOR J=1 TO 4
60   PRINT A(I,J);
70  NEXT J
80  PRINT
90 NEXT I
100 DATA 1,2,3,4,5,6,7,8,9,10,11,12
110 PRINT "THE MAT READ STATEMENT PASSED THE TEST"
120 PRINT "IF A MATRIX IS PRINTED HAVING 3 ROWS OF
    4 COLUMNS"
999 END
```

Sample Run

```
1   2   3   4
5   6   7   8
9  10  11   12
THE MAT READ STATEMENT PASSED THE TEST
IF A MATRIX IS PRINTED HAVING 3 ROWS OF 4 COLUMNS
```

Most MAT READ handling computers allow the array size to be established by the MAT READ statement if not more than 10 array elements are used. If more than 10 elements are required in an array, it must be DIMensioned.

For example,

```
110 DIM B(20,20)
120 MAT READ A(3,5)
130 MAT READ B(15,11)
```

To test this feature in your computer, omit line 20 in the TEST PROGRAM and change line 30 TO:

```
30 MAT READ A(3,4)
```

If your computer accepts this feature, the SAMPLE RUN should not change.

IF YOUR COMPUTER DOESN'T HAVE IT

If your computer does not have the MAT READ capability, it can be replaced by FOR-NEXT and READ statements.

Substitute the following lines in the TEST PROGRAM:

```
23 FOR I=1 TO 3
26  FOR J=1 TO 4
30    READ A(I,J)
33  NEXT J
36 NEXT I
```

Variations In Usage

None known.

Also See

```
MAT PRINT, MAT INPUT, READ, DATA, DIM, FOR
```

Statement

MAT TRN

MAT TRN is a statement used to form the transpose of a matrix (2 dimensional array). If A is an MxN array and B is an NxM array, then `MAT B=TRN(A)` forms matrix B in such a way that the first row of matrix A becomes the first column of matrix B, second row of A becomes second column of B, etc.

Test Program

```
10 REM * MAT TRN * TEST PROGRAM
20 DIM A(3,5), B(5,3)
30 FOR I=1 TO 3
40   FOR J=1 TO 5
50     A(I,J)=10*I+J
60   NEXT J
70 NEXT I
80 MAT B=TRN(A)
90 FOR J=1 TO 5
100   FOR I=1 TO 3
110     PRINT B(J,I);
120   NEXT I
130   PRINT
140 NEXT J
150 PRINT "'MAT TRN' PASSED THE TEST IF THE NUMBERS 11-15,"
160 PRINT "21-25, AND 31-35 ARE PRINTED IN 3 COLUMNS."
999 END
```

Sample Run

```
11 21 31
12 22 32
13 23 33
14 24 34
15 25 35
'MAT TRN' PASSED THE TEST IF THE NUMBERS 11-15,
21-25, AND 31-35 ARE PRINTED IN 3 COLUMNS.
```

The statement `MAT A=TRN(A)` is legal, but only if both dimensions of A are the same (i.e. A is a square matrix).

210

Variations In Usage

Some computers allow the word MAT to be optional. In those programs, Line 80 can be replaced by:

```
80 B=TRN(A)
```

IF YOUR COMPUTER DOESN'T HAVE IT

If your computer doesn't accept the MAT TRN statement, you can produce the transpose of an MxN matrix with:

```
76 FOR I=1 TO M
78  FOR J=1 TO N
80   B(J,I)=A(I,J)
82  NEXT J
84 NEXT I
```

Also See

The other MAT statements, DIM, FOR, NEXT

Statement

MAT ZER is used by some computers to set the value of each element of an array to 0. MAT ZER may be used to redimension the array as well, provided the number of cells in the redimensioned array is less than or equal to the number of cells originally reserved by the DIM statement.

For example, if array A is declared a 3x5 array, then MAT A=ZER stores fifteen 0's in 3 rows (with 5 in each row) while MAT A=ZER(2,6) stores twelve 0's in 2 rows (with 6 0's in each row).

Test Program #1

```
10 REM 'MAT ZER' TEST PROGRAM
20 DIM A(3,5)
22 REM START WITH SOME NON-ZERO VALUES
24 FOR I=1 TO 3
26  A(I,I)=I
28 NEXT I
30 MAT A=ZER
40 FOR I=1 TO 3
50  FOR J=1 TO 5
60   PRINT A(I,J);
70  NEXT J
80  PRINT
90 NEXT I
100 PRINT "'MAT ZER' PASSED THE TEST IF A"
110 PRINT "3X5 ARRAY OF ZEROS WAS PRINTED."
999 END
```

Sample Run

```
0 0 0 0 0
0 0 0 0 0
0 0 0 0 0
'MAT ZER' PASSED THE TEST IF A
3X5 ARRAY OF ZEROS WAS PRINTED.
```

Test Program #2

```
10 REM 'MAT ZER' REDIMENSION TEST PROGRAM
20 DIM A(3,5)
30 MAT A=ZER(2,6)
40 FOR I=1 TO 2
50  FOR J=1 TO 6
60   PRINT A(I,J);
70  NEXT J
80  PRINT
90 NEXT I
100 PRINT "'MAT ZER' PASSED THE REDIMENSION TEST IF A"
110 PRINT "2X6 ARRAY OF ZEROS WAS PRINTED"
999 END
```

Sample Run

```
0 0 0 0 0
0 0 0 0 0
'MAT ZER' PASSED THE REDIMENSION TEST IF A
2X6 ARRAY OF ZEROS WAS PRINTED
```

IF YOUR COMPUTER DOESN'T HAVE IT

If your computer doesn't allow MAT ZER, Line 30 can be replaced with nested FOR-NEXT loops:

```
22 FOR I=1 TO 3
26  FOR J=1 TO 5
30   A(I,J)=0
34  NEXT J
38 NEXT I
```

Also See

MAT CON, MAT IDN, DIM, FOR, NEXT

MAT = assigns the values stored in one array to the corresponding cells of another array. For example, MAT B=A copies the value of array A into array B. Most computers that accept MAT statements will dimension B to the same dimensions as A, provided sufficient space has been reserved by a DIM statement.

Test Program

```
10 REM * MAT ASSIGNMENT * TEST PROGRAM
20 DIM A(2,3), B(2,3)
30 FOR I=1 TO 2
40   FOR J=1 TO 3
50     READ A(I,J)
60   NEXT J
70 NEXT I
80 MAT B=A
90 FOR I=1 TO 2
100  FOR J=1 TO 3
110    IF B(I,J) <> A(I,J) THEN 160
120  NEXT J
130 NEXT I
140 PRINT "THE MAT ASSIGNMENT PASSED THE TEST"
150 GOTO 999
160 PRINT "THE MAT ASSIGNMENT FAILED THE TEST"
170 DATA 1, 2, 3, 4, 5, 6
999 END
```

Sample Run

```
THE MAT ASSIGNMENT PASSED THE TEST
```

Variations In Usage

Some computers allow the word MAT to be optional. In those programs, line 80 can be replaced by

```
80 B=A
```

IF YOUR COMPUTER DOESN'T HAVE IT

If your computer failed the MAT assignment test, use nested loops to copy the values of one array into another array. Substitute the following lines for line 80 in the TEST PROGRAM:

```
76 FOR I=1 TO 2
78   FOR J=1 TO 3
80     B(I,J) = A(I,J)
82   NEXT J
84 NEXT I
```

Also See

DIM, FOR, NEXT, READ, DATA, PRINT, MAT READ, MAT PRINT

Statement

The MAT + statement is used to add the corresponding elements of two arrays of the same size and store the results in a third array with the same dimensions. For example, MAT C=A+B will cause C(1,1) to contain A(1,1)+B(1,1). C(1,2) will contain A(1,2)+B(1,2), etc.

Test Program

```
10 REM 'MAT +' TEST PROGRAM
20 DIM A(2,3), B(2,3), C(2,3)
30 FOR I=1 TO 2
40   FOR J=1 TO 3
50     READ A(I,J)
60   NEXT J
70   FOR K=1 TO 3
80     READ B(I,J)
90   NEXT K
100 NEXT I
110 MAT C=A+B
120 FOR I=1 TO 2
130   FOR J=1 TO 3
140     PRINT C(I,J);
150   NEXT J
160   PRINT
170 NEXT I
180 PRINT "'MAT +' PASSED THE TEST IF  3  6  9"
190 PRINT "                           12  15  18
    WAS PRINTED"
200 DATA 2, 4, 6,  1, 2, 3
210 DATA 8,10,12,  4, 5, 6
999 END
```

Sample Run

```
 3  6  9
12  15  18
'MAT +' PASSED THE TEST IF  3  6  9
                           12  15  18  WAS PRINTED
```

Variations In Usage

Some computers permit the word MAT to be optional, much as LET is optional in most computers. In their programs, line 110 can be replaced by 110 C=A+B with the same results.

IF YOUR COMPUTER DOESN'T HAVE IT

If your computer didn't pass the test, matrix addition can be accomplished by replacing line 110 with:

```
106 FOR I=1 TO 2
108  FOR J=1 TO 3
110   C(I,J) = A(I,J) + B(I,J)
112  NEXT J
114 NEXT I
```

Also See

MAT -, MAT *, DIM, FOR, NEXT, MAT READ, MAT PRINT

Statement

The MAT − statement is used to subtract corresponding elements of two arrays of the same size and store the results in a third array with the same dimensions. For example, MAT C=A-B will cause C(1,1) to contain A(1,1) − B(1,1). C(1,2) will contain A(1,2) − B(1,2), etc.

Test Program

```
10 REM 'MAT -' TEST PROGRAM
20 DIM A(2,3), B(2,3), C(2,3)
30 FOR I=1 TO 2
40   FOR J=1 TO 3
50    READ A(I,J)
60   NEXT J
70   FOR K=1 TO 3
80    READ B(I,J)
90   NEXT K
100 NEXT I
110 MAT C=A-B
120 FOR I=1 TO 2
130   FOR J=1 TO 3
140    PRINT C(I,J);
150   NEXT J
160   PRINT
170 NEXT I
180 PRINT "'MAT -' PASSED THE TEST IF  1  2  3"
190 PRINT "                            4  5  6
    WAS PRINTED"
200 DATA 2, 4, 6,  1, 2, 3
210 DATA 8,10,12,  4, 5, 6
999 END
```

Sample Run

```
1  2  3
4  5  6
'MAT -' PASSED THE TEST IF  1  2  3
                            4  5  6  WAS PRINTED
```

Variations In Usage

Some computers allow the word MAT to be optional, much as LET is optional in most computers. In those programs, line 110 can be replaced by 110 C=A-B with the same results.

IF YOUR COMPUTER DOESN'T HAVE IT

If your computer didn't pass the test, matrix subtraction can be accomplished by replacing line 110 with:

```
106 FOR I=1 TO 2
108  FOR J=1 TO 3
110   C(I,J) = A(I,J) - B(I,J)
112  NEXT J
114 NEXT I
```

Also See

```
MAT +, MAT *, DIM, FOR, NEXT, MAT READ, MAT PRINT
```

Statement

The MAT * statement is used for two different kinds of multiplication.

In the form MAT B=(K)*A (called scalar multiplication) each element of array A is multiplied by the value of K and the result is stored in array B. K must be in parentheses and array B must have dimensions as array A.

The form MAT A=(K)*A is legal and stores the result of the multiplication back in array A.

Test Program #1

```
10 REM * SCALAR MULTIPLICATION TEST PROGRAM *
20 DIM A(2,3), B(2,3)
30 FOR I=1 TO 2
40   FOR J=1 TO 3
50     READ A(I,J)
60   NEXT J
70 NEXT I
80 K=10
90 MAT B=(K)*A
100 FOR I=1 TO 2
110   FOR J=1 TO 3
120     PRINT B(I,J);
130   NEXT J
140   PRINT
150 NEXT I
160 PRINT "'MAT *' PASSED THE TEST IF 10 20 30"
170 PRINT "                        40 50 60   WAS PRINTED"
180 DATA 1, 2, 3, 4, 5, 6
999 END
```

Sample Run

```
10 20 30
40 50 60
'MAT *' PASSED THE TEST IF 10 20 30
                        40 50 60 WAS PRINTED
```

MAT * can also be used to multiply one matrix, A, by another, B, provided that A has dimensions MxN and B has dimensions NxP (i.e. the second dimension of A must equal the first dimension of B). This is called Matrix Multiplication.

The result is stored in a matrix whose dimensions must be MxP. MAT A=A*B is illegal; however, MAT B=A*A is okay provided that A is a square matrix. (CAUTION: MAT C=B*A gives different results than MAT C=A*B.)

Test Program #2

```
10 REM * MATRIX MULTIPLICATION TEST PROGRAM *
20 DIM A(2,3), B(3,2), C(2,2)
30 FOR I=1 TO 2
40  FOR J=1 TO 3
50   READ A(I,J)
60  NEXT J
70 NEXT I
80 FOR I=1 TO 3
90  FOR J=1 TO 2
100   READ B(I,J)
110  NEXT J
120 NEXT I
130 MAT C=A*B
140 FOR I=1 TO 2
150  FOR J=1 TO 2
160   PRINT C(I,J);
170  NEXT J
180  PRINT
190 NEXT I
200 PRINT "'MAT *' PASSED THE TEST IF 10  14
210 PRINT "                      4  41  WAS PRINTED"
220 DATA 1,2,3,  4,5,0
230 DATA 1,4,  0,5,  3,0
999 END
```

Sample Run

```
10  14
4  41
'MAT *' PASSED THE TEST IF 10  14
                      4  41  WAS PRINTED
```

Variations In Usage

Some computers may allow the word MAT to be optional. In those programs, line 90 in TEST PROGRAM #1 can be replaced by

```
90 B=(K)*A
```

with the same results.

Also, line 130 in TEST PROGRAM #2 would be equivalent to

```
130 C=A*B
```

IF YOUR COMPUTER DOESN'T HAVE IT

If MAT ✳ is not available on your computer, you can accomplish both kinds of multiplication using nested FOR-NEXT loops. For scalar multiplication, replace line 90 in TEST PROGRAM #1 with

```
86 FOR I=1 TO 2
88  FOR J=1 TO 3
90   B(I,J)=K*A(I,J)
92  NEXT J
94 NEXT I
```

For matrix multiplication three extra loops are needed to replace Line 130:

```
122 FOR I=1 TO 2
124  FOR J=1 TO 2
126   C(I,J)=0
128   FOR K=1 TO 3
130    C(I,J) = C(I,J) + A(I,K) * B(K,J)
132   NEXT K
134  NEXT J
136 NEXT I
```

Also See

```
MAT +, MAT -, DIM, FOR, NEXT, MAT READ, MAT PRINT
```

The MAX function is used to determine which of two values is larger.

For example, Y=A MAX 5 assigns Y the value of A if it is larger than 5. Otherwise, Y becomes 5.

Test Program #1

```
10 REM 'MAX' TEST PROGRAM
20 A=12
30 Y=A MAX 5
40 IF Y=12 THEN 70
50 PRINT "'MAX' FAILED THE TEST"
60 GOTO 99
70 PRINT "'MAX' PASSED THE TEST"
99 END
```

Sample Run

```
'MAX' PASSED THE TEST
```

Micropolis BASIC uses MAX to compare two strings and return the string that would occur later in an alphabetical listing.

For example: MAX("ABC","XYZ") returns "XYZ".

Variations In Usage

Some computers use the form MAX(A,B) for the same purpose. A few computers can find the largest value in an array by using MAX. Example:
```
30 M=MAX(A)
```

IF YOUR COMPUTER DOESN'T HAVE IT

The MAXimum value (Y) of two numbers can be determined by the following formula:

```
Y= (A+B+ABS(A-B))/2
```

or by

```
30 Y=A
32 IF A>=B THEN 40
34 Y=B
```

The MAXimum value in an array can be determined by this program:

Test Program #2

```
10 DIM A(6)
20 FOR I=1 TO 6
30   READ A(I)
40 NEXT I
50 M=A(1)
60 FOR I=2 TO 6
70   IF M>=A(I) THEN 90
80   M=A(I)
90 NEXT I
100 PRINT "THE MAXIMUM VALUE IS";M
110 DATA 3,5,13,1,8,-3
999 END
```

Sample Run

```
THE MAXIMUM VALUE IS 13
```

Also See

```
ABS, MIN, >=
```

M.

MEM is usually used at the command level with a Print command to display the amount of unused bytes of MEMory remaining in the computer. MEM can also be used in a program statement.

Test Program

```
10 REM 'MEM' TEST PROGRAM
20 PRINT MEM; "BYTES OF MEMORY ARE
   REMAINING"
99 END
```

Sample Run *(Typical)*

```
13504 BYTES OF MEMORY REMAINING
```

(The amount of memory available will of course depend on the memory size of your computer.)

Alternate Spelling

M. is used by TRS-80 Level I as an abbreviation for MEM.

Variations In Usage

None known.

Also See

```
FRE, CLEAR
```

Function

MID

The MID$(string,n1,n2) function is used to isolate a specific number (n2) of string characters that are (n1) characters from the left-most character in the string.

For example, PRINT MID$("COMPUTER",4,3) prints the letters PUT, which are 3 MIDdle characters starting with the fourth string character from the left.

The string must be enclosed in quotes or assigned to a string variable. The number of characters and the starting position can be expressed as variables, numbers or arithmetic operations. A comma must separate each element in the MID$ function.

If the value of n1 or n2 is a decimal, the computer automatically converts to the integer value.

Test Program #1

```
10 REM 'MID$' TEST PROGRAM
20 A$="CONTESTANT"
30 B$=MID$(A$,4,4)
40 PRINT MID$("ATHENA",2,3)" 'MID$' FUNCTION PASSED
   THE ";B$
99 END
```

Sample Run

```
THE 'MID$' FUNCTION PASSED THE TEST
```

If the length (n2) is omitted, most BASICs will simply isolate the rest of the string. There are some, however, (e.g. TDL BASIC) that isolate only the character in the one specified position. Others don't allow values to be omitted.

Test Program #2

```
10 REM 'MID$(A$,N)' TEST PROGRAM
20 PRINT MID$("RODENT",3)
99 END
```

Did it print DENT, D or an error message?

MID$ is placed on the left side of the equal sign by some interpreters (e.g. BASIC-80, TDL BASIC, etc.) to modify the contents of a string variable. For example, 30 MID$(A$,3,5)=B$ replaces five characters of A$ with the first five characters of B$ starting at the third position from A$'s left. If B$ does not contain five characters, blanks are inserted in A$. If the length is omitted (5 in our example), all the rest of A$ is replaced by B$.

Test Program #3

```
10 REM 'MID$=' TEST PROGRAM
20 A$="CORPORATION"
30 MID$(A$,3,4)="MPUT"
40 PRINT "A COMPUTER WOULD SURE HELP THIS ";A$
99 END
```

Sample Run

```
A COMPUTER WOULD SURE HELP THIS COMPUTATION
```

Alternate Spelling

Some interpreters (e.g. DEC's BASIC-PLUS and Harris BASIC-V) accept MID in place of MID$ to isolate substrings.

IF YOUR COMPUTER DOESN'T HAVE IT

Most computers have ways of isolating substrings even if they don't have the MID$ function. SEG$ is used by some while SUBSTR is used by others.

Computers which require dimensioning of string variables (e.g. North Star, Hewlett-Packard, etc.) use subscripts to isolate the string characters. For example,

```
10 DIM A$(8)
20 A$="ABCDEFGH"
30 PRINT A$(3,5)
99 END
```

prints out CDE.

Sinclair ZX80 8K BASIC requires line 30 to read

```
30 PRINT A$(3 TO 5)
```

Variations In Usage

None known.

Also See

```
PRINT, RIGHT$, LEFT$, CHR$, SPACE$, STR$, STRING$,
INKEY$, SEG$
```

Function

The MIN function is used to determine which of two values is smaller.

For example, Y=A MIN 5 assigns Y the value of A if A is smaller than 5. Otherwise; Y = 5.

Test Program #1

```
10 REM 'MIN' TEST PROGRAM
20 A=2
30 Y=A MIN 5
40 IF Y=2 THEN 70
50 PRINT "'MIN' FAILED THE TEST"
60 GOTO 99
70 PRINT "'MIN' PASSED THE TEST"
99 END
```

Sample Run

```
'MIN' PASSED THE TEST
```

Variations In Usage

Some computers use the form MIN(A,B) for the same purpose. A few computers can find the smallest value in an array by using MIN. Example: 30 M=MIN(A)

Micropolis BASIC uses MIN to compare two strings and return the string that would occur earlier in an alphabetical listing.

For example: MIN("ABC","XYZ") returns "ABC".

IF YOUR COMPUTER DOESN'T HAVE IT

The MINimum value (Y) of two numbers can be determined by this formula:

```
Y= (A+B-ABS(A-B))/2
```

or by

```
30 Y=A
32 IF A<=B THEN 40
34 Y=B
```

The MINimum value in an array can be determined by this program:

Test Program #2

```
10 DIM A(6)
20 FOR I=1 TO 6
30  READ A(I)
40 NEXT I
50 M=A(1)
60 FOR I=2 TO 6
70  IF M<=A(I) THEN 90
80  M=A(I)
90 NEXT I
100 PRINT "THE MINIMUM VALUE IS ";M
110 DATA 3,5,13,1,8,-3
999 END
```

Sample Run

```
THE MINIMUM VALUE IS -3
```

Also See

```
ABS, MAX, <=
```

Function

MOD

X MOD Y is used in some computers (e.g. the H.P. 3000, COMPAL, Harris Computer Systems, and Apple) to compute the arithmetic remainder (MODulo) after the value X is divided by the value Y.

For example, PRINT 8 MOD 5 prints the number 3, which is the remainder of 8 divided by 5.

A few computers automatically integer the MODulo value.

For example, PRINT 10.5 MOD 4 may print the number 2 (the integer value of the 2.5 remainder).

Test Program

```
10 REM 'MOD' TEST PROGRAM
20 A = 13 MOD 5
30 IF A = 3 THEN 60
40 PRINT "THE MOD FUNCTION FAILED THE TEST"
50 GOTO 99
60 PRINT "THE MOD FUNCTION PASSED THE TEST"
99 END
```

Sample Run

```
THE MOD FUNCTION PASSED THE TEST
```

IF YOUR COMPUTER DOESN'T HAVE IT

MOD is handy but by no means irreplaceable. Here, step-by-step, is a way around it.

```
20 A = 13/5
22 A = A-INT(A)
24 A = INT(A*5)
```

A more general form of the equation is

```
20 A = INT(X - Y*INT(X/Y))
```

Substitute 13 for X and 5 for Y and try it in the TEST PROGRAM.

Variations In Usage

A few computers (e.g. the Harris BASIC-V) use MOD(X,Y) to compute the X MODulo Y value.

Also See

```
INT, FIX
```

NE is used in a few computers (e.g. the T.I. 990) as an abbreviation for the NEW command and the "not-equal" (<>) relational operator. It is recognized as NEW when used in the command mode, and as <> when used as a program statement.

Program #1 uses NE as the command NEW. For more information see NEW.

Test Program #1

```
10 REM 'NE(NEW)' TEST PROGRAM
20 PRINT "HELLO THERE"
99 END
```

Sample Run

LIST the program to ensure it has been entered as shown. Type NE to erase the TEST PROGRAM, then type LIST again to be certain the program has been "erased".

Program #2 uses NE as the "not-equal" relational operator. For more information see <>.

Test Program #2

```
10 REM 'NE (<>)' TEST PROGRAM
20 A=10
30 IF A NE 20 THEN 60
40 PRINT "THE NE OPERATOR FAILED THE TEST"
50 GOTO 99
60 PRINT "THE NE OPERATOR PASSED THE TEST"
99 END
```

Sample Run

```
THE NE OPERATOR PASSED THE TEST
```

Variations In Usage

None other known.

Also See

NEW, <>, <, >, <=, >=, =, EQ, GE, GT, LE, LT, IF-THEN

NE
N.

The NEW command erases the BASIC program(s) stored in memory. However, it does not erase the interpreter itself. NEW is normally used when a new program is to be entered into the computer and the existing program is to be deleted.

Test Program

```
10 REM 'NEW' COMMAND TEST PROGRAM
20 PRINT "HELLO THERE."
99 END
```

Sample Run

LIST the program to be sure it has been entered as shown. Check the remaining memory space with the PRINT MEMory command (or PRINT FRE(0), or other appropriate command).

Type NEW to erase the test program, then test for memory space again. There should be a corresponding increase in available memory.

To be certain the program has been "erased", double-check by typing LIST.

Some computers may use SCRATCH or SCR instead.

Alternate Spellings

A few computers accept NE or N. as abbreviations for NEW.

Variations In Usage

There are computers (e.g. Sinclair ZX80) that use NEW n to erase the program and at the same time set the amount of memory available for BASIC. If a machine language program is to be present in memory along with a BASIC program, it is good practice (maybe even necessary) to reserve the top portion of memory for the machine language program. n is a decimal number.

Also See

```
CLEAR, SCRATCH
```

The NEXT statement is used to return program execution to the preceding FOR statement which uses the same variable. When the range of the FOR statement is exceeded, the computer continues program execution at the line following the NEXT statement.

NEX
N.

For example:

```
10 FOR X=1 TO 3
20 NEXT X
99 END
```

The fourth time the NEXT statement is executed, the value of X is incremented to 4 which exceeds the FOR statement range of 3 causing the computer to "fall through" to line 99.

Test Program #1

```
10 REM 'NEXT' TEST PROGRAM
20 FOR X=1 TO 4
30 PRINT X,
40 NEXT X
50 PRINT
60 PRINT "THE 'NEXT' STATEMENT PASSED THE TEST."
99 END
```

Sample Run

```
1               2               3               4
THE 'NEXT' STATEMENT PASSED THE TEST.
```

Because NEXT statements return only to the preceding FOR statement which uses the same variable, it is possible with most computers to use "nested" FOR-NEXT statements. For more information see FOR.

Test Program #2

```
10 REM TEST PROGRAM WITH NESTED 'NEXT' STATEMENTS
20 FOR A=1 TO 3
30 FOR B=1 TO 4
40 PRINT A;B,
50 NEXT B
60 PRINT
70 NEXT A
80 PRINT "THE 'NEXT' STATEMENT PASSED THE TEST WHEN
   NESTED"
99 END
```

Sample Run

```
1   1              1   2              1   3              1   4
2   1              2   2              2   3              2   4
3   1              3   2              3   3              3   4
     THE  'NEXT'  STATEMENT  PASSED  THE  TEST  WHEN  NESTED
```

Many computers allow execution of a NEXT statement which does not contain a variable. In this case, the computer returns to the preceding FOR statement (regardless of its associated variable) so long as it has not exceeded its stated range.

To test for this feature, run the second TEST PROGRAM after removing the variables A and B from the NEXT statements in line 50 and 60. The sample run should remain the same.

Some computers allow NEXT to specify more than one variable. To end a triple nested loop, for example, NEXT K,J,I (with the variables in reverse order from the corresponding FOR statements) may be used.

Alternate Spellings

A few computers allow NEX and N. to be used as abbreviations for NEXT.

Variations In Usage

Some computers (e.g. DEC BASIC-PLUS-2) allow NEXT to be implied, *under certain circumstances*. The FOR is written, but not the NEXT.

Example: `30  PRINT  X,X*X  FOR  X=1  TO  5`

Also See

`FOR`

The NOFLOW command is used by Micropolis BASIC to disable its trace function (see FLOW). NOFLOW may be used as a program statement to turn the trace off at specified areas in the program.

Test Program

```
10 REM 'NOFLOW' TEST PROGRAM
20 PRINT "THE FIRST THREE LINES OF
   THIS PROGRAM"
30 NOFLOW
40 PRINT "ARE PRINTED WITH THE TRACE TURNED ON."
50 PRINT "THIS LINE IS PRINTED WITH THE TRACE TURNED OFF."
99 END
```

Sample Run

RUN the Test Program after typing the FLOW command.

```
<10> <20> THE FIRST THREE LINES OF THIS PROGRAM
<30> ARE PRINTED WITH THE TRACE TURNED ON.
THIS LINE IS PRINTED WITH THE TRACE TURNED OFF.
```

Variations In Usage

None known.

Also See

```
FLOW, NOTRACE, TRACE OFF, TROFF
```

NORMAL is used by the APPLE II as either a command or a statement to return the display to NORMAL mode. In this mode, all output from the computer is displayed as white characters on a black background. NORMAL is used following either FLASH or INVERSE, both of which create special display effects.

Test Program

```
10 REM 'NORMAL' TEST PROGRAM
20 INVERSE
30 PRINT "THIS IS INVERSE PRINTING,"
40 NORMAL
50 PRINT "BACK TO NORMAL"
99 END
```

To run this program, clear the screen and type RUN.

Sample Run

`THIS IS INVERSE PRINTING.`
BACK TO NORMAL

Variations In Usage

None known.

Also See

INVERSE, FLASH

NOT is used in IF-THEN statements as a logical operator to reverse the condition.

For example, IF NOT(A>5) THEN 60 reads, "if the value stored in A is NOT greater than 5, GOTO line 60".

Test Program #1

```
10 REM LOGICAL 'NOT' TEST PROGRAM
20 A=3
30 IF NOT(A>5) THEN 60
40 PRINT "'NOT' FAILED THE LOGICAL OPERATOR TEST"
50 GOTO 99
60 PRINT "'NOT' PASSED THE LOGICAL OPERATOR TEST"
99 END
```

Sample Run

```
'NOT' PASSED THE LOGICAL OPERATOR TEST
```

A few computers use NOT in string comparisons. For example, IF NOT(A$="YES" OR A$="NO") THEN 60 reads, "if the string stored in A$ is neither a YES nor a NO, program control goes to line 60".

Test Program #2

```
10 REM STRING LOGICAL 'NOT' TEST PROGRAM
20 PRINT "TYPE A YES OR A NO";
30 INPUT A$
40 IF NOT(A$="YES" OR A$="NO") THEN 70
50 PRINT "THANK YOU"
60 GOTO 99
70 PRINT A$;" IS NEITHER YES NOR NO!"
80 GOTO 20
99 END
```

Sample Run

```
TYPE A YES OR A NO? OK
OK IS NEITHER YES NOR NO!
TYPE A YES OR A NO? NO
THANK YOU
```

The NOT operator is used by some computers to form the binary complement (one's complement) of a number (i.e. each bit in the binary representation of the number is changed. All 0's become 1's and all 1's become 0's.)

Test Program #3

```
10 REM 'NOT' COMPLEMENT TEST PROGRAM
20 PRINT "ENTER A NUMBER BETWEEN -32768 AND 32767";
30 INPUT A
40 B=NOT(A)
50 PRINT "THE BINARY COMPLEMENT OF";A;"IS";B
60 GOTO 20
99 END
```

Sample Run *(using 5)*

```
ENTER A NUMBER BETWEEN -32768 AND 32767? 5
THE BINARY COMPLEMENT OF 5 IS -6
ENTER A NUMBER BETWEEN -32768 AND 32767?
```

IF YOUR COMPUTER DOESN'T HAVE IT

By changing the stated conditions, equivalent statements can be made without using NOT.

For example, NOT(A$="YES" OR A$="NO") is the same as A$<>"YES" AND A$<>"NO".

To form the binary complement of a number, use B=-(A+1).

Variations In Usage

None known.

Also See

AND, OR, XOR, IF-THEN

The NOTRACE command is used by the APPLE II BASIC to disable the trace function (see TRACE). NOTRACE may be used as a program statement to turn the trace off at specified areas in a program.

Test Program

```
10 REM 'NOTRACE' TEST PROGRAM
20 TRACE
30 PRINT "EACH LINE SHOULD BE TRACED"
40 NOTRACE
50 PRINT "BY THE 'TRACE' STATEMENT"
60 PRINT "UNTIL TURNED OFF BY THE 'NOTRACE' STATEMENT"
99 END
```

Sample Run

```
#30 EACH LINE SHOULD BE TRACED
#40 BY THE 'TRACE' STATEMENT
UNTIL TURNED OFF BY THE 'NOTRACE' STATEMENT
```

Variations In Usage

None known.

Also See

```
TRACE, TRACE OFF, TROFF, NOFLOW
```

Function

NUM is a function in some BASICs (e.g. Digital Group BASIC) that converts a numeric string into its numeric value. That is, a string of digits (including decimal point) is converted to the number it represents.

For example:

```
30 X = NUM("5.2")
40 PRINT X, X/2
```

stores 5.2 in X and prints 5.2 and 2.6. "5.2" cannot be used for computations since it is in "string" form. Converting the string to numeric form allows it to be included in calculations such as X/2. NUM is similar to the VAL function.

Test Program #1

```
10 REM 'NUM' TEST PROGRAM
20 A$="45.12"
30 A=NUM(A$)
40 PRINT "IF THE STRING ";A$;" IS CONVERTED TO THE
   NUMBER";A
50 PRINT "THEN THE NUM FUNCTION PASSED THE TEST."
99 END
```

Sample Run

```
IF THE STRING 45.12 IS CONVERTED TO THE NUMBER 45.12
THEN THE NUM FUNCTION PASSED THE TEST.
```

Some computers that have MAT INPUT (e.g. DEC PDP-11) use NUM to report how many items were typed into a list.

Test Program #2

```
10 REM 'NUM (MAT INPUT)' TEST PROGRAM
20 DIM N(20)
30 PRINT "TYPE A FEW NUMBERS SEPARATED BY COMMAS"
40 MAT INPUT N
50 S = 0
60 FOR I=1 TO NUM
70 S = S+N(I)
80 NEXT I
90 PRINT "THE AVERAGE OF";NUM;"VALUES IS";S/NUM
99 END
```

Sample Run *(typical)*

```
TYPE A FEW NUMBERS SEPARATED BY COMMAS
? 15, 34, 2, 8, 54, 19
THE AVERAGE OF 6 VALUES IS 22
```

Variations In Usage

None known.

Also See

```
VAL, MAT INPUT
```

Function

NUM$ is a function similar to STR$. It creates a **string** of numbers from a **numeric** expression.

For example, NUM$(25.6) converts the value 25.6 into the character string "25.6". The difference is that arithmetic operations can be performed on the numeric form while only string functions can be applied to the string form.

Test Program

```
10 REM 'NUM$' TEST PROGRAM
20 A = 123456
30 A$ = NUM$(A)
40 PRINT "IF THE NUMBER";A;"IS CONVERTED TO THE
   STRING ";A$
50 PRINT "THEN THE NUM$ FUNCTION PASSED THE TEST."
99 END
```

Sample Run

```
IF THE NUMBER 123456 IS CONVERTED TO THE STRING 123456
THEN THE NUM$ FUNCTION PASSED THE TEST.
```

Variations In Usage

None known.

Also See

STR$, VAL, ASC, CHR$

The ON ERROR GOTO statement is used to branch to an error subroutine when a program error is encountered, without stopping program execution. The ON ERROR GOTO statement must appear in the program before an execution error is anticipated. Any error encountered after the ON ERROR GOTO statement causes the computer to execute the line number listed in the ON ERROR GOTO statement.

ON ERR GOTO

Test Program

```
10 REM 'ON-ERROR-GOTO' TEST PROGRAM
20 ON ERROR GOTO 100
30 PRINT "ENTER A NUMBER AND ITS INVERSE WILL BE
   COMPUTED";
40 INPUT N
50 A=1/N
60 PRINT "THE INVERSE OF";N;"IS";A
70 GOTO 30
100 PRINT "THE INVERSE OF 0 CANNOT BE COMPUTED -
    TRY AGAIN"
110 RESUME 30
999 END
```

Sample Run *(using 4 and 0)*

```
ENTER A NUMBER AND ITS INVERSE WILL BE COMPUTED?4
THE INVERSE OF 4 IS .25
ENTER A NUMBER AND ITS INVERSE WILL BE COMPUTED? 0
THE INVERSE OF 0 CANNOT BE COMPUTED - TRY AGAIN
ENTER A NUMBER AND ITS INVERSE WILL BE COMPUTED?
```

*The error here was **division by zero**.)*

If ON ERROR GOTO 0 is executed during an ON ERROR GOTO subroutine, the error message is printed and program execution stops. Test this feature by adding the following line to the test program:

```
105 ON ERROR GOTO 0
```

A syntax error encountered by some computers causes the line containing the error to be printed by the edit feature after the ON ERROR GOTO statement has been executed and program execution has stopped. The computer is then in the Edit mode. To test this feature change line 50 in the TEST PROGRAM to:

```
50 ILLEGAL LINE
```

The RESUME statement is normally used to return to the main program from an ON ERROR GOTO subroutine.

Alternate Spelling

A few BASICs (e.g. APPLESOFT), have ON ERR GOTO instead of ON ERROR GOTO.

Variations In Usage

None known.

Also See

ERROR, RESUME, ERR, ERL

ON-GOSUB is a multiple subroutine branching scheme which incorporates a number of IF-GOSUB tests into a single statement.

ON-GOS.

For example, ON X GOSUB 100,200,300 instructs the computer to branch to subroutines starting at lines 100, 200 or 300 if the integer value of X is 1, 2, or 3 respectively. If INT X is less than 1 or more than 3 the tests in this ON-GOSUB example all fail. In some computers, execution then defaults to the next program line; in other computers, the program "crashes" and an error message is printed.

Test Program

```
10 REM 'ON-GOSUB' TEST PROGRAM
20 PRINT "ENTER THE NUMBER 1, 2 OR 3";
30 INPUT X
40 PRINT "THE ON-GOSUB STATEMENT";
50 ON X GOSUB 100,200,300
60 GOTO 20
100 REM SUBROUTINE #1
110 PRINT "BRANCHED TO SUBROUTINE #1"
120 RETURN
200 REM SUBROUTINE #2
210 PRINT "BRANCHED TO SUBROUTINE #2"
220 RETURN
300 REM SUBROUTINE #3
310 PRINT "BRANCHED TO SUBROUTINE #3"
320 RETURN
999 END
```

Sample Run

```
ENTER THE NUMBER 1, 2 OR 3? 1
THE ON-GOSUB STATEMENT BRANCHED TO SUBROUTINE #1
ENTER THE NUMBER 1, 2 OR 3? 2
THE ON-GOSUB STATEMENT BRANCHED TO SUBROUTINE #2
ENTER THE NUMBER 1, 2 OR 3? 3
THE ON-GOSUB STATEMENT BRANCHED TO SUBROUTINE #3
ENTER THE NUMBER 1, 2 OR 3?
```

Use the same TEST PROGRAM and try entering decimal values larger than 1 but smaller than 4.

Try values smaller than 1, then larger than 4.

IF YOUR COMPUTER DOESN'T HAVE IT

If your computer did not pass the ON-GOSUB test, substitute these lines:

```
45 IF X=1 GOSUB 100
50 IF X=2 GOSUB 200
55 IF X=3 GOSUB 300
```

(Be careful that the value of X is not changed in the subroutine called.) If this subroutine works, the intrinsic INT functions can be duplicated by substituting these lines:

```
45 IF INT(X)=1 GOSUB 100
50 IF INT(X)=2 GOSUB 200
55 IF INT(X)=3 GOSUB 300
```

For other tricks involving the ON-GOSUB statement, see ON-GOTO.

Alternate Spelling

TRS-80 Level I allows ON-GOS.

Variations In Usage

None known.

Also See

```
ON-GOTO, ON-ERROR-GOTO, GOTO-OF, GOSUB-OF, GOSUB
```

ON-GOTO is a multiple branching scheme which incorporates a number of IF-THEN tests into a single statement. For example, ON X GOTO 100,200,300 instructs the computer to branch to lines 100, 200, or 300 if the value of X is 1, 2, or 3 respectively. If X is less than 1 or more than 3.999 the tests in this ON-GOTO example all fail and execution defaults to the next program line.

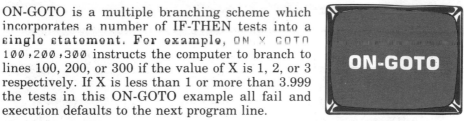

ON-GOT
ON-G.

The integer value of X cannot exceed the number of possible branches in the statement. If the value of X is a decimal, the computer automatically finds its integer value and selects the appropriate branching line number.

Test Program

```
10 REM 'ON(X)GOTO' TEST PROGRAM
20 PRINT "ENTER THE NUMBER 1, 2 OR 3"
30 INPUT X
40 PRINT "THE ON-GOTO STATEMENT";
50 ON X GOTO 100,200,300
60 PRINT "FAILED THE TEST"
70 GOTO 999
100 PRINT "BRANCHED TO LINE 100"
110 GOTO 20
200 PRINT "BRANCHED TO LINE 200"
210 GOTO 20
300 PRINT "BRANCHED TO LINE 300"
310 GOTO 20
999 END
```

Sample Run *(using 1, 2 and then 3)*

```
ENTER THE NUMBER 1,2 OR 3
? 1
THE ON-GOTO STATEMENT BRANCHED TO LINE 100
ENTER THE NUMBER 1, 2, OR 3
? 2
THE ON-GOTO STATEMENT BRANCHED TO LINE 200
? 3
THE ON-GOTO STATEMENT BRANCHED TO LINE 300
ENTER THE NUMBER 1, 2 OR 3
?
```

Using the same TEST PROGRAM, try values smaller than 1, then larger than 3.999.

Alternate Spellings

A few computers allow abbreviations of GOTO in the ON-GOTO statement. The PDP-8E allows ON X GOT while some Tiny BASICs allow ON X G.

IF YOUR COMPUTER DOESN'T HAVE IT

If the computer did not pass the ON-GOTO test, substitute these lines:

```
45 IF X=1 THEN 100
50 IF X=2 THEN 200
55 IF X=3 THEN 300
```

If this substitution works, the intrinsic INT functions can be duplicated by substituting these lines.

```
45 IF INT(X)=1 THEN 100
50 IF INT(X)=2 THEN 200
55 IF INT(X)=3 THEN 300
```

A TRICK

Errors might occur in prior rounding of the value X producing a value slightly lower than the expected integer value. The ON-GOTO statement can be protected from this shortcoming by slightly increasing the value X. For example:

```
ON X+.1 GOTO 100, 200, 300
```

If the value of X in this case had been rounded down to 1.99 instead of the expected value of 2.0, adding .1 puts X above 2(2.09), which is then rounded down to the desired 2.0, by the intrinsic integer function. If not, no harm is done.

Shifting The Base

When the value X is not 1, 2 or 3, an equation can take its place in order to make ON-GOTO usable. For example:

```
ON X-50 GOTO 100, 200, 300
```

branches to lines 100, 200 or 300 when the value of X is 51, 52 or 53 respectively.

Variations In Usage

Different interpreters may have a limit to the number of branching options (3 were used only for an example).

The ON-GOTO statement is also used with a few other key words to branch to another part of the program when a specified condition occurs.

ON END GOTO 2000 will send the program control to line 2000 when the program attempts to read more DATA than is stored in a disk or tape file. ON EOF(1) GOTO 2000 may be used for the same purpose by some computers.

ON ERROR GOTO 2000 transfers control to line 2000 on any error detected as will ON ERR GOTO 2000. See ON ERROR GOTO for more information.

Another variation of ON-GOTO is the ON X RESTORE statement. This will reset the data pointer to the start of a DATA line whose line number is in the list of numbers in the ON statement. Example: ON X RESTORE 200, 210, 220 will restore the DATA pointer to line 200 if X is 1, to 210 if X is 2 or to 220 if X is 3. See RESTORE for more information.

Also See

ON-GOSUB, ON-ERROR, GOTO-OF, GOSUB-OF, GOTO

OPTION is used in the Harris BASIC-V with the BASE statement to define the BASE (lowest) variable array element as any integer value from 0 to 10.

For example:

```
10 OPTION BASE=5
20 DIM A(10)
```

The OPTION BASE statement defines this array as having 6 elements [A(5) to A(10)].

If the OPTION BASE value is not specified, the computer assumes the BASE value to be 0.

For more information see BASE.

Test Program

```
10 REM 'OPTION' TEST PROGRAM
20 OPTION BASE=3
30 DIM A(5)
40 FOR X=3 TO 5
50 A(X)=X
60 NEXT X
70 OPTION BASE=0
80 FOR X=0 TO 2
90 A(X)=X
100 NEXT X
110 FOR X=0 TO 5
120 PRINT A(X);
130 NEXT X
140 PRINT "THE OPTION STATEMENT DID NOT CRASH"
999 END
```

Sample Run

```
 0   1   2   3   4   5 THE OPTION STATEMENT DID NOT CRASH
```

Variations In Usage

ANSI Standard BASIC specifies only OPTION BASE values 0 and 1, and an equal sign is not required following the word BASE.

Also See

BASE

OR is used with IF-THEN statements to create a "logical math" operator to test for multiple conditions.

For example, IF A=2 OR B=6 THEN 70 reads, "if the value of variable A equals 2 OR the value of variable B equals 6, OR both, the IF-THEN condition is met, and execution jumps to line 70."

Test Program #1

```
10 REM LOGICAL 'OR' TEST PROGRAM
20 A=8
30 B=6
40 IF A=2 OR B=6 THEN 70
50 PRINT "OR FAILED THE TEST AS A LOGICAL OPERATOR"
60 GOTO 99
70 PRINT "OR PASSED THE LOGICAL OPERATOR TEST"
99 END
```

Sample Run

```
OR PASSED THE LOGICAL OPERATOR TEST
```

A few computers allow the OR operator to be used to make compound tests on literal strings.

For example, IF A$="Y" OR A$="YES" THEN 80 reads, "If the string variable A$ contains either the letter Y OR the word YES, the IF-THEN condition is met and continues at line 80." Some computers allow the use of + in place of OR.

Test Program #2

```
10 REM STRING LOGICAL 'OR' TEST PROGRAM
20 A$="A"
30 B$="F"
40 IF A$="A" OR B$="B" THEN 70
50 PRINT "OR FAILED THE STRING LOGICAL OPERATOR TEST"
60 GOTO 99
70 PRINT" "OR PASSED THE STRING LOGICAL OPERATOR TEST"
99 END
```

Sample Run

```
OR PASSED THE STRING LOGICAL OPERATOR TEST
```

Some computers use the logical operator OR to determine if the conditions are met in either of two logical operators. If the condition of at least one of the operators is met, OR responds with a TRUE value (a -1 in most computers; check the user's manual for your system). When neither condition is met, OR responds with a FALSE value (the number 0).

For example, PRINT A=4 OR B>5 reads, "If A has a value of 4 OR the value stored in B is greater than 5, OR both, the computer will print the number -1." If neither condition is met, the computer will print a 0.

Test Program #3

```
10 REM 'OR' LOGICAL TEST PROGRAM
20 PRINT "ENTER A NUMBER FROM 1 TO 10";
30 INPUT A
40 B= A<1 OR A>10
50 IF B<>0 THEN 80
60 PRINT A; "IS A NUMBER BETWEEN 1 AND 10"
70 GOTO 20
80 PRINT A; "IS NOT GREATER THAN 0 AND LESS THAN 11"
90 GOTO 20
99 END
```

Sample Runs *(typical)*

```
ENTER A NUMBER FROM 1 TO 10? 6
 6 IS A NUMBER BETWEEN 1 AND 10
ENTER A NUMBER FROM 1 TO 10? 13
 13 IS NOT GREATER THAN 0 AND LESS THAN 11
```

The OR operator is used by a few computers to compute the binary logical OR of two numbers following the rules of Boolean Algebra. OR compares the binary forms of two numbers bit by bit. If either ORed bit is a 1, the computer outputs a 1.

For example:

```
0 OR 0 = 0
0 OR 1 = 1
1 OR 0 = 1
1 OR 1 = 1
```

Therefore, when the computer ORs one number with another, each number's bits are logically ORed with the other number's corresponding bits, producing a third number.

For example:

	DECIMAL	BINARY
	3	0011
(logical)	OR	
	5	0101
=	7	0111

In this example, the only time a 0 results is when both bits are 0.

Test Program #4

```
10 REM 'OR' BINARY LOGIC TEST PROGRAM
20 PRINT "ENTER A VALUE FOR X";
30 INPUT X
40 PRINT "ENTER A VALUE FOR Y";
50 INPUT Y
60 A = X OR Y
70 PRINT "THE LOGICAL 'OR' VALUE OF ";X;" AND ";Y;
   "IS ";A
80 GOTO 20
99 END
```

Sample Run *(using 6 and 10)*

```
ENTER A VALUE FOR X? 6
ENTER A VALUE FOR Y? 10
THE LOGICAL 'OR' VALUE OF 6 AND 10 IS 14
ENTER A VALUE FOR X?
```

Variations In Usage

The OR operator is sometimes used in a different form, OR(P\$,Q\$), to modify strings. If P\$ and Q\$ are strings, their contents will be ORed character by character with the results stored in P\$. If P\$ has fewer characters than Q\$, the remaining characters in Q\$ are ignored. If Q\$ has fewer characters, the remaining characters in P\$ are unchanged.

The WANG 2200B also accepts OR(A\$,B), where A\$ is a string and B is a hex constant. Each character of A\$ is ORed with the hex value B and the results stored in A\$.

Examples: If P\$ = "ABC" and Q\$ = "DEF", OR(P\$,Q\$) sets P\$ to "EGG". If A\$ = "DDD", OR(A\$,02) sets A\$ to "FFF"

Test Program #5

```
10 REM 'OR' STRING MODIFIER TEST PROGRAM
20 A$="ABC"
30 B$="LMN"
40 OR(A$,B$)
50 PRINT "OR PASSED THE TEST IF ";A$;"=MOO"
99 END
```

Sample Run

```
OR PASSED THE TEST IF MOO=MOO
```

IF YOUR COMPUTER DOESN'T HAVE IT

If you don't have the logical OR operator available on your computer, its effect can be simulated with subtraction and multiplication. Replace line 40 of Test Program #1 with:

```
40 IF (A-2) * (B-6) = 0 THEN 70
```

Also See

```
AND , XOR , NOT , + , *
```

PAUSE is a statement used by the Sharp/TRS-80 Pocket computer to display data in the window. PAUSE is like the PRINT statement except that a pause of 0.85 seconds is generated before the program resumes. (On the Pocket computer, PRINT stops the program until the user restarts it by pressing the ENTER key.)

Example: `PAUSE A$;F` displays the contents of A$ and the value of F next to each other.

`PAUSE J,K` displays the value of J at the left edge of the display and the value of K starting in column 13 of the 24 character screen.

The output can be formatted with USING. (See PRINT USING.)

Example: `PAUSE USING"#####.##";C` displays a number, C, chopped (not rounded) after 2 decimal places. The format specified by the USING clause stays in effect for all PRINT and PAUSE statements until another USING clause alters or cancels it. `PAUSE USING;N` cancels any existing format before printing the value of N.

Variations In Usage

A few BASICs (e.g. Processor Tech) use the statement PAUSE*n* to cause the program to PAUSE for *n* tenths of a second before continuing execution.

Test Program #1

```
10 REM 'PAUSE' TEST PROGRAM
20 PRINT "PAUSE PASSED THE TEST IF THIS"
30 PRINT "MESSAGE STAYS ON THE SCREEN FOR"
40 PRINT "FIVE SECONDS...."
50 PAUSE 50
60 PRINT "BEFORE THIS PART IS PRINTED."
99 END
```

Sample Run

```
PAUSE PASSED THE TEST IF THIS
MESSAGE STAYS ON THE SCREEN FOR
FIVE SECONDS....  (pause)
BEFORE THIS PART IS PRINTED.
```

IF YOUR COMPUTER DOESN'T HAVE IT

If your computer failed the test, you can build in a pause with a FOR-NEXT loop. By experimenting, the proper number of loops can be determined for the desired time lapse. Then substitute these lines for line 50:

```
50 FOR X=1 TO 1800
55 NEXT X
```

changing the 1800 to the number that causes your computer to PAUSE for five seconds.

Also See

PRINT, PRINT USING

The OUT statement is used to send a number (byte value) to a specified computer OUTput port.

The OUT statement format is OUT (port, byte).

The byte and port values must be positive integers or variables between 0 and 255. For example: OUT 255, 4 sends the binary equivalent of 4 (decimal) to port number 255.

Press the Play button on the cassette recorder and try this program.

Test Program #1 (Configured for TRS-80)

```
10 REM 'OUT' TEST PROGRAM
20 PRINT "ENTER '4' TO TURN ON THE CASSETTE RECORDER
   MOTOR"
30 INPUT X
40 OUT 255,X
50 PRINT "ENTER '0' TO TURN THE MOTOR OFF"
60 INPUT X
70 OUT 255,X
99 END
```

Sample Run

```
ENTER '4' TO TURN ON THE CASSETTE RECORDER MOTOR
? 4
ENTER '0' TO TURN THE MOTOR OFF
? 0
```

If the cassette recorder motor did not turn on, try this program to find which port and byte numbers work for your computer.

Test Program #2

```
10 REM 'OUT' SEARCH PROGRAM
20 FOR P=0 TO 255
30 FOR B=0 TO 255
40 PRINT "PORT#";P,
50 PRINT "BYTE#";B
60 OUT P,B
70 NEXT B
80 NEXT P
99 END
```

Variations In Usage

None known.

Also See

INP, PIN, PEEK, POKE

PDL is a special function used in APPLE II BASIC to indicate the settings of two game control units. The control units are identified as PDL(0) and PDL(1). (PDL is an abbreviation for Paddle and refers to control game "paddles".)

Test Program

```
10 REM 'PDL' TEST PROGRAM
20 A=PDL(0)
30 B=PDL(1)
40 PRINT "THE VALUE OF PDL(0) IS";A
50 PRINT "THE VALUE OF PDL(1) IS";B
60 PRINT "CHANGE THE CONTROL UNIT SETTINGS AND (RUN)
   AGAIN"
99 END
```

Sample Run *(typical)*

```
THE VALUE OF PDL(0) IS 13
THE VALUE OF PDL(1) IS 146
CHANGE THE CONTROL UNIT SETTINGS AND (RUN) AGAIN
```

Variations In Usage

None known.

Also See

```
GR, PLOT, COLOR, KEY$
```

Statement

PEEK is used to examine the contents of a specific address in the computer's memory.

For example, X=PEEK (18370) assigns the numeric value stored in memory address 18370 to the variable X.

The PEEK statement reports the contents of a memory address as a number between 0 and 255 (the range of values that can be held in an 8-bit memory cell). PEEK can be used with the POKE statement to read what POKE has POKEd into memory. The highest number address that can be PEEKed of course depends on the computer's memory size.

Check your computer's manual before executing this Test Program to determine that memory addresses 18368 to 18380 are reserved as a free memory. This avoids POKing data into memory addresses reserved for normal computer operation. If addresses 18368 to 18380 are not reserved as free memory in your computer, then select a group of 13 consecutive free memory addresses and change lines 20 and 60 in the TEST PROGRAM accordingly.

Test Program *(Configured for TRS-80)*

```
10 REM 'PEEK' TEST PROGRAM
20 FOR X=18368 TO 18380
30 READ Y
40 POKE X,Y
50 NEXT X
60 FOR X=18368 TO 18380
70 Y=PEEK(X)
80 PRINT CHR$(Y);
90 NEXT X
100 DATA 84,69,83,84,128,67,79,77,80,76,69,84,69
999 END
```

Sample Run

```
TEST COMPLETE
```

The PEEK and POKE statements are also used with the USR(X) statement to run machine language subroutines.

Variations In Usage

None known.

Also See

POKE, USR(X), SYSTEM, EXAM, FETCH, STUFF, FILL

Function

PI is used to represent the value of π (3.14159265).

Test Program

```
10 REM 'PI' TEST PROGRAM
20 R=6
30 C=2*PI*R
40 PRINT "THE CIRCUMFERENCE OF A
   CIRCLE"
50 PRINT "WITH A RADIUS OF 6 FEET
   IS";C;"FEET"
99 END
```

Sample Run

```
THE CIRCUMFERENCE OF A CIRCLE
WITH A RADIUS OF 6 FEET IS 37.6991 FEET
```

IF YOUR COMPUTER DOESN'T HAVE IT

If your computer does not have the PI capability, substitute the value 3.14159265 for it.

Variations In Usage

PI(X) in Harris BASIC-V computes the value of PI*X.

PIN is used by a few interpreters (e.g. Heath Benton Harbor BASIC) to read the decimal value of a byte of information at a specified computer port. The byte value can be any positive integer from 0 to 255.

For example, PRINT PIN(X) prints the decimal value of the byte at port X.

Test Program

```
10 REM 'PIN' TEST PROGRAM
20 FOR X=0 TO 255
30 PRINT "THE DECIMAL VALUE OF THE BYTE AT PORT#";
   X;"IS";PIN(X)
40 NEXT X
99 END
```

Sample Run *(Typical)*

```
THE DECIMAL VALUE OF THE BYTE AT PORT# 0 IS 255
                                        .
                                        .
                                        .
                                        .
                                        .
                                        .
                                        .
THE DECIMAL VALUE OF THE BYTE AT PORT# 255 IS 127
```

Alternate Word

See INP

Variations In Usage

None known.

Also See

INP, OUT, PEEK, USR, INPUT

Statement

PLOT (n1, n2) is used in APPLE II BASIC as a special feature to "turn on" or "light up" a colored graphics block in a predetermined grid on the screen. The color is determined by the COLOR statement. (See COLOR)

The grid block to be lit is specified by the two numbers following the PLOT statement. The first number (n1) specifies the column and the second number (n2) specifies the row.

For example, PLOT 10,25 instructs the computer to color a graphics block located in the 10th column and the 25th row (of the graphics grid).

To "turn off" individual graphics blocks, the color 0 (black) must be selected for each block. Executing the GR statement erases the entire screen (See GR).

The column number (n1) may range from 0 to 39 and the row number from 0 to 47, although only the rows 0 to 39 are within the graphics area. The bottom 8 graphics rows on the screen are reserved for TEXT. Each line of text requires 2 rows, making it possible to place 4 lines of text under the graphics display.

Test Program

```
10 REM 'PLOT' TEST PROGRAM
20 GR
30 COLOR = 4
40 PLOT 0,0
50 PLOT 39,0
60 PLOT 39,39
70 PLOT 0,39
99 END
```

Sample Run

If the computer accepted the PLOT statement, a green dot should appear at each corner of the screen.

Variations In Usage

None known.

Also See

GR, COLOR, TEXT, HLIN-AT, VLIN-AT, SET, RESET, POINT, DRAW

POINT

The POINT function is used with IF-THEN statements by the TRS-80 as a special feature to indicate whether or not a specific graphics block is "turned on".

The graphics block is specified by the X,Y coordinates enclosed in parentheses following the POINT function. For Level I a value of 1 is reported back when the block is lit. Level II gives back -1. Both report a 0 when the block is not lit.

Test Program

```
10 REM 'POINT' TEST PROGRAM
20 CLS
30 FOR X=20 TO 30 STEP 2
40 SET(X,8)
50 NEXT X
60 PRINT "POINT PASSED THE TEST IF NUMBERS 10101010101
    APPEAR"
70 FOR X=20 TO 30
80 A=0
90 IF POINT(X,8)=1 THEN A=1
100 PRINT A;
110 NEXT X
120 GOTO 120
999 END
```

Sample Run *(Level I)*

```
POINT PASSED THE TEST IF NUMBERS 10101010101 APPEAR
   1   0   1   0   1   0   1   0   1   0   1   0   1
```

To obtain the same results for Level II, change line 90 to

```
90 IF POINT(X,8)=-1 THEN A=1
```

Variations In Usage

None known.

Also See

```
SET, RESET, CLS, DOT
```

Statement

POKE is used to store integer values from 0 to 255 (decimal) in specified memory locations. For example, POKE 15360,65 places the ASCII number 65 (which is the letter 'A') in memory address 15360.

Check your computer's manual before running this test program to determine that memory addresses 15360 to 16383 are in the computer's CRT memory area, and can be POKEd without erasing memory dedicated to another use.

Test Program

```
10 REM 'POKE' TEST PROGRAM
20 REM USES CRT MEMORY ADDRESSES 15360 TO 16383
30 FOR Y=65 TO 90
40 FOR X=15360 TO 16383
50 POKE X,Y
60 NEXT X
70 NEXT Y
99 END
```

Sample Run

The computer passed this POKE test if the screen filled with letters from A to Z.

Variations In Usage

None known.

Also See

PEEK, FILL, STUFF, EXAM, FETCH

POP is a feature of Apple II BASIC. It "pops" the address of a GOSUB's line number off the top of a memory stack which stores it. When the program encounters a RETURN, it checks the stack to see where to resume execution, but gets fooled. Let's try that one again.

Each time a GOSUB is executed, its machine language address is stored in a special section of memory called a "push down" stack. The last value stored in this stack is the first value which will be read out and used up. A RETURN statement reads this top address "on the stack" to determine where to "return" program control after its GOSUB is completed.

In the TEST PROGRAM, the machine language address of Line 20 is stored on the top of the stack when the program GOSUBs to Line 50. When the GOSUB in Line 50 is executed, its address is piled on top of the line 20 address.

The POP statement in Line 80 "POPs" the address of Line 50 off the top of the stack and throws it away. When the RETURN statement in Line 90 goes to the stack to see where to resume execution, it finds the address of Line 20 instead of Line 50. Execution resumes at the end of Line 20, and moves on to Line 30.

POP may be used when a calculated result or an error condition requires branching to another place in the program, rather than RETURNing to the most recent GOSUB.

Test Program

```
10 REM 'POP' TEST PROGRAM
20 GOSUB 50
30 PRINT"'POP' PASSED THE TEST"
40 GOTO 99
50 GOSUB 80
60 PRINT "'POP' FAILED THE TEST"
70 GOTO 99
80 POP
90 RETURN
99 END
```

Sample Run

```
'POP' PASSED THE TEST
```

IF YOUR COMPUTER DOESN'T HAVE IT

If your computer failed the POP test, similar results can be produced by using "flags".

```
10 REM 'POOR MAN'S POP'
15 F=0
20 GOSUB 50
30 PRINT "RETURN TO HERE"
40 GOTO 99
50 GOSUB 80
55 IF F=1 THEN 70
60 PRINT "DON'T PRINT THIS"
70 RETURN
80 F=1
90 RETURN
99 END
```

Sample Run

```
RETURN TO HERE
```

Variations In Usage

None known.

Also See

```
GOSUB, RETURN, ON GOSUB, GOSUB OF
```

POS(*n*,A\$,B\$) is a string function that finds the starting position of the first occurence of string B\$ within string A\$. If B\$ is not found within A\$, POS = 0.

N is optional and is used to start the search at the *n*th character of A\$. If *n* is not used, the search begins at the first, or leftmost character in A\$.

Test Program #1

```
10 REM 'POS' TEST PROGRAM
20 A$ = "PROGRAM"
30 B$ = "RAM"
40 K = POS(A$,B$)
50 IF K<>5 THEN 110
60 B$ = "ROM"
70 K = POS(A$,B$)
80 IF K<>0 THEN 110
90 PRINT "'POS(A$,B$)' PASSED THE TEST"
100 GOTO 30999
110 PRINT "'POS(A$,B$)' FAILED THE TEST"
30999 END
```

Sample Run

```
'POS(A$,B$)' PASSED THE TEST
```

Test Program #2

```
10 REM 'POS(N,A$,B$)' TEST PROGRAM
20 A$ = "COMPUSOFT"
30 B$ = "O"
40 K = POS(4,A$,B$)
50 IF K=7 THEN 80
60 PRINT "'POS(N,A$,B$)' FAILED THE TEST"
70 GOTO 30999
80 PRINT "'POS(N,A$,B$)' PASSED THE TEST"
30999 END
```

Sample Run

```
'POS(N,A$,B$)' PASSED THE TEST
```

Variations In Usage

Some interpreters (e.g. Microsoft BASIC) use the POS(*n*) function to report the position of the cursor in the current print line. The value of *n* doesn't matter — it's just a "dummy" number.

Test Program #3

```
10 REM 'POS(N)' TEST PROGRAM
20 PRINT "THIS LINE HAS A CHARACTER COUNT OF";
30 K = POS(N)
40 PRINT K+3
99 END
```

Sample Run

```
THIS LINE HAS A CHARACTER COUNT OF 37
```

IF YOUR COMPUTER DOESN'T HAVE IT

If both tests #1 and #2 failed, try the INSTR and INDEX functions or use the subroutine listed under INSTR. To use this subroutine with Test Program #1 make these changes:

```
35 N = 1
40 GOSUB 30060
70 GOSUB 30060
```

For Test Program #2 make these changes:

```
35 N = 4
40 GOSUB 30060
```

Also See

```
INSTR, INDEX
```

The PRECISION statement is used in TDL BASIC to specify the maximum number of digits to be printed to the right of the decimal point by a PRINT statement. For example, 20 PRECISION 2 might be used in a program where the printed values are to represent dollars and cents. If the actual value is longer than the number of digits specified, the number is rounded to the desired number of places and the right most digits are not displayed.

Test Program

```
10 REM PRECISION TEST PROGRAM
20 PRECISION 4
30 X = 0.1234567
40 PRINT X
50 PRINT "PRECISION PASSED THE TEST IF 0.1235 WAS
   PRINTED"
99 END
```

Sample Run

```
 0.1235
PRECISION PASSED THE TEST IF 0.1235 WAS PRINTED
```

IF YOUR COMPUTER DOESN'T HAVE IT

If PRECISION isn't available on your computer, try the DIGITS statement in line 20.

The maximum number of digits after the decimal point can also be controlled by deleting line 20 and replacing line 40 with:

```
40 PRINT USING "##.####";X
```

If PRINT USING isn't available either, don't despair! Substitute

```
40 PRINT INT(X*10000 + .5)/10000
```

Variations In Usage

None known.

Also See

```
DIGITS, PRINT USING, IMAGE, FMT, INT
```

Command Statement

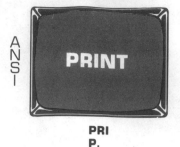

ANSI

PRINT

PRI
P.

PRINT has a wide range of uses. The most common is in program statements used to display variable values or whatever may be enclosed in quotes. For example, PRINT X prints the numeric value of the variable X, while PRINT "X" prints the letter X.

Most computers use PRINT both as a command (as you would on a standard calculator), and a program statement.

For example, the **command,** PRINT 4*12/(2+6) prints the answer 6.

Test Program #1

```
10 REM 'PRINT' TEST PROGRAM
20 PRINT "THE PRINT STATEMENT WORKS"
99 END
```

Sample Run

```
THE PRINT STATEMENT WORKS
```

A comma can be used in a PRINT statement to cause individual items to be printed in pre-established horizontal zones of about 16 spaces wide. Actual width of the print zones varies between computers.

For example, PRINT 1,2,3,4 prints in a format similar to;

```
1               2               3               4
```

For more information see ,(comma).

Test Program #2

```
10 REM 'PRINT' WITH COMMA TEST PROGRAM
20 PRINT "THE COMMA WORKED IN THE PRINT STATEMENT"
30 PRINT "IF THESE NUMBERS ARE PRINTED IN 4 ZONES"
40 PRINT 1,2,3,4
99 END
```

Sample Run

```
THE COMMA WORKED IN THE PRINT STATEMENT
IF THESE NUMBERS ARE PRINTED IN 4 ZONES
1               2               3               4
```

A semicolon works like a comma, but prints the output values packed tightly together, instead of in pre-established zones.

Change line 40 to read

```
40 PRINT 1;2;3;4
```

Run the Test Program again and note the new spacing.

The semicolon (;) is often used in PRINT statements to join together (concatenate) parts of words or sentences on one line.

For example, PRINT "H";"I" prints the word "HI".

For more information see ;(semicolon).

Test Program #3

```
10 REM 'PRINT' WITH SEMICOLON TEST PROGRAM
20 PRINT "IS THIS PRINTED ";
30 PRINT "ON ONE LINE?"
99 END
```

Sample Run

```
IS THIS PRINTED ON ONE LINE?
```

TAB(n) is used with the PRINT statement in a manner similar to the tab key on a typewriter. It inserts (n) spaces before the printed statement as specified by the value enclosed in parentheses. For more information see TAB.

The AT function is used with PRINT in the TRS-80 Level I BASIC (the @ operator is used by the TRS-80 Level II) to specify the PRINT statement's starting location. For more information see PRINT AT and @ .

PRINT USING is used by some computers as a special PRINT feature which allows numbers or strings to be printed USING a specified format.

For example, PRINT USING "*****.##";12.5 prints the number ***12.50.

For much more information see PRINT USING.

Some BASICs (e.g. North Star) place format information in the PRINT statement immediately after PRINT. For example,

PRINT %C10F2,P will print the value of P in a 10 column field with two digits following the decimal point (10F2).

C causes commas to be inserted to form 3-digit groupings. If P = 12345.678 then P will be printed as 12,345.68.

Other options for formatting are:
$(print leading dollar sign),
Z (suppress trailing zeros),
wEd (express number in exponential form with d digits to the right of the decimal. The w should be at least d+8), and
nI (integer mode with n digits maximum).

MAT PRINT prints the values stored in array variables.

For example,

```
10 DIM A(3)
20 MAT PRINT A
```

will print the values assigned to array variables A(1), A(2), and A(3). For more information see MAT PRINT.

PRINT# is used in the TRS-80 Level I BASIC to store data on cassette tape. To store more than one value with one PRINT# statement, the following format is used;

```
PRINT# A;",";B;",";C  etc.
```

To test this feature, set the cassette recorder to the Record mode and RUN this program.

Test Program #4

```
10 REM 'PRINT#' TEST PROGRAM
20 PRINT "DATA SHOULD BE RECORDING ON CASSETTE TAPE"
30 A$="TEST"
40 PRINT# A$;",";1;",";2;",";3
50 PRINT "PRINT# HAS COMPLETED THE DATA TRANSFER"
99 END
```

Sample Run

```
DATA SHOULD BE RECORDING ON CASSETTE TAPE
PRINT# HAS COMPLETED THE DATA TRANSFER
```

More advanced TRS-80 BASICs require a -1 following the PRINT# statement when used with a single recorder. If a second recorder is used, it is addressed by PRINT #-2, (etc.)

For example, PRINT#-1,A,B,C$ stores on tape drive #1 the values assigned to variables A, B and C$.

Test Program #5

Set the cassette recorder to the Record mode and RUN this program.

```
10 REM 'PRINT#' TEST PROGRAM
20 PRINT "DATA SHOULD BE RECORDING ON CASSETTE TAPE"
30 PRINT#-1,"TEST",1,2,3
40 PRINT "PRINT#-1 HAS COMPLETED THE DATA TRANSFER"
99 END
```

Sample Run

```
DATA SHOULD BE RECORDING ON CASSETTE TAPE
PRINT#-1 HAS COMPLETED THE DATA TRANSFER
```

To verify that the data was stored, rewind the tape, set the recorder to the Play mode and RUN this program.

```
10 REM * INPUT DATA FROM CASSETTE*
20 PRINT "THE COMPUTER SHOULD BE READING DATA FROM
   CASSETTE"
30 INPUT#-1,A$,A,B,C
40 PRINT "THE FOLLOWING DATA WAS READ FROM THE CASSETTE"
50 PRINT A$,A,B,C
99 END
```

Sample Run

```
THE COMPUTER SHOULD BE READING DATA FROM CASSETTE
THE FOLLOWING DATA WAS READ FROM THE CASSETTE
TEST            1               2               3
```

PRINT# is used by mini and maxi computers with file handling capability to store data in "files" on an external device such as disk or cassette. Each data file is identified by a number (file name) which is listed in the PRINT# statement to specify in which one the data is to be stored. The data can consist of numeric values or string characters.

For example, PRINT#3;A,B,"TESTING" stores the contents of variables A and B and the word "TESTING" in a file named #3. FILE#, INPUT# and READ# are used to assign file names and space for data storage, and to READ the data back out of file storage.

Alternate Spellings

A few computers allow shortened forms of the PRINT keyword. PRI is used by PDP-8E. Britain's Acorn ATOM, TRS-80 Level I, and other Tiny BASICs accept P.

In addition, several BASICs allow single-character substitutes for PRINT. Microsoft BASIC uses ?, North Star BASIC uses !, DEC BASIC-PLUS uses &, the ABC-80 from Sweden uses ; and Digital Group's MaxiBASIC uses #.

Also See

TAB, AT, @, PRINT USING, MAT PRINT, #, ,(comma),
;(semicolon), CUR, LIN, LPRINT, %, ?, &, !

PRINT AT is used by the TRS-80 Level I BASIC to indicate a PRINT statement's starting location. The AT value may be a number, numeric variable, or mathematical operation. A comma or semi-colon must be inserted between the AT value and the string. There are 1024 screen locations --- 16 rows of 64 horizontal addresses.

PRINT @
P.A.

For example:

```
10 PRINT AT 420, "HELLO"
20 PRINT AT (420);"HELLO"
```

Both lines print the word HELLO AT location 420. The parentheses are optional.

For more information see AT.

Test Program

```
10 REM 'PRINT AT' TEST PROGRAM
20 PRINT AT 128,"2. IF THIS LINE IS PRINTED AFTER LINE 1."
30 PRINT AT 0,"1. THE 'PRINT AT' STATEMENT PASSED THE TEST"
40 GOTO 40
99 END
```

Sample Run

```
1. THE 'PRINT AT' STATEMENT PASSED THE TEST
2. IF THIS LINE IS PRINTED AFTER LINE 1.
```

ALTERNATE SPELLINGS

Microsoft BASIC substitutes PRINT @ for PRINT AT and **requires** a comma after the location. Tiny BASICs accept P.A.

Variations In Usage

None known.

Also See

PRINT, AI, @, TAB

Statement

PRINT USING is used by computers of all sizes as a special PRINT feature which allows numbers or strings to be printed USING a variable format. PRINT USING is by far the most powerful (and complex) PRINT statement available in BASIC, so its many features will be covered here, one at a time. Not every feature is part of every computer, but the TEST PROGRAMS will quickly let you identify what yours can do. See your own computer's manual for other possible capabilities.

The pound sign (#) reserves a position for each digit in a number or numeric variable to the left and right of a decimal point. Zeros are automatically inserted if nothing exists to the right, making it valuable for financial printing. # always prints the decimal point in the same place, making it easier to examine rows of numbers. For more information see #.

Test Program #1

```
10 REM 'PRINT USING' TEST PROGRAM
20 PRINT "THE # OPERATOR PASSED THE PRINT USING TEST"
30 PRINT "IF THE FOLLOWING NUMBERS ARE PRINTED"
40 FOR X=1 TO 5
50 READ N
60 PRINT USING "#######.##";N
70 NEXT X
80 DATA 1.2,400,2400000,82450.5,-.25
99 END
```

Sample Run

```
THE # OPERATOR PASSED THE PRINT USING TEST
IF THE FOLLOWING NUMBERS ARE PRINTED
      1.20
    400.00
2400000.00
  82450.50
     -0.25
```

An asterisk (*) can be printed in all unused spaces to the left of a specified number's decimal point by placing a double asterisk (**) before the #. Its primary purpose is to prevent someone from increasing the size of a check printed by computer.

For example, PRINT USING "*******.##";234.25 will print ****234.25. This feature can be tested by making these changes to the TEST PROGRAM #1.

```
20 PRINT "THE ** OPERATOR PASSED THE PRINT USING TEST"
60 PRINT USING "********.##";N
```

Sample Run

```
THE ** OPERATOR PASSED THE PRINT USING TEST
IF THE FOLLOWING NUMBERS ARE PRINTED
*******1.20
*****400.00
*2400000.00
***82450.50
******-0.25
```

A $ sign can be printed before the number listed in the PRINT USING statement by inserting a double dollar sign ($$) before the # sign.

For example, PRINT USING "$$###.##";1.25 will print $1.25. To test this feature in your computer, make these changes to TEST PROGRAM #1:

```
20 PRINT "THE $$ OPERATOR PASSED THE PRINT USING TEST"
60 PRINT USING "$$#######.##";N
```

Sample Run

```
THE $$ OPERATOR PASSED THE PRINT USING TEST
IF THE FOLLOWING NUMBERS ARE PRINTED
       $1.20
     $400.00
 $2400000.00
   $82450.50
      -$0.25
```

It is possible to insert a comma between every third number to the left of the decimal point by using a comma between one or more left # signs. The position of the comma in the PRINT USING statement does **not** effect the position of the printed comma.

For example,

```
PRINT USING "#,####.##";12000
PRINT USING "####,#.##";12000
PRINT USING "#,##,#,#.##";12000
```

will each print the number 12,000.00.

To test this feature, make these changes to TEST PROGRAM #1.

```
20 PRINT "PRINT USING 'COMMA' PASSED THE TEST"
60 PRINT USING "#,#######.##";N
```

Sample Run

```
PRINT USING 'COMMA' PASSED THE TEST
IF THE FOLLOWING NUMBERS ARE PRINTED
        1.20
       400.00
  2,400,000.00
     82,450.50
        -0.25
```

A + sign placed to the **left** of the #'s causes a + sign to be printed **before** each positive number and a − sign before each negative number. If a + sign is placed to the **right** of the #'s, the computer prints a − sign to the **right** of all negative numbers, and a space is inserted to the right of all positive numbers.

For example,

```
PRINT USING "+####";123
PRINT USING "####+";-123
```

will print the numbers

```
+123
```

and `123-`

To test this feature, make these changes to TEST PROGRAM #1

```
20 PRINT "THE + OPERATOR PASSED THE PRINT USING TEST"
60 PRINT USING "+#######.##";N
```

Sample Run

```
THE + OPERATOR PASSED THE PRINT USING TEST
IF THE FOLLOWING NUMBERS ARE PRINTED
       +1.20
      +400.00
 +2400000.00
    +82450.50
       -0.25
```

Four exponentiation signs ($^{\wedge\wedge\wedge\wedge}$) can be used following a # to print numbers expressed in exponential or scientific notation. A few computers (e.g. the TRS-80) use ↑↑↑↑ instead.

For example, `PRINT USING "##^^^^";100` prints the number 1E + 02

Test Program #2

```
10 REM 'PRINT USING EXPONENTIATION' TEST PROGRAM
20 PRINT "PRINT USING '^^^^' PASSED THE TEST"
30 PRINT "IF THE NUMBER";123456
40 PRINT "IS PRINTED USING SCIENTIFIC NOTATION"
50 PRINT USING "##^^^^";123456
99 END
```

Sample Run

```
PRINT USING '^^^^' PASSED THE TEST
IF THE NUMBER 123456
IS PRINTED USING SCIENTIFIC NOTATION
 1E+05
```

Some computers (e.g. those with variations of the Microsoft BASIC) use the ! (enclosed in quotes) to print only the left-most character in a string or string variable listed in a PRINT USING statement.

For example, `PRINT USING "!";"WORD"` prints the letter W.

Test Program #3

```
10 REM 'PRINT USING !' TEST PROGRAM
20 PRINT "ENTER A SAMPLE WORD";
30 INPUT A$
40 PRINT "THE PRINT USING STATEMENT AND THE ! OPERATOR"
50 PRINT "PASSED THE TEST IF THE FIRST LETTER IN ";A$;" IS ";
60 PRINT USING "!";A$
99 END
```

Sample Run *(using HANDBOOK)*

```
ENTER A SAMPLE WORD? HANDBOOK
THE PRINT USING STATEMENT AND THE ! OPERATOR
PASSED THE TEST IF THE FIRST LETTER IN HANDBOOK IS H
```

Use of \\(backslash) permits printing only the left-most characters in strings. The number printed is determined by the number of spaces between the two \ signs. The computer also counts the two \ signs as character positions, therefore, no less than two characters can be specified by \\.

For example, `PRINT USING "\ \";"COMPUSOFT"` prints the first three letters COM because one space is included between the two \ signs (1 space + 2 backslashes = 3 letters). The TRS-80 uses the % sign instead of the \ sign.

Test Program #4

```
10 REM 'PRINT USING \' TEST PROGRAM
20 A$ = "TESTIFIED"
30 PRINT "THE PRINT USING STATEMENT ";
40 PRINT "AND THE \ OPERATOR PASSED THE ";
50 PRINT USING "\   \";A$
99 END
```

Sample Run

```
THE PRINT USING STATEMENT AND THE \ OPERATOR
  PASSED THE TEST
```

Most computers allow the PRINT USING operators, numbers and strings to be specified as variables. Line 10 contains the PRINT format and is called an Image Line.

For example,

```
10 A$="!"
20 B$="ABCD"
30 PRINT USING A$;B$
```

will print the letter A which is the left-most character assigned to string variable B$.

Test Program #5 shows how 3 different PRINT formats can be linked together by semicolons.

Test Program #5

```
10 REM 'PRINT USING VARIABLES' TEST PROGRAM
20 A$="**$####.##"
30 B$="\   \"
40 C$="TESTIMONIAL"
50 A=19.95
60 PRINT "THE BASIC HANDBOOK PASSED THE ";
70 PRINT USING A$;A;
80 PRINT USING B$;C$
99 END
```

Sample Run

```
THE BASIC HANDBOOK PASSED THE ****$19.95 TEST
```

The same results can be achieved by putting the entire format on one Image line, and on another line all variables to be printed. Delete lines 30 and 80 and change

```
20 A$="**$####.## \   \"
70 PRINT USING A$;A,C$
```

Or, better yet, delete lines 60 and 80 and change

```
20 A$="\                          \**$####.## \    \"
30 B$="THE BASIC HANDBOOK PASSED THE "
70 PRINT USING A$;B$,A,C$
```

(Note that commas can be used instead of semicolons after all but the
PRINT USING specifier.) Of course, the string image line must be executed
before its corresponding PRINT USING line.

Variations In Usage

Some computers (e.g. the DEC-10, and the Sperry/Univac VS/9) require that
when variables are printed in one line, and the PRINT USING format in an
image line, the image line must be addressed by number and must start
with a colon.

For example,

```
60 A = 12.34
70 B = 56.78
80 C$ = "MAIN FRAME"
90 PRINT USING 100,A,B,C$
100 :###.## $$$$.## 'CCCCCCCCC
```

will print

```
12.34  $56.78 MAIN FRAME
```

Test Program #6

```
10 REM 'PRINT USING LINE NUMBER' TEST PROGRAM
20 PRINT "THE PRINT USING STATEMENT PASSES THE TEST"
30 PRINT "IF THE NUMBER 125.50 IS PRINTED NEXT"
40 PRINT USING 50,125.5
50 :###.##
99 END
```

Sample Run

```
THE PRINT USING STATEMENT PASSES THE TEST
IF THE NUMBER 125.50 IS PRINTED NEXT
125.50
```

IF YOUR COMPUTER DOESN'T HAVE IT

Some of the features of PRINT USING are available even in BASICs without it. For example,

```
90 PRINT USING "#####.###";X
```

prints the value of X rounded to three places after the decimal. It can be
done by using DIGITS, instead. (See DIGITS.)

If DIGITS isn't available, a similar result is obtained by using

```
90 PRINT INT (X*1000+.5)/1000
```

To line up the decimal points in a column of numbers is more involved. To duplicate the effect of the PRINT USING statement in Test Program #1 we have to determine how many digits are to be printed before the decimal point. The common logarithm of the number can help here (See LOG10). $LOG10(10) = 1$, $LOG10(100) = 2$, $LOG10(1000) = 3$, etc. Therefore, to produce the same results as

```
60 PRINT USING "#######.##";N
```

substitute:

```
56 T=0
57 K=ABS(N)
58 IF K<.1 THEN 60
59 T=LOG10(K)
60 PRINT TAB(8-T); SGN(N)*INT(K*100+.5)/100
```

Even the floating dollar sign can be included by

```
60 PRINT TAB(7-T); "$"; SGN(N)*INT(K*100+.5)/100
```

Also See

```
PRINT, #, **, !, ↑ , +, _, %, IMAGE, FMT, DIGITS,
\ (backslash), $, &, :
```

RADIAN

RAD is used in a few computers (e.g. Cromemco 16K Extended BASIC) to make them perform trigonometric calculations in RADians instead of degrees. Most computers are in radian mode when powered up, but some also have the capability of calculating trig functions in degrees. If a DEG statement has been used in a program, RAD is needed to restore the computer to "normal" mode. One radian is approximately 57 degrees.

Test Program #1

```
10 REM 'RAD' TEST PROGRAM
20 DEG
30 D = SIN(30)
40 PRINT "THE SINE OF 30 DEGREES IS";D
50 RAD
60 R = SIN(30)
70 PRINT "THE SINE OF 30 RADIANS IS";R
99 END
```

Sample Run

```
THE SINE OF 30 DEGREES IS 0.5
THE SINE OF 30 RADIANS IS -0.988032
```

Alternate Spelling

Some computers (e.g. Sharp/TRS-80 Pocket) use RADIAN as the statement that sets the computer in radian mode for trig calculations.

Variations In Usage

A few BASICs (e.g. MAX BASIC) use RAD (*n*) as a function to convert a value (*n*) from degrees to radians.

Test Program #2

```
10 REM 'RAD FUNCTION' TEST PROGRAM
20 PRINT "ENTER AN ANGLE MEASURE (IN DEGREES)";
30 INPUT D
40 R = RAD(D)
50 PRINT "A MEASURE OF";D;" DEGREES IS EQUAL TO";R;"
   RADIANS"
99 END
```

Sample Run

```
ENTER AN ANGLE MEASURE (IN DEGREES) ?45
A MEASURE OF 45 DEGREES IS EQUAL TO 0.785398 RADIANS
```

IF YOUR COMPUTER DOESN'T HAVE IT

If your computer doesn't have the RAD function, it can be simulated by multiplying degree values by 0.0174533. To use this conversion factor in the second Test Program, replace line 40 with

```
40 R = D * 0.0174533
```

Also See

DEG, GRAD, ACS, ASN, ATN, COS, SIN, TAN

RANDOMIZE is used to "shuffle" or "reseed" a set of numbers (held in the computer) in a random order. These numbers are created as needed for selection by the RND function.

Placing RANDOMIZE in a program before the RND function causes the generation of a new set of random numbers for the RND function each time the program is run.

RANDOM
RAN

Test Program

```
10 REM 'RANDOMIZE' TEST PROGRAM
20 RANDOMIZE
30 FOR X=1 TO 8
40 PRINT RND,
50 NEXT X
99 END
```

Sample Run *(Typical)*

```
.250186      .975707      .775985      .544615
.890564      .227299      .408976      .771341
```

Each time the test program is run, a new set of random numbers should be printed. Be sure you have your own version of RND working before trying to include line 20.

Some BASICs (e.g. BASIC-80) expect a "seed" value to be included in the RANDOMIZE statement, such as RANDOMIZE 49817. If the seed is not included, the program stops and the user is prompted to enter a seed value from the keyboard.

Alternate Spellings

Several computers use the keyword RANDOM (e.g. TRS-80) instead of RANDOMIZE. Some (e.g. PDP-8E) accept RAN as a short form.

IF YOUR COMPUTER DOESN'T HAVE IT

If your computer doesn't have RANDOMIZE it may be that using a negative number with RND will "reseed" or start generating a new sequence of numbers. (See RND) If this is not the case, a simple procedure can be used with each program to cause new sequences of numbers for each run.

Replace line 20 of the Test Program with:

```
20 PRINT "ENTER A WHOLE NUMBER 'SEED' FOR RND";
22 INPUT S
24 FOR I=1 TO S
26 X=RND          'or RND(0)
28 NEXT I
```

287

and RUN the program several times using different numbers. The reason this works is that RND generates the same sequence of numbers each time the computer is turned on (each time RUN is typed on some computers). In effect, RND "reads" from the top of a list of random numbers each time the program is used. Our procedure causes the program to "throw away" the top of the list and start using the (S + 1)th entry. That allows different starting points for each seed value. It also allows for repeating a sequence by using the same seed value on different runs while testing out a new program.

Variations In Usage

None known.

Also See

RND

The READ statement is used to read data from a DATA line and assign that data to a variable.

READ

REA.
REA

Each time the READ statement is executed, data is read from a DATA line. The pointer then moves to the next item of data in the DATA line(s) and waits for another READ statement. When the last piece of data has been read from all DATA statements, the data pointer must be reset to the beginning of the DATA list before additional READ statements can be executed. (See RESTORE)

Test Program #1

```
10 REM 'READ' STATEMENT TEST PROGRAM
20 READ A
30 PRINT "THE READ STATEMENT WORKED IN LINE";A
40 DATA 20
99 END
```

Sample Run

```
THE READ STATEMENT WORKED IN LINE 20
```

Since computers allow more than one variable to be placed in one READ statement, each variable must be separated by a comma and the number of "reads" must not exceed the number of data items.

Test Program #2

```
10 REM 'MULTIPLE READ' STATEMENT TEST PROGRAM
20 READ A,B,C
30 D=A+B+C
40 PRINT "D=";D
50 PRINT "THE READ STATEMENT PASSED THE TEST IF D = 60"
60 DATA 10,20,30
99 END
```

Sample Run

```
D = 60
THE READ STATEMENT PASSED THE TEST IF D = 60
```

Most computers also allow strings to be read from DATA statements. Each time a string is read from the DATA statement, it must have a corresponding string variable in a READ statement.

Test Program #3

```
10 REM 'READ STRINGS' TEST PROGRAM
20 READ D$
30 PRINT "THE READ STATEMENT PASSED THE ";D$
40 DATA TEST
99 END
```

Sample Run

```
THE READ STATEMENT PASSED THE TEST
```

Many computers allow both numeric and string data to be read by the same READ statement and be contained in the same DATA line.

Test Program #4

```
10 REM 'MULTIPLE READ' STATEMENT TEST PROGRAM
20 READ A,B,C,D$
30 D=A+B+C
40 PRINT "THE READ STATEMENT PASSED THE TEST IN ";D$;D
50 DATA 2,8,10,LINE
99 END
```

Sample Run

```
THE READ STATEMENT PASSED THE TEST IN LINE 20
```

Alternate Spellings

Some computers allow abbreviations for READ. Computers using variations of Palo Alto Tiny BASIC accept REA. as READ while others (e.g. PDP-8E) accept REA as a short form.

Variations In Usage

None. The only other way to store and call up data is by inputting it through a keyboard or from off-line storage on tape, disc, etc.

Also See

```
DATA, RESTORE, ,(comma).
```

RECALL is used in the APPLE II computer as both a command and a statement to load an array of numeric values from cassette tape. A large array can be STOREd on tape under program control, then RECALLed by the same program or even another one. See STORE for additional information.

Example: `10 DIM A(3,3,3)`

`200 RECALL A`

will read up to 64 values (4*4*4) previously stored on a tape for future use. (Note the four values are 0, 1, 2 and 3.)

Test Program

```
10 REM 'RECALL' TEST PROGRAM
20 DIM A(25),B(25)
30 FOR I=1 TO 25
40 A(I)=I
50 NEXT I
60 STORE A
70 PRINT "REWIND TAPE AND SET TO PLAY - PRESS RETURN"
80 INPUT A$
90 RECALL B
100 FOR I=1 TO 25
110 PRINT B(I),
120 NEXT I
999 END
```

Sample Run

```
REWIND TAPE AND SET TO PLAY - PRESS RETURN
?
 1              2              3
 4              5              6
 7              8              9
10             11             12
13             14             15
16             17             18
19             20             21
22             23             24
25
```

Variations In Usage

None known.

Also See

STORE, CLOAD, DIM

REMARK

The REMark statement is used at the beginning of some program lines to make them serve as a "notebook" or "scratchpad" to hold comments about the program. The REM statement is not executed. Everything on a line beginning with REM is ignored by the computer.

If used in multiple statement lines, those statements preceding the REM statement will be executed, but everything following is ignored. If the REMarks require more than one program line, each such line must begin with REM.

Test Program

```
10 PRINT "'REM' TEST PROGRAM"
20 REM PRINT "REM FAILED THE TEST"
30 REM * REM FAILED THE TEST IF LINE 20 IS PRINTED*
40 PRINT "REM PASSED THE TEST"
99 END
```

Sample Run

```
'REM' TEST PROGRAM
REM PASSED THE TEST
```

Some computers allow either the REM or REMARK statement, while others accept only one.

Variations In Usage

None known.

Also See

'(apostrophe), !

RENUM
REN

RENUMBER is used in some computers (e.g. the Cromemco 16K Extended BASIC) to change the program line numbers. The line numbers used in GOTO, GOSUB, IF-THEN, ON-GOTO and ON-GOSUB statements are changed accordingly to maintain the same branching scheme.

If a number is not included in the RENUMBER statement, the computer automatically RE-NUMBERs each program line starting at line 10, and spacing the lines 10 numbers apart.

Test Program

```
2 REM 'RENUMBER' TEST PROGRAM
3 X=1
4 PRINT "IF EACH PROGRAM LINE ";
5 GOTO 10
6 PRINT "THE RENUMBER COMMAND ";
7 X=2
8 GOTO 12
10 PRINT "IS RENUMBERED"
12 ON X GOTO 6,14
14 PRINT "PASSED THE TEST."
16 END
```

RUN, to be sure it works.

Type the command RENUMBER and RUN again.

Sample Run

```
IF EACH PROGRAM LINE IS RENUMBERED
THE RENUMBER COMMAND PASSED THE TEST.
```

To verify that the program is RENUMBERed, LIST the program. It should appear:

```
10 REM 'RENUMBER' TEST PROGRAM
20 X=1
30 PRINT "IF EACH PROGRAM LINE ";
40 GOTO 80
50 PRINT "THE RENUMBER COMMAND ";
60 X=2
70 GOTO 90
80 PRINT "IS RENUMBERED"
90 ON X GOTO 50,100
100 PRINT "PASSED THE TEST."
110 END
```

RENUMBER n is used to renumber each program line starting with line number n and incrementing by 10. To test this feature on the Test Program, type `RENUMBER 20` and LIST the program. It should read:

```
20 REM 'RENUMBER' TEST PROGRAM
30 X=1
40 PRINT "IF EACH PROGRAM LINE ";
50 GOTO 90
60 PRINT "THE RENUMBER COMMAND ";
70 X=2
80 GOTO 100
90 PRINT "IS RENUMBERED"
100 ON X GOTO 60,110
110 PRINT "PASSED THE TEST."
120 END
```

RENUMBER n1,n2 is used to renumber each program line starting with line number n1 and incrementing by the value of n2. To test this feature on the Test Program, type `RENUMBER 50,20` and LIST the program. Now it should read:

```
50 REM 'RENUMBER' TEST PROGRAM
70 X=1
90 PRINT "IF EACH PROGRAM LINE ";
110 GOTO 190
130 PRINT "THE RENUMBER COMMAND ";
150 X=2
170 GOTO 210
190 PRINT "IS RENUMBERED"
210 ON X GOTO 130,230
230 PRINT "PASSED THE TEST."
250 END
```

RENUMBER n1,n2,n3 is used to renumber each program line starting with the old line number n3. Line number n3 is assigned line number n1, and the remaining line numbers are incremented by the value n2. To test this feature on the last Test Program, type `RENUMBER 500,10,90` and LIST the program. Does it look like this?

```
50 REM 'RENUMBER' TEST PROGRAM
70 X=1
500 PRINT "IF EACH PROGRAM LINE ";
510 GOTO 550
520 PRINT "THE RENUMBER COMMAND ";
530 X=2
540 GOTO 560
550 PRINT "IS RENUMBERED"
560 ON X GOTO 520,570
570 PRINT "PASSED THE TEST."
580 END
```

RENUMBER n1, n2, n3, n4 is used by a few computers to renumber the old program lines from line n3 to line n4. Line n3 is assigned line number n1 and those lines following (ending with line n4) are incremented by the value n2. To test this feature on the last Test Program, type RENUMBER 60,5,70,510 and LIST the program.

```
50 REM 'RENUMBER' TEST PROGRAM
60 X=1
65 PRINT "IF EACH PROGRAM LINE ";
70 GOTO 550
520 PRINT "THE RENUMBER COMMAND ";
530 X=2
540 GOTO 560
550 PRINT "IS RENUMBERED"
560 ON X GOTO 520,570
570 PRINT "PASSED THE TEST."
580 END
```

Alternate Spellings

Some computers accept short versions of RENUMBER such as RENUM and REN. TRS-80 Disk BASIC uses NAME. DEC computers use RESEQUENCE.

Variations In Usage

None known.

Also See

GOTO, GOSUB, IF-THEN, ON-GOTO, ON-GOSUB, LIST

The REPEAT$ function creates a character string containing a given set of characters repeated a specified number of times. For example, `REPEAT$ ("MICRO",4)` creates `MICROMICROMICROMICRO` and `REPEAT$("*",16)` generates `****************`.

Test Program

```
10 REM 'REPEAT$' TEST PROGRAM
20 PRINT "TYPE YOUR FIRST NAME";
30 INPUT N$
40 PRINT "NOW PICK A NUMBER FROM 2 TO 5";
50 INPUT M
60 A$ = REPEAT$(N$,M)
70 PRINT A$
99 END
```

Sample Run

```
TYPE YOUR FIRST NAME ? DAVID
NOW PICK A NUMBER FROM 2 TO 5 ? 3
DAVIDDAVIDDAVID
```

Also See

```
STRING$
```

Statement

R.

The RESET statement is used by the TRS-80 to "turn off" a graphics block in a predetermined grid on the screen.

The block to be "turned off" within the grid is specified by the X,Y coordinates enclosed in parentheses following the RESET statement. For example, RESET (5,8) instructs the computer to turn off a graphics block located in the 5th column and the 8th row of the graphics grid.

To turn on the graphics block, see SET.

Test Program

```
10 REM 'RESET' TEST PROGRAM
20 CLS
30 Y=1
40 FOR X=1 TO 100
50 SET (X,Y)
60 NEXT X
70 PRINT
80 PRINT "RESET PASSED THE TEST IF THE LINE DISAPPEARS"
90 FOR X=1 TO 100
100 RESET (X,Y)
110 NEXT X
999 END
```

Sample Run

```
RESET PASSED THE TEST IF THE LINE DISAPPEARS
```

Alternate Spelling

R. is used in Level I and Tiny BASIC as an abbreviation for RESET.

Variations In Usage

None known.

Also See

```
SET, CLS, POINT, CLRDOT
```

Execution of a RESTORE statement causes the DATA pointer to be "reset" back to the first piece of data in the first DATA line. This enables the computer to use data stored in DATA statements more than once.

Test Program #1

```
10 REM 'RESTORE' TEST PROGRAM
20 READ X
30 IF X=3 THEN 50
40 GOTO 20
50 RESTORE
60 READ X
70 IF X=1 THEN 100
80 PRINT "RESTORE FAILED THE TEST"
90 GOTO 999
100 PRINT "RESTORE PASSED THE TEST"
110 DATA 1,2,3
999 END
```

Sample Run

```
RESTORE PASSED THE TEST
```

Alternate Spellings

A few computers (e.g. TRS-80 Level I) allow RESTORE to be abbreviated REST. Others (e.g. DEC PDP-8E) accept RES as the short form of RESTORE.

Variations In Usage

Some interpreters allow resetting only the DATA in a specific DATA line by adding that DATA statement line number after a RESTORE statement. See line 100 below.

Test Program #2

```
10 REM 'RESTORE (LINE#)' TEST PROGRAM
20 READ X
30 PRINT X;
40 IF X=3 THEN 60
50 GOTO 20
60 READ X
70 PRINT X;
80 IF X=6 THEN 100
90 GOTO 60
100 RESTORE 180
110 READ X
120 IF X=4 THEN 150
```

```
130 PRINT "RESTORE FAILED THE TEST"
140 STOP
150 PRINT "RESTORE PASSED THE TEST"
160 GOTO 999
170 DATA 1,2,3
180 DATA 4,5,6
999 END
```

Sample Run

```
1  2  3  4  5  6 RESTORE PASSED THE TEST
```

There are computers (e.g. DEC-10) that can RESTORE numeric data and string data separately. RESTORE$ inserted in a program restores only the string data. RESTORE* is used when only the numeric values are to be reused.

Test Program #3

```
10 REM RESTORE$ TEST PROGRAM
20 READ X$
30 READ N
40 RESTORE$
50 READ T$
60 READ N
70 IF N=2 THEN 100
80 PRINT "IT DIDN'T WORK"
90 GOTO 999
100 PRINT "RESTORE$ PASSED THE ";T$
110 DATA TEST, 1, 2
999 END
```

Sample Run

```
RESTORE$ PASSED THE TEST
```

Also See

```
DATA, READ
```

The RESUME statement is used as the last statement in ON-ERROR-GOTO routines, telling the computer to RESUME program execution at a specified line number. The computer does not allow execution of the RESUME statement if it is not preceded by an ON-ERROR-GOTO statement. See ON-ERROR-GOTO for a Test Program using RESUME(line number). (Saves space not to duplicate it here.)

RESUME NEXT is used to branch to the line following the error and CONTinues program execution. To test for RESUME NEXT capability in your computer, change line 110 in the ON-ERROR-GOTO test program to:

```
110 RESUME NEXT
```

Sample Run (ON-ERROR-GOTO test program using RESUME NEXT) *(using 0)*

```
ENTER A NUMBER AND IT'S INVERSE WILL BE COMPUTED? 0
THE INVERSE OF 0 CANNOT BE COMPUTED - TRY AGAIN
THE INVERSE OF 0 IS 0
?
```

RESUME 0 and RESUME (without a line number or NEXT) are used to branch to the statement containing the error.

Test Program

```
10 REM 'RESUME' TEST PROGRAM
20 ON ERROR GOTO 100
30 PRINT "ENTER A POSITIVE NUMBER";
40 INPUT N
50 A=LOG(N)
60 PRINT "THE LOG OF";N;"IS";A
70 GOTO 30
100 PRINT "A NEGATIVE NUMBER IS NOT ALLOWED"
110 N=N*-1
120 RESUME 0
999 END
```

Sample Run *(using -4)*

```
ENTER A POSITIVE NUMBER? -4
A NEGATIVE NUMBER IS NOT ALLOWED
THE LOG OF 4 IS 1.38629
ENTER A POSITIVE NUMBER?
```

To test RESUME (without a line number or NEXT) capability in your computer, change line 120 in the above Test Program to:

```
120 RESUME
```

and RUN. The Sample Run should not change.

Variations In Usage

None known.

Also See

ON-ERROR-GOTO, ERL, ERR

The RETURN statement is used in conjunction with the GOSUB statement. It is used as the last statement in a subroutine; it tells the computer to return to the line containing the GOSUB statement and continue program execution from that point.

RETURN

A
N
S
I

The computer will not allow execution of the RETURN statement if it was not preceded by a GOSUB statement.

RET.
RET
R.

Test Program

```
10 REM 'RETURN' STATEMENT TEST PROGRAM
20 GOSUB 50
30 PRINT "WAS ACCEPTED,"
40 GOTO 99
50 PRINT "THE RETURN STATEMENT ";
60 RETURN
70 PRINT "WAS NOT ACCEPTED,"
99 END
```

Sample Run

```
THE RETURN STATEMENT WAS ACCEPTED,
```

Alternate Spellings

Various abbreviations are used, including RET. (TRS-80 Level I), RET (DEC PDP-8E), and R. (Acorn ATOM).

Variations In Usage

None known.

Also See

```
GOSUB, ON-GOSUB, IF-GOSUB, GOSUB-OF
```

Function

RIGHT

The RIGHT$(string,n) function is used to isolate a specific number (n) of string characters, counting from the right-most character in the string.

For example, `PRINT RIGHT$("COMPUSOFT",4)` prints the letters SOFT, which are the right 4 characters in COMPUSOFT, which is a string.

The string must be enclosed in quotes or assigned to a string variable. The number (n) of characters can be expressed as a variable, number or arithmetic operation. A comma must separate the string from the number.

If the value of (n) is a decimal, the computer automatically finds its integer value.

Test Program

```
10 REM 'RIGHT$' TEST PROGRAM
20 A$="CONTEST"
30 B$=RIGHT$(A$,4)
40 PRINT "THE ";RIGHT$("ALRIGHT",5);"$ FUNCTION PASSED
   THE ";B$
99 END
```

Sample Run

```
THE RIGHT$ FUNCTION PASSED THE TEST
```

Alternate Spelling

The RIGHT function is used in some computers (e.g. those using MAX BASIC).

Variations In Usage

A few BASICs use RIGHT$(A$,N) to isolate the substring of A$ that begins in position N. Everything to the right of that point is included. For example, `RIGHT$("CHOCOLATE",6)` returns LATE since L is in the sixth position.

Also See

```
PRINT, LEFT$, MID$, CHR$, SPACE$, STR$, STRING$, INKEY$,
INSTR, SEG$
```

RND is a function used by nearly all computers to produce RaNDom numbers. Actual variation in usage between computers is as wide as any word in the BASIC language.

Most computers use RND(*n*) to tell it to create a random decimal number between 0 and 1. Very few (e.g. DEC and APF) comply with the ANSI rule which requires that RND shall be used alone, without (*n*). ANSI further requires that the same sequence of numbers created shall repeat itself each time RND is used (for debugging purposes) unless the BASIC word RANDOMIZE is included in the program, to "reshuffle the deck".

Some computers, (e.g. Apple Integer and TRS-80 Level I) have a limited "Integer BASIC". They use RND(N) to generate random integer numbers between certain minimum and maximum values of the particular machine, typically -32768 to +32767.

Ordinarily, each time RND is used, the computer will "deliver" a different number. It is common, however, to find the value of N used to specify HOW the RND function will operate.

For example: if N is given a negative value, it may be "reseeding" the random number generator. That means, it's directing that a new SEQUENCE of numbers be created each time the negative number is changed. If the same negative number is repeated, the same sequence of numbers will be repeated. Forcing this repetition is valuable for program troubleshooting.

Other computers use a negative N to make the VALUE repeat itself. In this case, N must be positive for RND to operate "normally".

If the value of N is greater than 1, a few computers (e.g. Sinclair ZX80 and TRS-80) deliver a positive whole number between 1 and the value of N.

Determining exactly what RND is doing in a program will avoid a lot of "cut and try". Your computers reference manual is the best source of information about how your specific computer can use RND.

Test Program #1

```
10 REM 'RND' TEST PROGRAM
20 FOR X=1 TO 8
30 PRINT RND,
40 NEXT X
99 END
```

Sample Run *(Typical)*

```
.627633          .358479          .137551          .127641
.125054          .809923          .888076          .787762
```

RND(0) is used by some computers to specify the same operation as RND.

Test Program #2

```
10 REM 'RND(0)' TEST PROGRAM
20 FOR X=1 TO 8
30 PRINT RND(0),
40 NEXT X
99 END
```

Sample Run *(Typical)*

```
.862675          .735285          .476059          .55141
.245708          .242171          .968336          .721014
```

While RND(n) generates a random number, in some computers RND(0) repeats the last number generated by the random number generator.

Test Program #3

```
10 REM 'RND(0) AS A REPEAT' TEST PROGRAM
20 PRINT "RND(1)"
30 FOR X=1 TO 4
40 PRINT RND(1),
50 NEXT X
60 PRINT "RND(0)"
70 FOR Y=1 TO 4
80 PRINT RND(0),
90 NEXT Y
99 END
```

Sample Run *(Typical)*

```
RND(1)
 .592453         .245804          .118263          .961308
RND(0)
 .961308         .961308          .961308          .961308
```

A few computers create a random integer between 1 and the value of n when n is greater than 1 (e.g. TRS-80).

RND(n) automatically integers the value of n.

Test Program #4

```
10 REM 'RND' TEST PROGRAM
20 N=10
30 FOR X=1 TO 4
40 PRINT RND(N),
50 NEXT X
99 END
```

Sample Run *(Typical)*

```
8              7              2              9
```

A TRICK

If your computer is one that generates random numbers > 0 and < 1 and you need a random integer number from 0 to 9, then try this trick.

```
PRINT INT(10*RND)
```

A random number from 1 to 10 can be printed with this trick.

```
PRINT INT(10*RND+1)
```

The general form for generating random integers from A to B is

```
INT(RND*(B-A+1)+A)
```

Also See

```
RANDOMIZE
```

Command
Statement

RUN

RU
R.

The RUN command instructs the computer to execute the program or programs held in memory, starting with the lowest line number. With many computers, a line number may be included after the RUN command to specify a starting line other than the first one (e.g. RUN 40).

Test Program

```
10 REM 'RUN' TEST PROGRAM
20 PRINT "THIS PRINTING STARTED AT LINE 20."
30 GOTO 99
40 PRINT "THIS PRINTING STARTED AT LINE 40."
99 END
```

Sample Run

After entering the RUN Command, the computer should display:

```
THIS PRINTING STARTED AT LINE 20.
```

By adding the number 40 to the RUN command, RUN40 or RUN 40, the computer should start at line 40 and print the following message:

```
THIS PRINTING STARTED AT LINE 40.
```

While most computers use RUN strictly as a command at the monitor level, a few will accept RUN as a program statement. Those computers using Microsoft Disk BASIC accept RUN as a form of the CHAIN statement. (See CHAIN.) For example, 570 RUN "PROG:1" loads a program named PROG from disk #1 and RUNs it.

Alternate Spellings

Some computers (e.g. TI 990) use the abbreviation RU. Computers using Tiny BASIC accept R.

Also See

CHAIN

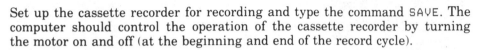

SAVE is used in a few computers (e.g. the APPLE II BASIC and the Commodore PET) to record programs from computer memory to cassette tape or disk.

For more information see CSAVE.

Test Program

```
10 REM 'SAVE' TEST PROGRAM
20 PRINT "THIS PROGRAM TESTS THE SAVE FEATURE"
99 END
```

Set up the cassette recorder for recording and type the command SAVE. The computer should control the operation of the cassette recorder by turning the motor on and off (at the beginning and end of the record cycle).

Once the program is recorded on cassette tape, type NEW (or whatever is required) to erase the program from memory. Load the program from tape back into the computer (see LOAD). List the program to verify that the program held in the computer's memory is identical to that originally entered (see LIST).

Sample Run

```
THIS PROGRAM TESTS THE SAVE FEATURE
```

Variations In Usage

Some computers with disk storage capability use SAVE to copy programs in computer memory to disk memory. A file name is required.

Example:

```
SAVE "TEST"
```

Also See

```
LOAD, CSAVE, CLOAD, LIST
```

Command
Statement

SCRATCH

SCR

As a command, SCRATCH erases the program from memory and resets all variables to zero. It is equivalent to NEW as used on other computers. (See NEW for more information.)

Test Program

```
10 REM 'SCRATCH' COMMAND TEST PROGRAM
20 PRINT "THIS IS A TEST"
99 END
```

Sample Run

LIST the program to be sure it has been entered into memory. Type SCRATCH, then LIST it again. The program should be gone. A check of the amount of memory available both before and after SCRATCHing should show an increase in space when the program is gone.

Alternate Spelling

SCR is sometimes accepted as an abbreviation for SCRATCH.

Variations In Usage

Some systems (e.g. DEC-10) use SCRATCH as a statement to prepare a disk file to accept output from the computer. Previous contents of that file are erased (SCRATCHed) so new data can be printed in it.

For example,

```
100 SCRATCH #1
```

erases the contents of a file that has been opened on device #1, and sets the pointer to its first record. The next PRINT #1 statement (or equivalent) will print data in the first record of that file.

Other BASICs (e.g. Micropolis BASIC) use SCRATCH as a command to delete files from a disk directory. In this application, SCRATCH must be followed by a file specification.

Example:

```
SCRATCH "1:FILE,GROUP"
```

Also See

NEW, CLEAR, ERASE

Function

SCRN is used in APPLE II BASIC as a special feature to indicate the color of a graphics block on the screen. The computer has the capability of displaying 16 colors (numbered from 0 to 15). For a complete color listing, see COLOR.

The graphics block is specified by the X,Y coordinates enclosed in parentheses following SCRN. The X value represents the column number and the Y value represents the row number. These values may range from 0 to 39 for X and 0 to 47 for Y.

Test Program

```
10 REM 'SCRN' TEST PROGRAM
20 GR
30 COLOR=11
40 PLOT 20,10
50 IF SCRN(20,10)=11 THEN 80
60 PRINT "THE SCRN FUNCTION FAILED THE TEST"
70 GOTO 99
80 PRINT "THE SCRN FUNCTION PASSED THE TEST"
99 END
```

Sample Run

```
THE SCRN FUNCTION PASSED THE TEST
```

Variations In Usage

None known.

Also See

```
COLOR, PLOT, GR, POINT
```

SEG$ extracts a segment of a string from a string variable. SEG$ has three arguments: the string variable, the starting position in the string, and the number of characters in the substring.

SEG

Example: IF A$="COMPUTER", THEN PRINT SEG$(A$,4,3) prints PUT.

Test Program

```
10 REM * SEG$ TEST PROGRAM *
20 A$="CONTESTANT"
30 B$=SEG$(A$,4,4)
40 IF B$<>"TEST" THEN 70
50 PRINT "SEG$ PASSED THE ";B$
60 GOTO 99
70 PRINT "SEG$ FAILED THE TEST"
99 END
```

Sample Run

```
SEG$ PASSED THE TEST
```

SEG$ can be used to simulate LEFT$ and RIGHT$. SEG$(A$,1,4) is equivalent to LEFT$(A$,4), while SEG$(A$,LEN(A$)-3,3) is equivalent to RIGHT$(A$,3).

Alternate Spelling

A few computers use SEG.

IF YOUR COMPUTER DOESN'T HAVE IT

If neither SEG$ nor SEG is available on your computer, try MID$ in the test program. If that doesn't work, some computers that require a DIM statement for all strings (e.g. Hewlett-Packard) will accept A$(4,7) as the substring in positions 4 through 7.

Variations In Usage

None known.

Also See

MID$, LEFT$, RIGHT$, DIM

Statement

S.

The SET statement is used by the TRS-80 to "turn on" or "light up" a graphics block in a predetermined grid on the screen.

The block to be lit, within the grid, is specified by the X,Y coordinates enclosed in parentheses following the SET statement. For example, SET (5,8) instructs the computer to SET a graphics block located in the 5th column and the 8th row of the graphics grid.

To turn off the graphics block, see RESET.

Test Program

```
10 REM 'SET' TEST PROGRAM
20 PRINT "ENTER X COORDINATE";
30 INPUT X
40 PRINT "ENTER Y COORDINATE";
50 INPUT Y
60 SET(X,Y)
70 PRINT "SET PASSED THE TEST"
80 PRINT "IF A LIGHT APPEARED AT (X,Y) COORDINATE
   (";X;",";Y;")."
99 END
```

Sample Run *(Using 65 and 40)*

```
ENTER X COORDINATE? 65
ENTER Y COORDINATE? 40
SET PASSED THE TEST
IF A LIGHT APPEARED AT (X,Y) COORDINATE (65,40).
```

Alternate Spelling

Some computers (e.g. TRS-80 Level I) allow S. as an abbreviation.

Variations In Usage

None known.

Also See

RESET, SETDOT

The SETDOT statement is used by Sweden's ABC-80 as a graphics feature to "turn on" a graphics block on the display screen. The block to be "turned on" is specified by the L,C coordinates following the SETDOT statement where L determines the line (0 to 71 in graphics mode) and C determines the column (2 to 79 in graphics mode).

For example, SETDOT 9,15 causes the computer to turn on the block located in the tenth row and sixteenth column from the upper left corner. To turn off the graphics block see CLRDOT.

Test Program

```
10 REM 'SETDOT' TEST PROGRAM
20 PRINT CHR%(12)                    'CLEARS SCREEN
30 PRINT "SETDOT PASSED THE TEST IF A LINE APPEARS"
40 FOR T=1 TO 2000 : NEXT T
50 PRINT CHR%(12)
60 FOR R=0 TO 23                     'LINES 60, 70 AND
70 PRINT CUR(R,0);CHR%(151);         '80 SET THE SCREEN
80 NEXT R                            'IN GRAPHICS MODE.
90 R=5
100 FOR C=2 TO 35
110 SETDOT R,C
120 NEXT C
130 FOR T=1 TO 2000 : NEXT T
140 PRINT CHR%(12)
999 END
```

Sample Run

```
SETDOT PASSED THE TEST IF A LINE APPEARS
```

Variations In Usage

None known.

Also See

SET, CLRDOT, RESET, ☒

Function

SGN tells us the sign of a number. If its sign is negative we get a -1. If it is zero, a 0, and a 1 if it is positive.

For example, `PRINT SGN(-8), SGN(0), SGN(4)` prints:

    -1   0   1

Test Program

```
10 REM 'SGN' FUNCTION TEST PROGRAM
20 X = 5
30 T = SGN(X)
40 IF T=1 THEN 70
50 PRINT "'SGN' FAILED THE TEST"
60 GOTO 99
70 PRINT "'SGN' PASSED THE TEST"
30999 END
```

Sample Run

```
'SGN' PASSED THE TEST
```

Variations In Usage

None known.

IF YOUR COMPUTER DOESN'T HAVE IT

If your computer failed the SGN test, substitute the following subroutine:

```
30000 GOTO 30999
30080 REM * SGN FUNCTION SUBROUTINE * INPUT X, OUTPUT T
30082 T = 0
30084 IF X=0 THEN 30092
30086 T = 1
30088 IF X>0 THEN 30092
30090 T = -1
30092 RETURN
```

and change Test Program line 30 to

```
30 GOSUB 30080
```

Also See

ABS

The SIN(A) function computes the Sine of the angle A, when that angle is expressed **in Radians, (not in degrees)**. One radian — approximately 57 degrees.

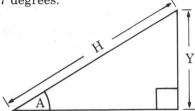

A N S I

SIND
SING

Sine (SIN) is defined as the ratio of the length of the side opposite the angle in question to the length of the hypotenuse. This formula applies only to right triangles: $SIN(A)=Y/H$

The opposite of SIN is ARCSIN. ARCSIN finds the value of the angle when its SIN, or ratio of sides (Y/H), is known. See ASN for more information.

Test Program

```
10 REM 'SINE' TEST PROGRAM
20 PRINT "ENTER AN ANGLE (EXPRESSED IN RADIANS)";
30 INPUT R
40 Y=SIN(R)
50 PRINT "THE SINE OF A";R;"RADIAN ANGLE IS";Y
30999 END
```

Sample Run *(using 1)*

```
ENTER AN ANGLE (EXPRESSED IN RADIANS)? 1
THE SINE OF A 1 RADIAN ANGLE IS .841471
```

To convert angles from degrees to radians, multiply the angle in degrees times .0174533.

For example, R=SIN(A*.0174533)

To convert angles from radians to degrees, multiply radians times 57.29578.

Some computers also allow entry of the angle in either degrees or grads (100 grads = 90 degrees). These computers use the function SIND for degrees and SING for grads. Changing Line 40 should produce .0174524 with SIND and .0157073 with SING.

IF YOUR COMPUTER DOES NOT HAVE IT

If your interpreter does not have the SINe capability, the following sub-routine can be substituted to compute the Sine in radians.

```
30000 GOTO 30999
30360 REM * SINE SUBROUTINE * INPUT X IN RADIANS,
      OUTPUT Y
30362 REM ALSO USES C AND Z INTERNALLY
30364 X=X*57.29578
30366 IF X=0 THEN 30408
30368 Z=ABS(X)/X
30370 C=X
30372 X=Z*X
30374 IF X<360 THEN 30378
30376 X=X-INT(X/360)*360
30378 IF X<=90 THEN 30398
30380 X=X/90
30382 Y=INT(X)
30384 X=(X-Y)*90
30386 ON Y GOTO 30388,30392,30396
30388 X=90-X
30390 GOTO 30398
30392 X=-X
30394 GOTO 30398
30396 X=X-90
30398 X=Z*X/57.29578
30400 IF ABS(X)<2.48616E-4 THEN 30408
30402 Y=X*X
30404 Y=(((((Y/72-1)*Y/42+1)*Y/20-1)*Y/6+1)*X
30406 GOTO 30410
30408 Y=X
30410 X=C/57.29578
30412 RETURN
```

And be sure to make these TEST PROGRAM changes:

```
35 X=R
40 GOSUB 30360
```

To find the SINE of an angle (expressed in Degrees) either delete line 30364 or change line 40 to:

```
40 GOSUB 30366
```

Variations In Usage

Some (rare) interpreters convert everything to degrees automatically.

Also See

```
TAN, COS, ATN, ACS, ASN, SINH
```

SINH(N) is a function that calculates the hyperbolic sine of a number. Hyperbolic functions express relationships based on a hyperbola, similar to the way trigonometric functions are identified on a circle.

SNH

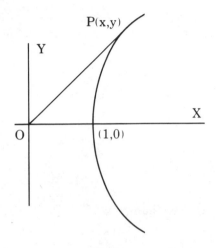

If, on the unit hyperbola (i.e. the graph of X*X − Y*Y = 1), a line is drawn from the origin to a point ,P, of the curve (see diagram), a region is formed with area N/2. SINH(N) will give the value of the Y coordinate of the point of intersection. (COSH(N) will give the value of X.)

Unlike the trig functions, N does **not** name the measure of an angle and, therefore, is not naming degrees or radians. N can be any real number, positive or negative.

Test Program

```
10 REM 'SINH' TEST PROGRAM
20 PRINT "ENTER A VALUE";
30 INPUT N
40 S=SINH(N)
50 PRINT "THE HYPERBOLIC SINE OF";N;"IS";S
30999 END
```

Sample Run *(for input of 1)*

```
ENTER A VALUE? 1
THE HYPERBOLIC SINE OF 1 IS 1.1752
```

IF YOUR COMPUTER DOESN'T HAVE IT

If your computer doesn't accept SINH, you can compute the value by substituting the EXP function, as follows:

```
40 S=.5 * (EXP(N)-EXP(-N))
```

If your computer doesn't have the EXP function either, substitute the following subroutine, instead. The subroutine program found under EXP must be included here.

```
30000 GOTO 30999
30450 REM * SINH SUBROUTINE * INPUT N, OUTPUT S
30452 REM ALSO USES A, B, E, L AND X INTERNALLY
30454 X=N
30456 GOSUB 30200
30458 S=E
30460 X=-N
30462 GOSUB 30200
30464 S=.5*(S-E)
30466 RETURN
```

To use this subroutine, make the following change in TEST PROGRAM:

```
40 GOSUB 30450
```

Alternate Spelling

Harris BASIC-V uses SNH for the SINH function.

Variations In Usage

None known.

Also See

```
COSH, TANH, EXP
```

SLEEP is used by the HARRIS BASIC-V to suspend program execution for a specified number of tenths of seconds.

For example, SLEEP 300 causes the computer to pause 30 seconds before continuing program execution.

Test Program

```
10 REM 'SLEEP' TEST PROGRAM
20 PRINT "THE COMPUTER SHOULD PRINT THE FOLLOWING LINE"
30 SLEEP 150
40 PRINT "AFTER SLEEPING 15 SECONDS"
99 END
```

Sample Run

```
THE COMPUTER SHOULD PRINT THE FOLLOWING LINE
```
                    (15 second pause)
```
AFTER SLEEPING 15 SECONDS
```

IF YOUR COMPUTER DOESN'T HAVE IT

Insert a FOR-NEXT loop to "burn up" computer time. Test your computer to see how many loops it executes per second. A micro-computer may perform as few as several hundred, while a big mainframe may execute 50,000 or more. Replace line 30 in the Test Program (assuming your computer executes 1000 loops per second) with:

```
30 FOR L=1 TO 15000
35 NEXT L
```

Variations In Usage

None known.

Also See

WAIT

Command

SKIPF is used by a few computers (e.g. Sharp/ TRS-80 Pocket) to advance the cassette tape to the end of a file. In other words, use SKIPF to SKIP a File.

If the SKIPF command is given without a file name, the current file is skipped and the tape stops at its end. If a file name is specified, for example

```
SKIPF "A"
```

the computer searches the tape for file "A" and stops at its end. If file "A" is not found, an I/O ERROR is printed on the screen.

SKIPF can be used to display a directory of the programs on a tape by specifying a non-existent file name in the command. Each file name encountered in the search is displayed on the screen until the tape ends and an I/O ERROR message is displayed.

Also See

CLOAD, CSAVE.

The SPACE$(*n*) function is used to insert a specified number (*n*) of spaces.

For example, `PRINT SPACE$(20);"HELLO"` prints 20 spaces followed by the word HELLO.

SPACE$

Most computers with SPACE$(*n*) capability require the value (*n*) to be greater than 0 and less than 256.

SPACE
SPA
SPC

Test Program

```
10 REM 'SPACES' TEST PROGRAM
20 A$=SPACE$(10)
30 PRINT "IF THE FOLLOWING LINE CONTAINS 10 LEADING SPACES"
40 PRINT A$;"THE SPACE$ FUNCTION PASSED THE TEST"
99 END
```

Sample Run

```
IF THE FOLLOWING LINE CONTAINS 10 LEADING SPACES
          THE SPACE$ FUNCTION PASSED THE TEST
```

IF YOUR COMPUTER DOESN'T HAVE IT

If your computer uses STRING$, try `20 A$=STRING$(10," ")` in the Test Program. Then try `20 A$=STRING$(10,32)`. The second number is the ASCII number for a space.

In most cases, SPACEs can be inserted by **careful** use of the TAB function. Remember, SPACE$ counts from the present cursor position while TAB always counts from the left margin.

For example, `40 PRINT TAB(10);"THE SPACE$ FUNCTION PASSED THE TEST"` will accomplish the same thing, and a variable could have been used instead of the number 10.

Where a variable isn't needed, simple enclosure of spaces between quotes will also work.

For example, `40 PRINT"          THE SPACE$ FUNCTION PASSED THE TEST"`

Alternate Spellings

Several other words are used for the SPACE$ function. Among them are SPACE (used by MAX BASIC), SPA (Hewlett-Packard 2000) and SPC (Benton Harbor BASIC).

Variations In Usage

None known.

Also See

TAB, STRING$

The SQR(*n*) function computes the square root of any positive number (*n*)

SQR

A
N
S
I

SQRT

Test Program

```
10 REM 'SQR' TEST PROGRAM
20 PRINT "THE SQUARE ROOT OF 225
   IS";
30 PRINT SQR(225)
40 PRINT "'SQR' PASSED THE TEST IF
   THE RESULT IS 15"
30999 END
```

Sample Run

```
THE SQUARE ROOT OF 225 IS 15
'SQR' PASSED THE TEST IF THE RESULT IS 15
```

Alternate Spelling

SQRT is used by computers such as the DEC-10 and NORTH STAR to indicate the square root function.

IF YOUR COMPUTER DOESN'T HAVE IT

If the computer failed the Test Program substitute the following subroutine:

```
30000 GOTO 30999
30020 REM * SQUARE ROOT SUBROUTINE * INPUT X, OUTPUT Y
30022 REM ALSO USES VARIABLES W AND Z INTERNALLY
30024 IF X=0 THEN 30048
30026 IF X>0 THEN 30032
30028 PRINT "ROOT OF NEGATIVE NUMBER?"
30030 STOP
30032 Y=X/4
30034 Z=0
30036 W=(X/Y-Y)/2
30038 IF W=0 THEN 30050
30040 IF W=Z THEN 30050
30042 Y=Y+W
30044 Z=W
30046 GOTO 30036
30048 Y=0
30050 RETURN
```

To use this subroutine in the TEST PROGRAM, make these Test Program changes:

```
25 X=225
30 GOSUB 30020
35 PRINT Y
```

Variations In Usage

None known.

The STEP function is used to specify the size between steps in a FOR-NEXT statement. The STEP value can be positive, negative or sometimes even a non-integer decimal value. When a STEP value is not specified, the value of +1 is automatically assumed.

STE
ST
S.

Test Program #1

```
10 REM 'STEP' TEST PROGRAM
20 PRINT "WHEN THE STEP VALUE IS 2,
   X=";
30 FOR X=1 TO 10 STEP 2
40 PRINT X;
50 NEXT X
99 END
```

Sample Run

```
WHEN THE STEP VALUE IS 2, X= 1  3  5  7  9
```

The following program tests the interpreter's ability to handle negative STEP values.

Test Program #2

```
10 REM 'NEGATIVE STEP' TEST PROGRAM
20 PRINT "WHEN THE STEP VALUE IS -2, X=";
30 FOR X=10 TO 1 STEP -2
40 PRINT X;
50 NEXT X
99 END
```

Sample Run

```
WHEN THE STEP VALUE IS -2, X= 10  8  6  4  2
```

Test program #3 checks the interpreter's ability to handle non-integer decimal STEP values.

Test Program #3

```
10 REM 'NON-INTEGER STEP' TEST PROGRAM
20 PRINT "WHEN THE STEP VALUE IS .5, X=";
30 FOR X=1 TO 5 STEP .5
40 PRINT X;
50 NEXT X
99 END
```

Sample Run

```
WHEN THE STEP VALUE IS .5, X= 1   1.5   2   2.5   3   3.5   4
   4.5   5
```

A variable is accepted as the STEP value by some interpreters. For example, FOR X=1 TO 30 STEP A causes the value of X to be incremented by the value of variable A each time the corresponding NEXT statement is executed.

Test Program #4

```
10 REM 'VARIABLE STEP' TEST PROGRAM
20 PRINT "ENTER A STEP VALUE (BETWEEN 1 AND 10)"
30 INPUT S
40 PRINT "THE VALUE OF X=";
50 FOR X=1 TO 10 STEP S
60 PRINT X;
70 NEXT X
99 END
```

Sample Run *(Using 3)*

```
ENTER A STEP VALUE (BETWEEN 1 AND 10)
? 3
THE VALUE OF X= 1   4   7   10
```

Alternate Spellings

STE is used in the PDP-8E, ST in the TI 990, and S. in the TRS-80 Level I.

IF YOUR COMPUTER DOESN'T HAVE IT

If STEP is not intrinsic, or not powerful enough, it can be easily simulated in ascending FOR-NEXT statements. Omit STEP S from line 50 in the last test program, and add the following lines:

```
45 Y=1
60 PRINT Y;
65 Y=Y+S
67 IF Y>10 GOTO 99
```

Inserting these lines immediately before the corresponding NEXT statement allows incrementing X by any integer or decimal fraction you wish.

Also See

```
FOR, NEXT
```

The STOP statement is used to STOP execution of the program and place the computer in the command or immediate mode. It can be placed at any point within a program, but is not usually used in place of the END statement.

Some computers will stop the program at the line which contains the STOP statement, while others jump to the line containing the END statement.

Many computers with interpreters (but not usually compilers) print the line number where the program stopped, and allow continuation of program execution via the CONTINUE command (see CONT).

ANSI

STO
ST.
S.

Test Program

```
10 REM 'STOP' TEST PROGRAM
20 PRINT "SEE THE STOP STATEMENT IN ACTION"
30 STOP
40 PRINT "THE STOP STATEMENT FAILED THE TEST"
99 END
```

Sample Run

```
SEE THE STOP STATEMENT IN ACTION
BREAK AT LINE 30
```

Alternate Spellings

STO is used in the PDP-8E and Tektronix 4050 series. ST. and S. in the TRS-80 Level I.

Variations In Usage

Trying to use both STOP and END in the same program can be unusually frustrating unless you know your machine's capabilities. Some machines (e.g. Varian) require physical intervention (push a button) before RUNning, after hitting a program STOP.

Others (mostly large machines) allow an unlimited number of STOPs, but only one END. Others allow an unlimited number of ENDs, but no STOPs. Most micros allow trouble-free mixing of STOPs and ENDs.

With care, the STOP/END problem can almost always be resolved and programs easily converted.

Also See

```
CONT, END, GO
```

Statement
Command

STORE is used in the APPLE II computer as both a command and a statement to save an array of numeric values on cassette tape. A large array can be placed on tape under program control, then RECALLed by the same program or by another program. See RECALL for additional information.

Example: 10 DIM A(3,3,3)

$\qquad$ 200 STORE A

will store 64 values (4*4*4) on tape for future use. (Note: The four values are 0, 1, 2 and 3.)

Test Program

```
10 REM 'STORE' TEST PROGRAM
20 DIM A(25),B(25)
30 FOR I=1 TO 25
40 A(I)=I
50 NEXT I
60 STORE A
70 PRINT "REWIND TAPE AND SET TO PLAY - PRESS RETURN"
80 INPUT A$
90 RECALL B
100 FOR I=1 TO 25
110 PRINT B(I),
120 NEXT I
999 END
```

Sample Run

```
REWIND TAPE AND SET TO PLAY - PRESS RETURN
?
1           2           3
4           5           6
7           8           9
10          11          12
13          14          15
16          17          18
19          20          21
22          23          24
25
```

Variations In Usage

None known.

Also See

RECALL, CSAVE, DIM

The STRING$(*n*,ASCII code) function is used with the PRINT statement to print an ASCII character (*n*) number of times.

For example, PRINT STRING$(10,65) prints the ASCII character A(ASCII code 65) ten times.

STRING$

STRING
STR

Test Program #1

```
10 REM 'STRING$' TEST PROGRAM
20 PRINT STRING$(18,42);
30 PRINT "STRING$ FUNCTION";
40 PRINT STRING$(18,42)
99 END
```

Sample Run

```
*********STRING$ FUNCTION*********
```

Variations In Usage

Some computers (e.g. the TRS-80) allow string characters (enclosed in quotes) or string variables in the STRING$ function.

For example, 10 PRINT STRING$(10,"A")

prints the letter A ten times.

```
10 A$="B"
20 PRINT STRING$(5,A$)
```

prints the letter B five times.

Test Program #2

```
10 REM 'STRING$' TEST PROGRAM
20 PRINT "ENTER ANY LETTER, NUMBER OR SYMBOL";
30 INPUT A$
40 PRINT STRING$(20,",");
50 PRINT STRING$(20,A$)
99 END
```

Sample Run

```
ENTER ANY LETTER, NUMBER OR SYMBOL? X
,,,,,,,,,,,,,,,,,,,,XXXXXXXXXXXXXXXXXXXX
```

Alternate Spellings

Some computers accept STRING or STR in place of STRING$.

IF YOUR COMPUTER DOES NOT HAVE IT

If your computer does not allow the STRING$ function, it can be simulated by finding the ASCII character in the ASCII table (see Appendix A) which matches the ASCII code listed in the STRING$ function. Then place that character in a PRINT statement the number of times specified by the first number in the STRING$ function.

For example:

```
10 PRINT STRING$(12,45)
```

can be replaced with:

```
10 PRINT "------------"
```

or

```
10 FOR N=1 TO 12
15 PRINT "-";
20 NEXT N
```

Also See

PRINT, ASC, CHR$, LEN, MID$, LEFT$, RIGHT$, STR$, VAL

The STR$(*n*) function is used to convert a numeric value (*n*) into a string. The value (*n*) may be expressed as a number or a numeric variable.

For example,

```
10 A$=STR$(35)
20 PRINT A$
```

prints the number 35 as a string. The computer automatically allows room before the number for its sign. In the event the number is positive, that space is left blank.

Conversion of a number to a string via the STR$ function allows its manipulation using string modifiers (e.g. LEFT$, RIGHT$, MID$, ASC, etc.)

Test Program

```
10 REM 'STR$' TEST PROGRAM
20 A = 123
30 A$ = STR$(A)
40 PRINT "IF THE NUMBER";A;"IS CONVERTED TO THE
   STRING";A$
50 PRINT "THEN THE STR$ FUNCTION PASSED THE TEST."
99 END
```

Sample Run

```
IF THE NUMBER 123 IS CONVERTED TO THE STRING 123
THEN THE STR$ FUNCTION PASSED THE TEST.
```

Variations In Usage

None known.

Also See

```
ASC, CHR$, LEN, LEFT$, MID$, RIGHT$, STRING$, VAL NUM$
```

Statement

STUFF is used in the Digital Group Opus 1 and Opus 2 BASIC to insert integer values between 0 and 255 into specified memory locations.

For example, STUFF 3000,65 places the decimal value 65 in memory address 3000.

The FETCH function can be used with STUFF to check what STUFF has stored into memory. (Some computers use PEEK or EXAM instead.)

Computers vary in the amount of available memory and memory addresses that can be STUFFed without erasing memory dedicated to other purposes. Check your computer's manual before running this Test Program to determine that addresses 15001 to 15010 are non-critical memory locations. If they are already dedicated, select 10 other consecutive addresses.

Test Program

```
10 REM 'STUFF' TEST PROGRAM
20 FOR X=1 TO 10
30 STUFF 15000+X,X
40 NEXT X
50 FOR X=15001 TO 15010
60 Y=FETCH(X)
70 PRINT Y;
80 NEXT X
90 PRINT
100 PRINT "'STUFF' PASSED THE TEST IF #1 THRU #10 ARE
    PRINTED"
999 END
```

Sample Run

```
 1  2  3  4  5  6  7  0  9  10
'STUFF' PASSED THE TEST IF #1 THRU #10 ARE PRINTED
```

IF YOUR COMPUTER DOESN'T HAVE IT

If your computer failed the Test Program, try the Test Programs found in POKE and FILL.

Variations In Usage

None known.

Also See

POKE, FILL, PEEK, FETCH, EXAM

SWAP is used by several computers (e.g. INTELLEC, SWTP, COMPUCORP) to switch the values of two variables or array elements.

For example, SWAP(A,B) results in the original value of A being stored in B and the former value of B being stored in A. SWAP is very useful for arranging array values in an ascending or descending order.

Test Program

```
10 REM 'SWAP' TEST PROGRAM
20 PRINT "ENTER TWO VALUES (SEPARATED BY COMMAS)"
30 INPUT A,B
40 IF A<=B THEN 60
50 SWAP (A,B)
60 PRINT A;" IS LESS THAN OR EQUAL TO ";B
70 GOTO 20
99 END
```

Sample Run

```
ENTER TWO VALUES (SEPARATED BY COMMAS)
? 3,7
3 IS LESS THAN OR EQUAL TO 7
ENTER TWO VALUES (SEPARATED BY COMMAS)
? 9,1
1 IS LESS THAN OR EQUAL TO 9
ENTER TWO VALUES (SEPARATED BY COMMAS)
?
```

IF YOUR COMPUTER DOESN'T HAVE IT

If SWAP doesn't work with your computer, try EXCHANGE in line 50. If neither is available, the values can be switched by replacing line 50 with:

```
48 T=A
50 A=B
52 B=T
```

Also See

```
EXCHANGE
```

Command
Statement

SYSTEM

SYS

The SYSTEM command is used by some computers to allow machine language data (object code) to be loaded from cassette tape or disc into the computer. These computers may also use SYSTEM as a program statement.

When the computer executes the line containing the SYSTEM statement, or when SYSTEM is typed on the terminal, the computer changes to the monitor mode and prints an asterisk followed by a question mark (*?) or some other cryptic symbol. This signal indicates the computer is ready to accept the object file from disc or tape.

Place an object code tape in the cassette player and set it to the PLAY mode. Type the object file name and RETURN. The cassette recorder's motor is controlled by the computer, which turns it on and off before and after the load cycle. The cassette should "play back" the data into the computer. When the data is loaded in the computer, another *? is displayed.

To execute the object file routine, type a slash (/) followed by a memory starting address. If the / is entered without the starting address, then execution begins at the address specified in the object file.

Alternate Spellings

The Commodore PET, DEC – 10, and Sperry Univac System/9 use SYS as an abbreviation for SYSTEM.

Variations In Usage

The SYSTEM command is similar to the ESC (escape) key on many keyboards. Both place the command in the System, Executive or monitor mode.

Also See

PEEK, POKE, MON

T.

The TAB function is used with PRINT statements in a manner similar to the TAB key on a typewriter. When the PRINT statement is followed by TAB() the computer inserts a number of spaces (enclosed in parentheses) before the statement to be printed. The TAB value must always be positive and should be less than the number of spaces allowed per line.

If more than one TAB statement is used in one line, the numbers must get progressively larger and allow room inbetween for that which is to be printed. If insufficient room is allowed between TABs, they will be overrun, just like on a typewriter.

The value may be expressed as a number, PRINT TAB(5); a variable, PRINT TAB(X); or an expression, PRINT TAB(2X+Y). TAB() should be followed by a semicolon or comma, but it depends upon the interpreter.

Test Program

```
10 REM 'TAB' FUNCTION TEST PROGRAM
20 PRINT TAB(5); "TAB 5"
30 X = 10
40 PRINT TAB(X); "TAB 10"
50 PRINT TAB(6*X/5+8); "TAB 20"
999 END
```

Sample Run

```
    TAB 5
        TAB 10
            TAB 20
```

The maximum value your computer can TAB can be quickly determined by adding the following lines to the Test Program:

```
60 PRINT "TYPE IN A TAB VALUE";
70 INPUT T
80 PRINT TAB(T); "TAB";T
90 GOTO 60
```

The TAB value entered in line 70 will cause line 80 to print the TAB value following the same number of spaces.

Alternate Spelling

Computers using variations of Tiny BASIC accept T. as an abbreviation for TAB.

Variations In Usage

None known.

IF YOUR COMPUTER DOESN'T HAVE IT

There is no completely satisfactory replacement for TAB, but there are several ways to obtain printouts which may be acceptable. Assume an original PRINT series:

```
200 PRINT TAB(10);"THE";TAB(20);"QUICK";TAB(30);"BROWN";
210 PRINT TAB(40);"FOX"
```

The TAB values are simple numbers and could be replaced by:

```
200 PRINT"          THE          QUICK     BROWN       FOX"
```

or, less accurately:

```
200 PRINT "THE","QUICK","BROWN","FOX"
```

or

A combination of inserting spaces and automatic zone spacing.

A third, and generally less satisfactory, method of arriving at a usable printout involves combining the carriage return suppressing ability of the semicolon (;), the automatic zoning of the comma (,), and inserted spaces. In some interpreters (compilers) however this can create a remarkably messy situation.

Also See

PRINT, PRINT USING, PRINT AT, ,(comma), ;(semicolon), SPACE$

The TAN(A) function computes the Tangent of the angle A when that angle is expressed **in radians** (*not in degrees*). One radian = approximately 57 degrees.

TAND
TANG

A
N
S
I

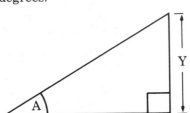

Tangent (TAN) is defined as the ratio of the length of the side opposite the angle being investigated to the length of the side adjacent to it.

```
TAN(A)=Y/X
```

The opposite of TAN is ARCTAN (ATN). ARCTAN finds the value of the angle when its TAN, or ratio of sides (Y/X) is known.

Test Program

```
10 REM 'TAN' TEST PROGRAM
20 PRINT "ENTER AN ANGLE (EXPRESSED IN RADIANS)";
30 INPUT R
40 Y=TAN(R)
50 PRINT "THE TANGENT OF A";R;"RADIAN ANGLE IS";Y
30999 END
```

Sample Run (*using 1*)

```
ENTER AN ANGLE (EXPRESSED IN RADIANS)? 1
THE TANGENT OF A 1 RADIAN ANGLE IS 1.55741
```

To convert values from degrees to radians, multiply the angle in degrees times .0174533. For example, `R=TAN(A*.0174533)` To convert values from radians to degrees, multiply the angle in radians times 57.29578.

Some computers accept the measure of the angle in degrees or grads (100 grads = 90 degrees), These computers use the function TAND for degrees and TANG for grads. Changing Line 40 should produce .0174451 with TAND and .0157092 with TANG.

IF YOUR COMPUTER DOESN'T HAVE IT

If your interpreter has the SINe and COSine capability but not TANgent, substitute SIN(A)/COS(A) for TAN(A).

If your interpreter does not have SINe, COSine or TANgent capability, the following subroutine can be substituted to compute the TANgent in radians.

The subroutine programs found under SIN and COS **must** be added to this one to make it work (saves space not to duplicate them here).

```
30000 GOTO 30999
30300 REM *TANGENT SUBROUTINE * INPUT X IN RADIANS,
      OUTPUT Y
30302 REM ALSO USES A, B, C, D, W AND Z INTERNALLY
30304 X=X*57.29578
30306 A=X
30308 GOSUB 30336
30310 IF ABS(Y)>1E-8 THEN 30316
30312 PRINT "TANGENT UNDEFINED"
30314 STOP
30316 B=Y
30318 X=A
30320 GOSUB 30366
30322 Y=Y/B
30324 X=A/57.29578
30326 RETURN
```

and be sure to make the following Test Program changes:

```
35 X=R
40 GOSUB 30300
```

To find the TANGENT of an angle (expressed in **degrees**), either delete line 30304 or change line 40 to:

```
40 GOSUB 30306
```

Variations In Usage

Some (rare) interpreters convert everything to degrees automatically.

Also See

SIN, COS, ATN, ASN, ACS, TANH

TNH

TANH(N) is a function that calculates the hyperbolic tangent of a number. Hyperbolic functions express relationships based on a hyperbola similar to the way trigonometric functions are identified on a circle.

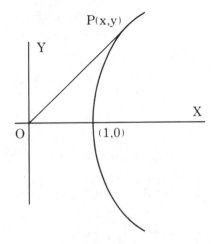

If, on the unit hyperbola (i.e. the graph of X*X − Y*Y = 1), a line is drawn from the origin to a point P, on the curve (see diagram), a region is formed with an area N/2. TANH(N) will give the slope of the line drawn. [COSH(N) gives the value of the X coordinate of the point of intersection and SINH(N) gives the value of Y.]

Unlike the trig functions, N does **not** name the measure of an angle and, therefore, is not in degrees or radians. N can be any real number, positive or negative but TANH(N) is always between -1 and 1.

Test Program

```
10 REM 'TANH' TEST PROGRAM
20 PRINT "ENTER A VALUE";
30 INPUT N
40 T=TANH(N)
50 PRINT "THE HYPERBOLIC TANGENT OF ";N;"IS";T
30999 END
```

Sample Run *(using the value .5)*

```
ENTER A VALUE? .5
THE HYPERBOLIC TANGENT OF .5 IS .462117
```

IF YOUR COMPUTER DOESN'T HAVE IT

If your computer doesn't accept TANH, you can compute the value by substituting the EXP function, as follows:

```
40 T=1-2*EXP(-N)/(EXP(N)+EXP(-N))
```

If your computer doesn't have EXP function either, substitute the following subroutine, instead. The subroutine program found under EXP must also be included.

```
30000 GOTO 30999
30470 REM * TANH SUBROUTINE * INPUT N, OUTPUT T
30472 REM ALSO USES A, B, E, L AND X INTERNALLY
30474 X=N
30476 GOSUB 30200
30478 T=E
30480 X=-N
30482 GOSUB 30200
30484 T=1-2*E/(T+E)
30486 RETURN
```

To use this subroutine, make the following change in Test Program:

```
40 GOSUB 30470
```

Alternate Spelling

Harris BASIC-V uses TNH for the TANH function.

Variations In Usage

None known.

Also See

```
SINH, COSH, EXP
```

TAPPEND is used by some interpreters (e.g. Percom) to combine a program from cassette tape with one already in memory. It stands for Tape APPEND.

The line numbers of the program statements being brought into memory must be larger than the last line number already in memory.

Test Program

To test TAPPEND, store this short program on tape as PROG2.

```
1000 PRINT "THESE LINES ARE"
1010 PRINT "FROM PROG2"
1020 END
```

Then type NEW or SCRATCH to erase the program and type this PROG1:

```
10 REM 'TAPPEND' TEST PROGRAM PROG1
20 PRINT "THESE LINES ARE"
30 PRINT "FROM PROG1"
40 PRINT "     BUT..."
```

Then type TAPPEND PROG2 and RUN.

Sample Run

```
THESE LINES ARE
FROM PROG1
      BUT...
THESE LINES ARE
FROM PROG2
```

Also See

```
APPEND, CLOAD, CSAVE, TLOAD, TSAVE
```

TEXT is used in APPLE II BASIC as both a command and a program statement to change the computer's operation from the graphics mode to the normal TEXT (narrative) mode.

Test Program

```
10 REM 'TEXT' TEST PROGRAM
20 TEXT
30 PRINT "THE 'TEXT' STATEMENT DID NOT CRASH"
40 END
```

Sample Run

```
THE 'TEXT' STATEMENT DID NOT CRASH
```

Variations In Usage

TEXT is used in computers with MAXBASIC to specify designated variables as string variables. For example, TEXT A,F,M defines variables A,F and M as string variables.

Also See

GR, DEFSTR, $

THEN is used with the IF statement to indicate the next operation the computer is to perform when the condition of the IF statement is met.

For more information see IF-THEN.

THE
T.

Test Program

```
10 REM 'THEN' TEST PROGRAM
20 X=10
30 IF X=10 THEN 60
40 PRINT "'THEN' FAILED THE TEST"
50 GOTO 99
60 PRINT "'THEN' PASSED THE TEST"
99 END
```

Sample Run

```
'THEN' PASSED THE TEST
```

Alternate Spellings

THE is allowed by the PDP-8E computer and T. by TRS-80 Level I.

Variations In Usage

None known.

Also See

IF-THEN

345

Command
Function

TIME

TIM
TI

TIME is used as a special feature in some computers to indicate the elapsed time in seconds or fractions of seconds from a known reference point in time.

Most "time-shared" machines count time from 12:00 midnight until the following midnight, while "stand-alone" machines count from the moment the computer is turned on until it is turned off.

For example, PRINT TIME may print a number similar to 017230 indicating the total computer run time in some cryptic units.

Computers vary in their unit of time measurement. The Commodore PET increments the TIME value at a rate of 60 times per second, those using MAX BASIC increment at a rate of 1000 times per second, and the DEC BASIC-PLUS-2 increments at a rate of one count per second.

Some computers (e.g. the Commodore PET) report elapsed TIME as a six-digit number, and this value cannot be changed or reset to zero except by turning off the computer.

Test Program

```
10 REM 'TIME' TEST PROGRAM
20 A=TIME
30 PRINT "TIME IS MARCHING ON"
40 FOR X=1 TO 2000
50 NEXT X
60 B=TIME
70 IF B>A THEN 100
80 PRINT "THE TIME FUNCTION FAILED THE TEST"
90 GOTO 999
100 PRINT "'TIME' PASSED THE TEST - ELAPSED TIME =";B-A
999 END
```

Sample Run (typical)

```
TIME IS MARCHING ON
'TIME' PASSED THE TEST - ELAPSED TIME = 270
```

Alternate Spellings

TIM is used by some computers (e.g. DEC-10) while others (e.g. Commodore PET) use TI.

Variations In Usage

The DEC BASIC-PLUS-2 uses the following TIME variations:

TIME(0) indicates the total elapsed time in seconds since midnight.

For example, 100 PRINT TIME(0) may print a value similar to 25128 indicating 25,128 seconds have elapsed since midnight.

TIME(1%) indicates the total elapsed program time in tenths of seconds.

For example, 100 PRINT TIME(1%) may print a value similar to 85 indicating the program ran 8.5 seconds before printing TIME(1%).

TIME(2%) indicates the total elapsed time in minutes that a terminal was connected to a time share system.

For example, 10 PRINT TIME(2%) may print a value similar to 130 indicating 130 minutes have elapsed since the terminal was connected to the time share system.

The Hewlett Packard 2000F TIME-SHARED BASIC uses TIME as a command to print the elapsed time since the terminal was logged onto the system, and the total accumulated account time.

For example, if the command TIME is typed, it will print a report similar to this;

```
CONSOLE TIME = 5 MINUTES, TOTAL TIME = 2045 MINUTES,
```

Also See

TIME$, CLK$

Command
Function

TI$

TIME$ is used by some computers (e.g. the Commodore PET and the DEC BASIC-PLUS-2) to indicate the time of day.

The PET reports the time in hours (0 -24), minutes, and seconds as a six digit number (hhmmss). The TIME$ value is "set" by assigning a six digit number (enclosed in quotes) to TIME$.

For example, TIME$="144500" sets the time at 144500 (which is the same as 2:45 p.m.). The time advances in one second increments from the time the computer is turned on (TIME$ is initialized at 000000), and from the moment it is assigned a new value.

Test Program

```
10 REM 'TIME$' TEST PROGRAM
20 PRINT "THE CURRENT TIME IS";TIME$
30 PRINT "THE TIME$ FUNCTION PASSED THE TEST"
40 PRINT "IF A SIX DIGIT NUMBER IS PRINTED"
99 END
```

Sample Run *(typical)*

```
THE CURRENT TIME IS 012536
THE TIME$ FUNCTION PASSED THE TEST
IF A SIX DIGIT NUMBER IS PRINTED
```

Alternate Spelling

TI$ is used by the Commodore PET as an abbreviation for TIME$.

Variations In Usage

DEC BASIC-PLUS-2 uses TIME$(0%) to indicate the time of day in hours and minutes, leaving off the seconds.

For example, PRINT TIME$(0%) will print a time in the format 14:32. The computer automatically inserts the colon between the hours and minutes. Also, DEC BASIC-PLUS-2 uses TIME$(n) to indicate the time (n) minutes before midnight. For example: PRINT TIME$(61) prints 22:59.

Also See

```
TIME, CLK$
```

The TLOAD command is used by PERCOM BASIC to LOAD a program into the computer from cassette tape.

Test Program

Enter this program into the computer from the keyboard, and store it on cassette tape. (See TSAVE for details.)

```
10 REM 'TLOAD' TEST PROGRAM
20 PRINT "THIS PROGRAM TESTS THE TLOAD FEATURE"
99 END
```

Once the program is recorded on cassette tape, erase the computer's memory with NEW (or SCRATCH or whatever is appropriate).

Rewind the tape, then set the recorder to the PLAY mode and type the TLOAD command.

When the recorder stops, LIST the program to verify that the program loaded matches the program above (see LIST). If all looks well, RUN.

Sample Run

```
THIS PROGRAM TESTS THE TLOAD FEATURE
```

Variations In Usage

None known.

Also See

```
CLOAD, LOAD, TSAVE, LIST, NEW, SCRATCH
```

Function

The TOP function in the ACORN ATOM computer identifies the address of the first byte of unused memory.

For example, PRINT TOP will print the beginning address (in hexadecimal) of the available memory. If you know the starting address (SA) of your program, then PRINT TOP - SA will report how large the program is.

Test Program

```
10 REM 'TOP' TEST PROGRAM
20 IF TOP=0 THEN 50
30 PRINT "FREE MEMORY STARTS AT ";TOP
40 GOTO 99
50 PRINT "TOP FAILED THE TEST"
99 END
```

Sample Run

```
FREE MEMORY STARTS AT 285A
```

The exact address will depend on the size of computer and the amount of memory currently being used.

Variations in Usage

None known.

Also See

FRE(0), MEM

The TRACE command is used in APPLE II BASIC to activate a feature which prints program line numbers as each one is executed by the computer. It is used as a trouble-shooting aid. This feature is disabled by the NOTRACE command.

TRACE may also be used as a program statement to allow tracing only specific sections of programs.

Test Program

```
10 REM 'TRACE' TEST PROGRAM
20 PRINT "'TRACE' TRACES EACH LINE"
30 TRACE
40 GOTO 90
50 PRINT "UNTIL TURNED OFF BY"
60 NOTRACE
70 PRINT "THE 'NOTRACE' STATEMENT"
80 GOTO 110
90 PRINT "THAT FOLLOWS THE 'TRACE' STATEMENT"
100 GOTO 50
110 PRINT "AS ILLUSTRATED BY THIS LINE"
999 END
```

Sample Run

```
'TRACE' TRACES EACH LINE
#40#90 THAT FOLLOWS THE 'TRACE' STATEMENT
#100#50 UNTIL TURNED OFF BY
#60 THE 'NOTRACE' STATEMENT
AS ILLUSTRATED BY THIS LINE
```

Variations In Usage

None known.

Also See

NOTRACE, TRON, TRACE ON, FLOW

The TRACE OFF command is used in Motorola BASIC to disable the trace function (see TRACE ON). TRACE OFF may be used as a program statement to turn the trace off at specified areas in the program.

Test Program

```
10 REM 'TRACE OFF' TEST PROGRAM
20 TRACE ON
30 PRINT "EACH LINE SHOULD BE TRACED"
40 TRACE OFF
50 PRINT "BY THE 'TRACE ON' STATEMENT"
60 PRINT "UNTIL TURNED OFF BY THE 'TRACE OFF' STATEMENT"
99 END
```

Sample Run

```
<30> EACH LINE SHOULD BE TRACED
<40> BY THE 'TRACE ON' STATEMENT
UNTIL TURNED OFF BY THE 'TRACE OFF' STATEMENT
```

Variations In Usage

None known.

Also See

TRACE ON, NOTRACE, TROFF, NOFLOW

The TRACE ON command is used in Motorola BASIC to activate a feature which prints program line numbers as each one is executed by the computer. It is used as a trouble-shooting aid. This tracing feature is disabled by the TRACE OFF command.

TRACE ON may be used as a program statement to trace only specified sections of a program.

Test Program

```
10 REM 'TRACE ON' TEST PROGRAM
20 PRINT "'TRACE ON' TRACES EACH LINE"
30 TRACE ON
40 GOTO 90
50 PRINT "UNTIL TURNED OFF BY"
60 TRACE OFF
70 PRINT "THE 'TRACE OFF' STATEMENT"
80 GOTO 110
90 PRINT "THAT FOLLOWS THE 'TRACE ON' STATEMENT"
100 GOTO 50
110 PRINT "AS ILLUSTRATED BY THIS LINE"
999 END
```

Sample Run

```
'TRACE ON' TRACES EACH LINE
<40> <90> THAT FOLLOWS THE 'TRACE ON' STATEMENT
<100> <50> UNTIL TURNED OFF BY
<60> THE 'TRACE OFF' STATEMENT
AS ILLUSTRATED BY THIS LINE
```

Variations In Usage

None known.

Also See

```
TRACE OFF, TRACE, TRON, FLOW
```

TROFF (trace off) is a command which disables the trace feature found in many interpreters (e.g. TRS-80). TROFF may also be used as a program statement to turn the trace off at specific areas in the program.

Test Program

Type the TRON command, then RUN this test program:

```
10 REM 'TROFF' TEST PROGRAM
20 PRINT "THE FIRST THREE LINES OF THIS PROGRAM"
30 TROFF
40 PRINT "ARE PRINTED WITH THE TRACE TURNED ON."
50 PRINT "THIS LINE IS PRINTED WITH THE TRACE TURNED OFF."
99 END
```

Sample Run

```
<10> <20> THE FIRST THREE LINES OF THIS PROGRAM
<30> ARE PRINTED WITH THE TRACE TURNED ON.
THIS LINE IS PRINTED WITH THE TRACE TURNED OFF.
```

Variations In Usage

None known.

Also See

```
TRON, NOTRACE, NOFLOW, TRACE OFF
```

The TRON (trace on) command is used to activate an analytical tool which prints program line numbers as each line is executed by the computer. This trace feature is disabled by the TROFF or NEW commands. TRON is intended to be used as a program tracing and troubleshooting aid.

Test Program

```
10 REM 'TRON' TEST PROGRAM
20 GOTO 50
30 PRINT "OF THIS TEST PROGRAM,"
40 GOTO 70
50 PRINT "TRON TRACES EACH LINE"
60 GOTO 30
70 PRINT "END OF TEST PROGRAM,"
99 END
```

Sample Run

Type TRON before running the test program.

```
<10><20><50> TRON TRACES EACH LINE
<60><30>OF THIS TEST PROGRAM,
<40><70>END OF TEST PROGRAM,
<99>
```

TRON may also be used as a program statement to trace specific sections of programs. To test this feature, type TROFF to be sure the "trace" is off, then add the following line to the test program and RUN it.

```
35 TRON
```

Sample Run

```
TRON TRACES EACH LINE
OF THIS TEST PROGRAM,
<40><70>END OF TEST PROGRAM,
<99>
```

Variations In Usage

None known.

Also See

```
TROFF, NEW, FLOW, TRACE, TRACE ON
```

Command

The TSAVE command is used by PERCOM BASIC to store the program in computer memory on cassette tape. For more information see CSAVE.

Test Program

```
10 REM 'TSAVE' TEST PROGRAM
20 PRINT "THIS PROGRAM TESTS THE TSAVE FEATURE"
99 END
```

Set up the cassette recorder for recording and type the command TSAVE. The computer should control the operation of the cassette recorder by turning the motor on and off (at the beginning and end of the SAVE cycle).

Once the program is recorded on cassette tape, type NEW (or SCRATCH or whatever is appropriate) to erase the program from memory. Load the program from tape back into the computer (see TLOAD). LIST the program to verify that the program held in the computer's memory is identical to that originally entered (see LIST).

Sample Run

```
THIS PROGRAM TESTS THE TSAVE FEATURE
```

Variations In Usage

None known.

Also See

```
CSAVE, SAVE, TLOAD, LIST, NEW, SCRATCH
```

UNTIL is used as both a modifier and a statement. As a modifier, some computers (e.g. DEC PDP-11) use UNTIL to make statements conditional.

For example, 60 X=X+Y UNTIL X>100 causes the value of Y to be added to the value of X repeatedly until the sum is greater than 100. It's like having its own built-in FOR-NEXT loop. Of course, if X and Y have values such that the sum will not reach 100 (X=1 and Y=-5 for instance) the program will never leave line 60.

Test Program

```
10 REM 'UNTIL' TEST PROGRAM
20 PRINT "TYPE 4 OR 5 NUMBERS (ONE AT A TIME)"
30 PRINT "THE LAST ONE BEING ZERO"
40 INPUT X
50 S=S+X
60 GOTO 40 UNTIL X=0
70 PRINT "THE SUM OF THE NUMBERS TYPED IN IS";S
99 END
```

Sample Run

```
TYPE 4 OR 5 NUMBERS (ONE AT A TIME)
THE LAST ONE BEING ZERO
? 23
? 82
? 47
? 125
? 6
? 0
THE SUM OF THE NUMBERS TYPED IN IS 283
```

Some computers (e.g. DEC PDP-11) use UNTIL in a special form of FOR statement. Example: 50 FOR X=1 STEP 3 UNTIL X*X >100*X+35. Notice the statement does not have a terminating value (as in FOR X=1 TO 20) but ends only when a specified condition has been achieved.

UNTIL is used as a statement by a few computers (e.g. the Acorn ATOM) to terminate a loop created by the DO statement. Example:

```
10 DO X=X+1
20 PRINT X, X*X, SQR(X)
30 UNTIL X=12
```

Also See

```
WHILE, FOR
```

Function

USER

The USR function executes a machine language routine stored in the computer's memory. The machine language routine can be entered into memory from the keyboard using the POKE statement or from tape or disk using a SYSTEM command.

The USR function can be used in programs similar to any other "built in" function.

For example, `10 PRINT USR(N)` will print the value that is computed by the user's machine language routine.

If a machine language routine which computes the square root of N, is stored in the computer's memory, then the computer will print the square root of the number N.

To test for the USR function, you must load a machine language routine into the computer (at appropriate addresses) using the POKE statement or SYSTEM command. Refer to your computer's Manual for specific instructions in the use of this special function on your machine.

Alternate Spelling

Some computers use USER in place of USR.

Also See

`POKE, SYSTEM`

The VAL function is used to convert numbers which are written as strings back into numeric notation. VAL has the effect of stripping off the quotes or dollar sign.

For example:

```
10 A$="35"
20 PRINT VAL(A$)
```

prints the number 35 as a numeric value.

Test Program #1

```
10 REM 'VAL' TEST PROGRAM
20 A$="45.12"
30 A=VAL(A$)
40 PRINT "IF THE STRING ";A$;" IS CONVERTED TO THE
   NUMBER";A
50 PRINT "THEN THE VAL FUNCTION PASSED THE TEST."
99 END
```

Sample Run

```
IF THE STRING 45.12 IS CONVERTED TO THE NUMBER 45.12
THEN THE VAL FUNCTION PASSED THE TEST.
```

CAUTION: Some BASICs do not interpret a string such as " -45" (a plus or minus sign preceded by blanks) as a numeric value. If this is a problem on your computer, a 0 is displayed when PRINT VAL(" -45") is executed. Include the following lines in each program where this is a problem:

```
200 IF LEFT$(A$,1)<>" " THEN 230
210 A$ = RIGHT$(A$,LEN(A$)-1)
220 GOTO 200
230 A = VAL (A$)
```

Variations In Usage

Some computers (e.g. Microsoft variations) allow combinations of numbers and letters with the VAL function, but the numbers must precede the letters. If they don't, the VAL function produces a 0 indicating it did not find a number as the first character.

For example, PRINT VAL("123ABC") prints the number 123.

Test Program #2

```
10 REM 'VAL WITH MIXED STRING' TEST PROGRAM
20 A$="12 O'CLOCK"
30 A=VAL(A$)
40 PRINT "IF THE STRING ";A$;" IS CONVERTED TO THE
   NUMBER";A
50 PRINT "THE VAL FUNCTION ACCEPTED NUMBERS MIXED
   WITH LETTERS."
99 END
```

Sample Run

```
IF THE STRING 12 O'CLOCK IS CONVERTED TO THE NUMBER 12
THE VAL FUNCTION ACCEPTED NUMBERS MIXED WITH LETTERS.
```

Also See

STR$, ASC, CHR$, LEN, LEFT$, MID$, RIGHT$, STRING$

VARPTR is a function used by some BASICs (e.g. Microsoft BASIC) to locate the memory address of a variable. It stands for VARiable PoinTeR.

```
A = VARPTR(X)
```

assigns to A the ADDRESS of the first memory cell used to store the **value** of variable X. To see **what** is stored in location A, type `PRINT PEEK(A)`. The meaning given to what we find depends on the type of variable X represents.

If X is an **integer** variable (see DEFINT and %), location A holds the **Least** Significant Byte (LSB) of the value of **X**. Location $A+1$ holds the **Most** Significant Byte (MSB) of the value of X. VARPTR works correctly if MSB*256 + LSB = X.

Test Program #1

```
10 REM 'VARPTR' TEST PROGRAM
20 X% = 32737
30 A = VARPTR(X%)
40 PRINT "'VARPTR' PASSED THE TEST IF";
50 PRINT PEEK(A+1)*256+PEEK(A);"EQUALS";X%
99 END
```

Sample Run

```
'VARPTR' PASSED THE TEST IF 32737 EQUALS 32737
```

When VARPTR is used with a STRING variable, A is the memory location were the **length** of the string is stored. The next two memory cells, $A+1$ and $A+2$, hold the LSB and MSB of the **starting** address for the string.

VARPTR can be used with string variables to make the strings available to USR routines. Example: `T = USR(VARPTR(A$))` passes the first of the three addresses to the machine-language routine.

VARPTR can also be used to exchange the contents of two string variables. Study this Test Program carefully:

Test Program #2

```
10 REM 'VARPTR(A$)' TEST PROGRAM
20 READ F$,L$
30 DATA FIRST,LAST
40 PRINT "THE ";F$;" SHALL BE ";L$
50 A=VARPTR(F$)
60 B=VARPTR(L$)
70 F1=PEEK(A)
80 F2=PEEK(A+1)
90 F3=PEEK(A+2)
100 L1=PEEK(B)
110 L2=PEEK(B+1)
120 L3=PEEK(B+2)
130 POKE B,F1
140 POKE B+1,F2
150 POKE B+2,F3
160 POKE A,L1
170 POKE A+1,L2
180 POKE A+2,L3
190 PRINT "AND THE ";F$;", ";L$

999 END
```

Sample Run

```
THE FIRST SHALL BE LAST
AND THE LAST, FIRST
```

VARPTR can also be used with single-precision and double-precision variables. The number returned is the **address** of the first of four storage cells containing the single precision value. (Eight storage cells are required for double precision.) Since these numbers are usually stored in a "normalized exponential form", it is impractical to "reconstruct" their value the way we did in Test Program #1.

VARPTR is most often used to simply locate the address of a variable so that address can be passed to a machine-language routine.

IF YOUR COMPUTER DOESN'T HAVE IT

If VARPTR failed the tests try PTR or ADR.

Variations In Usage

None known.

Also See

```
PEEK, POKE, USR, DEFINT, %
```

VLIN-AT is used in APPLE II BASIC to display a Vertical LINe AT a specified column on the screen.

The vertical line length is determined by two numbers following the VLIN statement. These numbers indicate the bounds between which the line will exist. The line may be any length between rows 0 and 39.

The number following AT is the column number which the line must occupy. This number may range from 0 to 39.

For example, VLIN 10,30 AT 20 tells the computer to draw a vertical line from row 10 to row 30 AT column 20.

The GRaphics statement must be executed before the computer can accept the VLIN-AT statement (see GR). The line's color is determined by the COLOR statement (see COLOR).

Test Program

```
10 REM 'VLIN-AT' TEST PROGRAM
20 GR
30 Y=0
40 FOR X=0 TO 39
50 COLOR = Y
60 VLIN 0,39 AT X
70 Y=Y+1
80 IF Y<16 THEN 100
90 Y=0
100 NEXT X
999 END
```

Sample Run

If the computer accepted the VLIN-AT statement, the screen should be filled with 39 vertical lines of various colors.

APF BASIC does not use AT in its VLIN statement. The statement equivalent to the example above is simply VLIN 10, 30, 20. The shape and color to be used are declared in SHAPE and COLOR statements prior to execution of VLIN.

Variations In Usage

None known.

Also See

GR, COLOR, PLOT, HLIN-AT, TEXT

VTAB (vertical tab) is used by APPLE II BASIC to specify the vertical location on the screen for a PRINT statement. VTAB values from 1 to 24, representing the screen's 24 lines, are accepted.

For example, VTAB 12 specifies the PRINT starting point as the 12th line down on the screen.

Test Program

```
10 REM 'VTAB' TEST PROGRAM
20 PRINT "ENTER A VTAB VALUE FROM 1 TO 24";
30 INPUT N
40 VTAB N
50 PRINT "VTAB PASSED THE TEST IF THIS IS PRINTED ON
   LINE";N
99 END
```

Sample Run (using 5)

```
ENTER A VTAB VALUE FROM 1 TO 24? 5
```



```
VTAB PASSED THE TEST IF THIS IS PRINTED ON LINE 5
```

IF YOUR COMPUTER DOESN'T HAVE IT

The easiest way to cause printing to start a certain number of lines down the screen is to first clear it [by a long series of PRINT statements in succession, or with a series of ASCII "line feeds" or CLS (clear screen)]. Check your ASCII chart to find your proper "N" for PRINT CHR$(N).

Then, again using PRINTs or an ASCII character, move down the screen the desired number of lines before printing.

Variations In Usage

None known.

Also See

TAB, PRINT-AT, PRINT, ASC, CHR$, HOME, LIN

WAIT is used by some computers (e.g. those using MAX-BASIC) to suspend program execution for a specified time.

For example, WAIT 30 tells the computer to wait 30 seconds before executing the next statement.

A few computers WAIT a fractional value (e.g. 1/10 or 1/1000) of the specified time.

For example, WAIT 10000 requires computers with ADDS BASIC to WAIT 1000 seconds while the VARIAN 620 will WAIT 10 seconds.

This program allows you to check your computer's WAIT capability.

Test Program #1

```
10 REM 'WAIT TIME PERIOD' TEST PROGRAM
20 PRINT "ENTER A UNIT OF TIME FOR THE COMPUTER TO WAIT";
30 INPUT T
40 PRINT "THE COMPUTER IS WAITING FOR";T;"UNITS OF TIME"
50 WAIT T
60 PRINT "THE WAIT STATEMENT PASSED THE TEST"
99 END
```

Sample Run *(using 60)*

```
ENTER A UNIT OF TIME FOR THE COMPUTER TO WAIT? 60
THE COMPUTER IS WAITING FOR 60 UNITS OF TIME

THE WAIT STATEMENT PASSED THE TEST
```

For a time delay alternative, substitute the following FOR-NEXT loop for WAIT in TEST PROGRAM #1. The value of T will require adjustment for your computer to produce the same amount of delay as the WAIT statement.

```
50 FOR X=1 TO T
55 NEXT X
```

WAIT is used by some other computers (e.g. those using a Microsoft BASIC) to suspend program execution until the byte value at a specified computer port meets the conditions established by two byte values listed after WAIT.

For example, WAIT 30, 2, 5 tells the computer to WAIT until a non-zero value is produced when the byte value at port 30 is eXclusive ORed with the byte value 5, and the resultant value is logically ANDed with the byte value of 2. (Oh well ... back to bird watching.) When this condition is met, program execution continues at the next statement. If this condition is not met, the keyboard BREAK, MONITOR, ESCAPE (or whatever works) key can be pressed to get out of the WAIT condition.

Each value listed in the WAIT statement must be between 0 and 255 (the range of values that can be held in an 8 bit memory cell). When the last byte value (5 in the example above) is omitted from the WAIT statement, the computer assumes its value to be 0.

In the above example, the byte value at port 30 must have its 2-bit "turned on" before the computer continues program execution, as illustrated by this table.

PORT VALUE	3rd BYTE VALUE		2nd BYTE VALUE		
1	0	1	1	0	0
2	1	0	1	1	1
4	0	1	1	0	0
8	0	0	0	0	0
16	0	0	0	0	0
32	0	0	0	0	0
64	0	0	0	0	0
128	0	0	0	0	0
2	XOR	5 =	7 AND	2 =	2

Some computers (e.g. Processor Technology Extended Cassette BASIC) WAIT until the byte value at the specified computer port, ANDed with the second byte value, is EQUAL to the third byte value.

For example, WAIT 120, 255, 6 has the computer WAIT until the byte value at port 120 is equal to 6 as shown in this table.

PORT VALUE	2nd BYTE VALUE	3rd BYTE VALUE
1	0	1	0
2	1	1	1
4	1	1	1
8	0	1	0
16	0	1	0
32	0	1	0
64	0	1	0
128	0	1	0
6	AND 255	=	6

Test Program #2

```
10 REM 'WAIT FOR PORT CONDITION' TEST PROGRAM
20 PRINT "THE COMPUTER IS WAITING FOR ONLY BIT 1 TO
   BE SET"
30 PRINT "IN PORT 20 (THE DECIMAL VALUE OF 2)"
40 WAIT 20, 255, 2
50 PRINT "BIT 1 IN PORT 20 IS SET"
99 END
```

Sample Run

```
THE COMPUTER IS WAITING FOR ONLY BIT 1 TO BE SET
IN PORT 20 (THE DECIMAL VALUE OF 2)
BIT 1 IN PORT 20 IS SET
```

If you are unable to set bit 1 in port 20, then press the keyboard BREAK key (or whatever works) to escape from this condition.

Some computers can use WAIT as a command.

IF YOUR COMPUTER DOESN'T HAVE IT

If your computer has the INP capability, but does not have WAIT, substitute INP for WAIT in TEST PROGRAM #2, using these changes:

```
40 IF INP(20)=2 THEN 50
45 GOTO 40
```

Also See

```
INP, FOR, NEXT, XOR, AND
```

WHILE is the beginning statement in a series
which are executed repeatedly until a certain
condition is false. The loop which begins with
WHILE must be closed by a WEND, ENDLOOP,
or THEN statement. Example:

```
100 WHILE X<>0
110    INPUT X
120    S=S+X
130 WEND
140 PRINT "SUM =";S
```

As long as the condition (X<>0) is true, lines 110
and 120 will be executed again and again. When a
0 is entered, execution breaks out of the loop and drops to line 140.

Test Program

```
10 REM 'WHILE' TEST PROGRAM
20 L$ = "FIRST"
30 WHILE L$<>"LAST"
40 READ X, Y, L$
50 PRINT "X*Y =";X*Y
60 WEND
70 PRINT "WHILE PASSED THE TEST"
80 DATA 3, 20, MORE
95 DATA 16, 40, MORE
100 DATA 12, 32, LAST
999 END
```

Sample Run

```
X*Y = 60
X*Y = 640
X*Y = 384
WHILE PASSED THE TEST
```

Some BASICs use WHILE in conjunction with DO to form conditional loops.
Line 30 becomes 30 DO WHILE L$<>"LAST" and line 60 is replaced by
60 DOEND.

Other BASICs (e.g. DEC BASIC-PLUS) use WHILE as a modifier of other
statements, making them conditional. For example, to find the largest
power of two that is less than 10000 use:

```
10 X = 1
20 X = X*2 WHILE X<10000
30 PRINT X
99 END
```

IF YOUR COMPUTER DOESN'T HAVE IT

Conditional loops can be constructed with IF statements if your computer does not have a WHILE statement. Deleting lines 20 and 30 of the Test Program and changing line 60 to 6Ø IF L$<>"LAST" THEN 4Ø should produce the same results as in the SAMPLE RUN.

Also See

UNTIL, FOR, IF

XDRAW is a statement used by the Apple II to erase a shape previously drawn on the screen.

XDRAW can also be used to draw the shape. XDRAWing it a second time erases it without erasing the background.

Example: XDRAW 2 AT 135,78 will draw shape number 2 (from the user's shape table) at location 135 (horizontal) and 78 (vertical).

XDRAW always uses the complement of the color currently at each point of the shape. Otherwise XDRAW has the same features as DRAW. See DRAW for more information.

Variations In Usage

None known.

Also See

DRAW

Operator

XOR

XRA

XOR is used in IF-THEN statements as the "eXclusive OR" logical operator. For example, IF A=3 XOR B=3 THEN 80 reads, "if A has a value of 3 OR B has a value of 3, but not both of them, the IF-THEN condition is true and execution jumps to line 80".

See OR for more details. XOR is the same as OR with one exception; if both conditions are met, XOR says the test fails, usually by sending us a 0.

Test Program #1

```
10 REM LOGICAL 'XOR' TEST PROGRAM
20 A=6
30 B=8
40 IF A=3 XOR B=8 THEN 70
50 PRINT "'XOR' FAILED THE TEST AS A LOGICAL OPERATOR"
60 GOTO 99
70 IF A=6 XOR B=8 THEN 90
80 PRINT "'XOR' PASSED THE LOGICAL OPERATOR TEST"
85 GOTO 99
90 PRINT "'XOR' FAILED THE 'EXCLUSIVE OR' TEST"
99 END
```

Sample Run

```
'XOR' PASSED THE LOGICAL OPERATOR TEST
```

Alternate Spelling

NORTH STAR IBASIC uses XRA as the exclusive OR operator.

IF YOUR COMPUTER DOESN'T HAVE IT

If your computer allows OR, AND, and NOT but lacks XOR and XRA replace line 40 of Test Program #1 with

```
40 IF (A=3 OR B=8) AND NOT (A=3 AND B=8) THEN 70
```

For computers having none of the logical operators the following Test Program offers a way to simulate XOR.

Test Program #2

```
10 REM 'XOR' SIMULATION
20 PRINT "TYPE IN TWO NUMBERS BETWEEN 1 AND 10"
30 INPUT A,B
40 IF ·(A-3)*(B-8)<>0 THEN 90
50 IF A-3<>0 THEN 70
60 IF B-8=0 THEN 90
70 PRINT "EITHER A=3 OR B=8, BUT NOT BOTH"
80 GOTO 20
90 PRINT "BOTH CONDITIONS ARE TRUE OR BOTH ARE FALSE"
100 GOTO 20
999 END
```

Sample Run

```
TYPE IN TWO NUMBERS BETWEEN 1 AND 10
? 3,5
EITHER A=3 OR B=8, BUT NOT BOTH
TYPE IN TWO NUMBERS BETWEEN 1 AND 10
? 3,8
BOTH CONDITIONS ARE TRUE OR BOTH ARE FALSE
```

Also See

OR, AND, NOT, +, *

Operator

Pairs of quotation marks (") are used in PRINT statements to enclose letters, numbers or characters to be printed. If the quotes are omitted, the computer recognizes the letters as variables and prints whatever values are assigned to them.

For example, `PRINT "A"` prints the letter "A". While `PRINT A` prints the value assigned to variable A.

Quotes can be used to print numbers without the usual space for their + or − sign. It can insert extra spaces by enclosing them.

For example,

```
10 PRINT "      THE NUMBER";
20 PRINT "10"
```

will print

```
      THE NUMBER10
```

Quotes **cannot** be "nested" inside other quotes. The computer is unable to distinguish which one is the end of the actual PRINT statement.

For example, `PRINT "I SAID "HELLO" TO HIM"` will not work. An apostrophe is usually substituted for the inside quotes in these cases.

For example, `PRINT "I SAID 'HELLO' TO HIM"`

Test Program #1

```
10 REM 'QUOTED (")' PRINT STATEMENT TEST PROGRAM
20 A=5
30 B=10
40 PRINT "A+B=";A+B
50 PRINT "THE QUOTATION MARKS PASSED THE PRINT TEST."
99 END
```

Sample Run

```
A+B= 15
THE QUOTATION MARKS PASSED THE PRINT TEST.
```

Quotes can be used with most newer computers to allow the INPUT statement to serve in both a PRINT and INPUT capacity at the same time.

Test Program #2

```
10 REM 'QUOTED (")'INPUT STATEMENT TEST PROGRAM
20 INPUT "ASSIGN A VALUE TO VARIABLE X";X
30 PRINT "THE VALUE OF X IS";X
99 END
```

Sample Run *(using 5)*

```
ASSIGN A VALUE TO VARIABLE X? 5
THE VALUE OF X IS 5
```

Some computers require quotes around strings in DATA statements, while others require them only when the string is preceded by, encloses, or is followed by a blank, comma or colon. For more information see DATA.

Test Program #3

```
10 REM 'QUOTED (")'DATA STATEMENT TEST PROGRAM
20 DATA " DATA STATEMENT "
30 READ A$
40 PRINT "QUOTES IN";A$;"PASSED THE TEST"
99 END
```

Sample Run

```
QUOTES IN DATA STATEMENT PASSED THE TEST
```

Quotes are used with CSAVE and CLOAD in MICROSOFT BASIC to assign a specific name to the program recorded on cassette tape.

For example,

```
CSAVE "A"
CLOAD "A"
```

will record a program on cassette tape, naming it "A", then will load only the program named "A" back into the computer. For more information and test procedures see CLOAD and CSAVE.

TRS-80 Level I BASIC uses quotes in the PRINT# statement to record data on cassette tape.

For example, `PRINT#A;",";B;",";C` will store the values assigned to variables A, B and C on cassette tape. For more information and TEST PROGRAMS see PRINT.

Also See

`PRINT , TAB , ;`(semicolon), `,`(comma), `DATA , READ , CSAVE , CLOAD`

Operator

ANSI

The Comma is an operator with a wide range of uses. One of the more common is with the PRINT statement, where it causes individual items to be printed in pre-established horizontal zones. For example, PRINT 1,2,3,4 prints each number in a separate zone.

Each zone usually allows a maximum of sixteen characters. The number of zones allowed on each line varies from 4 to 8, depending on screen (or printer), line width.

Test Program #1

```
10 REM TEST PROGRAM USING 'COMMA' FOR ZONING
20 PRINT "THE FOLLOWING LINE WILL PRINT IN 4 ZONES"
30 PRINT 1,2,3,4
40 PRINT "THE FOLLOWING LINES SHOW YOUR AVAILABLE ZONES"
50 PRINT 1,2,3,4,5,6,7,8,9,10,11,12,13,14,15,16
99 END
```

Sample Run *(4 zone per line display, 64 characters maximum per line)*

```
THE FOLLOWING LINE WILL PRINT IN 4 ZONES
1               2               3               4
THE FOLLOWING LINES WILL SHOW YOUR AVAILABLE ZONES
1               2               3               4
5               6               7               8
9               10              11              12
13              14              15              16
```

The COMMA is also used to separate elements in array fields. Example, A(I,J,K). The COMMA separates I, J, and K into individual elements within this three-dimension array.

Test Program #2

```
10 REM TEST PROGRAM USING 'COMMA' IN 2 DIMENSION ARRAY
20 A(1,1)=5
30 PRINT "A(1,1) =";A(1,1)
40 PRINT "LINE 20 PASSED THE TEST IF A(1,1) = 5."
99 END
```

Sample Run

```
A(1,1)= 5
LINE 20 PASSED THE TEST IF A(1,1) = 5,
```

The COMMA is used in a similar manner in DATA, DIM, INPUT, ON-GOTO, and READ statements to separate items of data.

This program tests the COMMA's capability in INPUT and PRINT statements.

Test Program #3

```
10 REM 'COMMA' TEST PROGRAM
50 PRINT "ENTER THREE NUMBERS";
60 INPUT A,B,C
100 PRINT "NUMBER 1 =";A,2;"=";B,3;"=";C
999 END
```

Sample Run *(using 11,12,13)*

```
ENTER THREE NUMBERS? 11,12,13
NUMBER 1 = 11    2 = 12              3 = 13
```

To test the COMMA's capability in READ and DATA statements, add these lines to the last TEST PROGRAM.

```
80 READ D,E,F
100 PRINT "NUMBER";D;"=";A,E;"=";B,F;"=";C
110 DATA 1,2,3
```

Run the program. The SAMPLE RUN should remain the same.

To test COMMA capability in the ON-GOTO statement, add these lines:

```
30 FOR X=1 TO 3
40 ON X GOTO 50,80,100
70 GOTO 90
90 NEXT X
```

Run the program, and again the sample run should remain the same.

The computer's COMMA capability in DIM statements can be checked by adding this line:

```
20 DIM A(1),B(2),C(3)
```

The addition of this line should not change the SAMPLE RUN.

For other applications of the COMMA see PRINT USING, AT and @.

Variations In Usage

Some computers (e.g. those with Palo Alto Tiny BASIC) use the COMMA in LET statements similar to the way most computers use the COLON, and it's use in the PRINT and INPUT statements can be modified with the # and − operators.

Also See

DATA, DIM, INPUT, ON-GOTO, AT, @, PRINT USING, READ

The period (.) is used as a decimal point by nearly all computers except those having only integer BASIC.

The Period is used in MICROSOFT BASIC (and others) to cause the computer to LIST or EDIT the last program line entered, listed or which caused an error in program execution.

Test Program

```
10 REM ',(PERIOD)' TEST PROGRAM
20 PRINT "THE PERIOD FOLLOWING THE LIST COMMAND"
30 PRINT "SHOULD LIST THE LAST LINE YOU ENTER"
99 END
```

Sample Run

Type the command: LIST. (if you omit the period following LIST, the entire program will of course be LISTed). The computer should print:

```
99 END
```

Add the following line to the TEST PROGRAM:

```
40 PRINT "THE PERIOD PASSED THE TEST"
```

Type the command: EDIT. (including the period).

If your computer has this EDIT capability, the computer will print the number 40 followed by a cursor. This indicates the computer is in the EDIT mode and is ready to modify line 40 (the last line entered).

Variations In Usage

Several computers (e.g. the TRS-80 Level I and other variations of Tiny BASIC) use the period as part of word abbreviations.

For example, the letter I is normally used as a variable, but I. can be used as an abbreviation for INPUT or INTeger depending on how it is used in the program. In addition, P. = PRINT, R. = RUN, L. = LIST, etc.

Also See

```
EDIT, LIST, INPUT, INT
```

ANSI

A semicolon is used in PRINT statements to allow several printed sections to be joined together (concatenated) onto one line. For example, PRINT "H";"I" is printed as HI.

Test Program #1

```
10 REM 'SEMICOLON' STRING TEST PROGRAM
20 PRINT "IF THIS SENTENCE IS PRINTED ";
30 PRINT "ON ONE LINE, THE TEST PASSED."
99 END
```

Sample Run

```
IF THIS SENTENCE IS PRINTED ON ONE LINE, THE TEST PASSED.
```

When a SEMICOLON is used to separate the printing of numeric values or numeric variables, a space is often automatically inserted before each number to make room for its + or − sign. An additional space is automatically inserted after the number since it's assumed that such a space is always required. This feature can cause programming difficulties when trying to get a special print format. (Apple II and DEC-10 do not use this automatic feature.)

For example, PRINT 1;2;3 may be printed with two spaces between each number.

Test Program #2

```
10 REM 'SEMICOLON' TEST PROGRAM WITH NUMERICS
20 A=5
30 PRINT "STUDY THE SPACING BETWEEN EACH OF THE NUMBERS."
40 PRINT 1;"2";"3";4;A;"6"; -7
50 PRINT "12345678901234567890"
99 END
```

Sample Run

```
STUDY THE SPACING BETWEEN EACH OF THE NUMBERS.
 1 23 4  5 6-7
12345678901234567890
```

Variations In Usage

A few interpreters insert a space between strings being concatenated. This (rare) feature eliminates the need for inserting the space after the letter "D" in line 20 of the first TEST.

Also See

COMMA, PRINT USING, TAB

Operator

The COLON allows placing more than one statement on a single program line.

For example, `10 PRINT "SAMPLE LINE":`
`LET A=10: GOTO 99` holds three separate statements ... PRINT, LET and GOTO in one program line, number 10.

Test Program #1

```
10 REM 'COLON (:) OPERATOR' TEST PROGRAM
20 PRINT "THIS TEST";:FOR X=1 TO 5000:
   NEXT X: PRINT" IS COMPLETE"
99 END
```

Sample Run

```
THIS TEST (PAUSE) IS COMPLETE
```

GOTO, IF-GOTO, IF-THEN, ON-GOTO and other branching statements should be the last statement on a multiple statement line to prevent branching out of it before the entire line is executed.

For example, in the line

```
10 FOR X=1 TO 10:NEXT X:GOTO 100:PRINT "THE LOST WORDS"
```

The computer executes the GOTO statement and branches to line 100 before it has a chance to execute the PRINT statement. There is no way to PRINT "THE LOST WORDS".

Most computers do not allow DATA statements in multiple statement lines. Others (e.g. IMSAI) do not execute statements on the same line if they follow a GOSUB statement even though a RETURN directs execution back to that line.

Be especially careful when using IF-THEN statements in multiple statement lines. If there are statements following the IF-THEN on the same line, some BASICs (e.g. Microsoft BASIC) will execute them only if the condition is true. Others (e.g. North Star BASIC) will execute the rest of the statement unless branching has taken place. To see which way your computer responds try this short program.

Test Program #2

```
10 A = 1
20 IF A =2 THEN 30:PRINT "EXECUTES THE REST":GOTO99
30 PRINT "IGNORED THE REST"
99 END
```

The COLON is also used by some computers (e.g. DEC-10) as the first character of the image line referred to in a PRINT USING statement.

For example:

```
120 :$$######.##
130 PRINT USING 120, C
```

produces the same result as 130 PRINT USING "$$######.##", C

IF YOUR COMPUTER DOESN'T HAVE IT

Many computers have no provision for writing more than one program statement on a numbered line. Others that do however, may use a backslash (\) instead of a colon. A very few use a semicolon.

Variations In Usage

None known.

Also See

```
\, ;, GOTO, IF-THEN, IF-GOTO, ON-GOTO,
PRINT USING, IMAGE
```

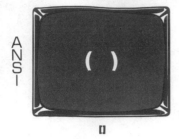

Operator

ANSI

( )

[]

Parentheses are used in arithmetic operations to determine the order in which math operations are performed. Math operations enclosed within parentheses are performed before those outside the parentheses. If a math operation is enclosed in parentheses which is in turn enclosed within another set of parentheses (and so on), the computer first performs those operations "buried the deepest". When there is a "tie", the operation to the left is executed first.

For example, A=5+(((2*4)-2)*3). The computer performs this math operation in the following sequence:

A = 5+((8-2)*3) = 5+(6*3) = 5+18 = 23

Test Program #1

```
10 REM '() PARENTHESES' TEST PROGRAM
20 A=(10*(5-3))/2
30 PRINT "A =";A
40 PRINT "THE PARENTHESES PASSED THE TEST IF A = 10"
99 END
```

Sample Run

```
A = 10
THE PARENTHESES PASSED THE TEST IF A = 10
```

Parentheses are required with some "logical math" operators to identify the two statements being compared. They are essential with TRS-80 Level I and other Tiny BASIC's.

For example, IF (A=8) * (B=6) THEN 80

For more information see * and AND.

Parentheses are also used to enclose the elements in DIM statements and array variables. For more information see DIM.

Test Program #2

```
10 REM '() PARENTHESES' TEST PROGRAM USING DIM AND ARRAYS
20 DIM A(5,5)
30 A(1,1)=20
40 PRINT "() PASSED THE TEST IN LINES";A(1,1);"AND";A(1,1)+10
99 END
```

Sample Run

```
() PASSED THE TEST IN LINES 20 AND 30
```

Most computers with built in functions use Parentheses to enclose the numbers or letters to be manipulated.

For example, LOG(10)

Most computers that use parentheses but not brackets ([]) allow parentheses to substitute for brackets without ill effect.

For example,

```
[(A*B)/C]
```

can be written

```
((A*B)/C)
```

Also See

```
*, +, AND, OR, DIM
```

Operator

The @ Operator is used by a few computers (e.g. TRS-80 Level II) to specify a starting location on the video screen for a PRINT statement. Its value should be from 0 to 1023 and must be followed by a comma. For example, PRINT @ 475,"HELLO" prints the word HELLO on the CRT starting at grid position 475.

Test Program

```
10 REM "@" PRINT MODIFIER TEST PROGRAM
20 PRINT @ 128, "2, IF THIS LINE IS PRINTED AFTER LINE 1,"
30 PRINT @ 0, "1, THE @ OPERATOR PASSED THE TEST"
40 GOTO 40
99 END
```

Sample Run

```
1, THE @ OPERATOR PASSED THE TEST
2, IF THIS LINE IS PRINTED AFTER LINE 1,
```

IF YOUR COMPUTER DOESN'T HAVE IT

If your computer does not use the @ operator as a PRINT modifier, this feature can be simulated by using an appropriate number of PRINT statements (to activate line feeds) and spaces or TAB's to arrive at the same location on the CRT.

Variations In Usage

The @ (AT) operator is used by some computers (e.g. North Star) to erase the last line displayed on the screen and execute a carriage return. For example, type 10 REM LINE DELETION TEST (but don't hit the ENTER or RETURN key) and press the @ key. The line should be erased and the cursor should return to the left margin.

The same operation can be accomplished on some computers by pressing the RUB (rub out), SCR (scratch), ← (left arrow) or SND (send) key, or by pressing the ENTER (or RETURN) key before and after typing the number of the line to be deleted.

Each of the commands used by the Exatron Stringy Floppy System includes a prefix of the @symbol. Example: @NEW, @SAVE, @LOAD.

Also See

PRINT, AT, PRINT AT, DELETE

The # (number sign) is used to specify individual variables as being of "double-precision". Double precision variables are capable of storing numbers containing 17 digits (only 16 digits are printed). Single-precision variables are accurate to 6 digits.

The # sign must be placed after a variable to define it as having double-precision, each time that variable is used in the program. If the # sign is found with a variable that is listed in DEFSNG or DEFINT statements (within the same program), the double precision character (#) temporarily over-rides their action and declares the variable to be of double-precision.

Test Program #1

```
10 REM '#' DOUBLE PRECISION OPERATOR TEST PROGRAM
20 DEFSNG A,B
30 A=1.234567890123456
40 B#=1.234567890123456
50 IF A=B# THEN 100
60 PRINT "A =";A
70 PRINT "B# =";B#
80 PRINT "THE # SIGN PASSED THE DOUBLE PRECISION TEST"
90 GOTO 999
100 PRINT "THE # SIGN FAILED THE DOUBLE PRECISION TEST"
999 END
```

Sample Run

```
A = 1.23457
B# = 1.234567890123456
THE # SIGN PASSED THE DOUBLE PRECISION TEST
```

The # is used by a few computers as a shorthand symbol for the PRINT statement. For more information see PRINT.

Test Program #2

```
10 REM '#' TEST PROGRAM
20 #"THE # SIGN PASSED THE PRINT TEST"
99 END
```

Sample Run

```
THE # SIGN PASSED THE PRINT TEST
```

The # operator is used by a few computers as the relational operator "not-equal-to" (<>).

For example, IF A#B THEN 100 tells the computer to branch to line 100 if the value of variable A is not equal to variable B.

The # operator is used in the PRINT USING statement by most computers using a Microsoft BASIC to indicate the PRINT position for each digit in a number or numeric variable. If the PRINT USING statement contains more # signs than the number of digits in a number, the computer prints a space for each unused # sign to the left of the decimal point, and a zero for each unused # sign to the right of the decimal point.

For example, 10 PRINT USING "#####.###";12.5 will print the number 12.500 with 3 blank spaces printed to the left of the number 1 in place of the 3 unused # signs.

For more information see PRINT USING.

Test Program #3

```
10 REM '#' PRINT USING TEST PROGRAM
20 PRINT "ENTER A VALUE FOR VARIABLE N";
30 INPUT N
40 PRINT "THE NUMBER";N;"IS PRINTED AS";
50 PRINT USING "####.##" ;N
99 END
```

Sample Run (using 12.5)

```
ENTER A VALUE FOR VARIABLE N? 12.5
THE NUMBER 12.5 IS PRINTED AS   12.50
```

Computers with file handling capability use the # operator in such statements as INPUT#, PRINT#, READ#, CLOSE#, and others to indicate a device number to store data and retrieve data from external memory such as disc and cassette tape.

Test Program #4 *(stores data on TRS-80 Level II cassette tape)*

Set the cassette recorder to the RECORD mode and RUN this program.

```
10 REM 'PRINT#' TEST PROGRAM
20 PRINT "DATA SHOULD BE RECORDING ON CASSETTE TAPE"
30 PRINT#-1, "TEST" ,1,2,3
40 PRINT "PRINT# HAS COMPLETED THE DATA TRANSFER"
99 END
```

Sample Run

```
DATA SHOULD BE RECORDING ON CASSETTE TAPE
PRINT# HAS COMPLETED THE DATA TRANSFER
```

To test the computer's READ# capability, rewind the cassette tape, set the recorder to the Play mode, erase memory and RUN the next Test Program.

Test Program #5 *(enters data from cassette into the computer)*

```
10 REM 'INPUT#' TEST PROGRAM
20 PRINT "THE COMPUTER SHOULD NOW READ DATA FROM
   CASSETTE"
30 INPUT#-1,A$,A,B,C
40 PRINT "THE INPUT# STATEMENT PASSED THE TEST IF"
50 PRINT A$;A;B;C;"IS PRINTED"
99 END
```

Sample Run

```
THE COMPUTER SHOULD NOW READ DATA FROM CASSETTE
THE INPUT# STATEMENT PASSED THE TEST IF
TEST 1  2  3 IS PRINTED
```

In large time-sharing systems (e.g. the DEC-10), one program can access a number of different data files, each of which is given a name and stored on disc. A statement in the program gives a number to each file it will be using, and that file is referred to by number, not name. The # sign then literally means "number" – – – the file number(name) from which DATA is to be READ, INPUT, PRINTed or otherwise processed.

Example:

```
30 FILE #1,"TESTING"
80 READ #1,A,B,C,D,E
```

etc.

Also See

DEFDBL, DEFSNG, DEFINT, !, %, PRINT, REM, PRINT USING, READ#, < >

A
N
S
I

The $ symbol following a letter or letter/number combination is used to declare that variable to be a string variable.

Information declared a string variable in a program statement must usually be enclosed in quotation marks. For example, A$ = "THE BASIC HANDBOOK." If an INPUT statement is used to assign the information entered to a string variable, then quotes are not usually required. (See INPUT and READ.)

Test Program #1

```
10 REM '$' TEST PROGRAM WITH STRING STATEMENT
20 A$ =" LINE 20"
30 PRINT "THIS COMPUTER PASSED THE '$' TEST IN";A$
99 END
```

Sample Run

```
THIS COMPUTER PASSED THE '$' TEST IN LINE 20
```

The number of characters that can be assigned to a string variable is limited by the computer's interpreter. Most computers with string capability accept at least 16 characters, and some as many as 255.

Some computers (e.g. Hewlett-Packard) require you to reserve memory space for each separate string with a DIM statement [e.g. 10 DIM A$(50)]. (See DIM and CLEAR.)

The following program demonstrates the assignment of characters to the variable A$ (pronounced "A string"):

Test Program #2

```
10 REM '$' INPUT STRING WITH LENGTH TEST PROGRAM
20 PRINT "ENTER A KNOWN QUANTITY OF CHARACTERS"
30 INPUT A$
40 PRINT "COUNT THE NUMBER OF CHARACTERS PRINTED BELOW"
50 PRINT A$
99 END
```

Sample Run *(Typical)*

The "character string" shown in the sample run is 10 characters long:

```
ENTER A KNOWN QUANTITY OF CHARACTERS
?  1234567890
COUNT THE NUMBER OF CHARACTERS PRINTED BELOW
1234567890
```

If all the characters were printed and no error message appeared, RUN again and add perhaps 10 more characters. If that prints, continue the process until characters start being chopped off the end, or an error message appears.

Most computers which can handle strings allow all the letters of the alphabet to serve as string variable designators. A few computers allow only a few. (e.g. Radio Shack TRS-80 LEVEL I allows only two strings, A$ and B$ and they cannot be compared against each other.)

The next program tests the full range (A and Z) of alphabet characters allowed by your computer.

Test Program #3

```
10 REM '$' (STRING) VARIABLE TEST PROGRAM
20 A$="LINE 20,"
30 PRINT "A$ PASSED THE TEST IN ";A$;
40 Z$=" AND Z$ IN LINE 40"
50 PRINT Z$
99 END
```

Sample Run

```
A$ PASSED THE TEST IN LINE 20, AND Z$ IN LINE 40
```

Many string handling computers allow combinations of letters, numbers and symbols to specify string and numeric variables. Each variable must start with a letter, but frequently only the first several (usually 2) alphanumeric characters are recognized and processed by the interpreter. For example, AB34K$ and ABYN8$ (if accepted), are usually processed as the same string variable (AB$) since the first two letters are identical. A little experimenting will quickly show your machine's capability.

Test Program #4

```
10 REM '$' (STRING NAME) TEST PROGRAM
20 ABCDE$="TEST STRING"
30 PRINT "ABXYZ$ = ";ABXYZ$
40 PRINT "AB123$ = ";AB123$
50 PRINT "ONLY THE FIRST TWO LETTERS OF THE STRING
   NAME"
60 PRINT "WERE RECOGNIZED IF THE TWO STRINGS ARE
   IDENTICAL"
99 END
```

Sample Run

```
ABXYZ$ = TEST STRING
AB123$ = TEST STRING
ONLY THE FIRST TWO LETTERS OF THE STRING NAME
WERE RECOGNIZED IF THE TWO STRINGS ARE IDENTICAL
```

Words that are intrinsic Statements or Functions cannot be used as string or numeric variables. For example, SPRINTS$ may be an illegal string variable because it contains the word "PRINT". Refer to your owner's manual for a list of "reserved words" that cannot be used in your computer's programs.

Most computers that accommodate strings, permit string comparison. That is, one string or string variable can be compared, character by character, against another string or string variable using relational operators. Strings must be enclosed in quotation marks when compared to a string variable.

Test Program #5

```
10 REM '$' (STRING) COMPARISON TEST PROGRAM
20 READ A$
30 IF A$="WHOA" THEN 60
40 PRINT A$,
50 GOTO 20
60 PRINT "STRINGS CAN BE COMPARED."
70 DATA ONE, TWO, WHOA
99 END
```

Sample Run

```
ONE             TWO             STRINGS CAN BE COMPARED.
```

Variations In Usage

The British Acorn ATOM uses $ as a prefix for string variables ($A instead of A$).

Some computers (e.g. Apple II) use $ as a prefix to indicate a machine address and/or a hexadecimal number. Example: $8A = 138 decimal.

Also See

DEFSTR, CHR$, FRE(string), INKEY$, LEN, LEFT$, MID$, RIGHT$, STR$, STRING$, VAL, LET, DATA, READ, DIM, CLEAR, TEXT, &, ⋈ (sol)

Operator

The ! (exclamation mark) is used to specify individual variables as being of "single-precision". Single precision variables are capable of storing numbers containing no more than 7 digits (only 6 digits are printed). Double-precision means having 17 digit precision.

Since variables are automatically single precision, the ! operator is used in programs to change a variable back to single precision after it has been declared double-precision by a previous DEFDBL statement or # operator.

Test Program #1

```
10 REM '!' SINGLE PRECISION OPERATOR TEST PROGRAM
20 DEFDBL X,N
30 N=1234.56789012345
40 X=N
50 PRINT "DOUBLE PRECISION VARIABLE X=";X
60 X!=N
70 PRINT "SINGLE PRECISION VARIABLE X! =";X!
80 PRINT "THE '!' SINGLE PRECISION OPERATOR PASSED
   THE TEST"
99 END
```

Sample Run

```
DOUBLE PRECISION VARIABLE X = 1234.56789012345
SINGLE PRECISION VARIABLE X! = 1234.57
THE '!' SINGLE PRECISION OPERATOR PASSED THE TEST
```

The ! operator is also used by some computers (e.g. those using the Microsoft BASIC) in the PRINT USING statement to allow only the left-most character in a string to be printed.

For example, PRINT USING"!";"COMPUSOFT" should print the letter "C".

For more information see PRINT USING and the next Test Program.

Test Program #2

```
10 REM '! STRING SPECIFIER' TEST PROGRAM
20 PRINT "ENTER A SAMPLE WORD";
30 INPUT A$
40 PRINT "THE FIRST LETTER IN THE WORD ";A$;" IS ";
50 PRINT USING "!";A$
99 END
```

Sample Run *(using HANDBOOK)*

```
ENTER A SAMPLE WORD? HANDBOOK
THE FIRST LETTER IN THE WORD HANDBOOK IS H
```

Variations In Usage

Some interpreters (e.g. the COMPUMAX BASIC) use ! as an abbreviation for REMark.

Test Program #3

```
10 PRINT "'! (REMARK) ' TEST PROGRAM"
20 ! PRINT " THE ! SIGN FAILED THE REM TEST"
30 REM THE ! SIGN FAILED THE REMARK TEST IF LINE 20 IS
   PRINTED
40 PRINT "THE ! SIGN PASSED THE TEST"
99 END
```

Sample Run

```
'! (REMARK)' TEST PROGRAM
THE ! SIGN PASSED THE TEST
```

NORTH STAR BASIC uses ! as a substitute for PRINT.

Also See

DEFDBL, DEFSNG, #, PRINT USING, DEFINT, CSNG, CDBL, PRINT, CINT, %

Operator

% is used by some computers (e.g. those using Microsoft BASIC) to define variables as integers. When the % sign is placed to the right of a variable, that variable is then only capable of storing integer values.

For more information on the use of the INTeger function see INT.

Test Program #1

```
10 REM '% INTEGER OPERATOR' TEST PROGRAM
20 I%=2.864
30 IF I%=2 THEN 60
40 PRINT "THE % INTEGER OPERATOR FAILED THE TEST"
50 GOTO 99
60 PRINT "THE % INTEGER OPERATOR PASSED THE TEST"
99 END
```

Sample Run

```
THE % INTEGER OPERATOR PASSED THE TEST
```

The % operator is used by some computers (e.g. those using Microsoft BASIC) in the PRINT USING statement. It causes the printing of as many left-most characters in a string as there are spaces between two % signs. The computer also counts the two % signs, therefore no less than two characters can be specified. (To specify one character in the string, see the ! operator.)

For example, PRINT USING "% %";"ABCDEFGHI" should print the first four letters "ABCD" because two spaces were included between the % signs (2 spaces + 2 % signs = 4 letters). For more information see PRINT USING.

Test Program #2

```
10 REM '%' STRING SPECIFIER TEST PROGRAM
20 A$"TESTIMONIAL"
30 PRINT "THE % OPERATOR PASSED THE STRING SPECIFIER ";
40 PRINT USING "%  %";A$
99 END
```

Sample Run

```
THE % OPERATOR PASSED THE STRING SPECIFIER TEST
```

Some computers use the % sign in the PRINT USING statement to "flag" a number as having exceeded the limits of the field specifier (#).

For example, PRINT USING "###.#";1234.56 should print the number %1234.6. The entire number on the left side of the decimal point is printed when it exceeds the field specifier limits. If the number on the right side of the decimal point exceeds the field specifier, it is rounded off. For more information see PRINT USING.

Test Program #3

```
10 REM '%' PRINT USING OVERFLOW TEST PROGRAM
20 A=123.45
30 PRINT "THE PRINT USING STATEMENT CHANGED #";A;"TO ";
40 PRINT USING "##.#" ;A
99 END
```

Sample Run

```
THE PRINT USING STATEMENT CHANGED # 123.45 TO %123.5
```

Also See

INT, CINT, DEFINT, CSNG, CDBL, DEFSNG, DEFDBL, PRINT USING, IMAGE, FORMAT, !, #, &, \ (backslash)

Operator

The ? (question mark) is used by many computers (e.g. those with variations of Microsoft BASIC) as an abbreviation for PRINT. Most (but not all) automatically change the ? sign to the word "PRINT" when the program is LISTed.

For more information see PRINT.

Test Program #1

```
10 REM '? (PRINT)' TEST PROGRAM
20 ? "THE ? SIGN PASSED THE PRINT TEST"
99 END
```

Sample Run

```
THE ? SIGN PASSED THE PRINT TEST
```

The computer may use ? as the INPUT prompt, indicating it is waiting for you to enter some data or an answer. Execution resumes when the ENTER or RETURN key is pressed.

For more information see INPUT.

Test Program #2

```
10 REM '?' (INPUT REQUEST) TEST PROGRAM
20 PRINT "THE ? SIGN PASSED THE TEST"
30 PRINT "IF THE FOLLOWING LINE CONTAINS THE ? SIGN"
40 INPUT A
99 END
```

Sample Run

```
THE ? SIGN PASSED THE TEST
IF THE FOLLOWING LINE CONTAINS THE ? SIGN
?
```

Some computers (e.g. those with a Microsoft BASIC) use the ? sign with the CLOAD command to compare a program stored in the computer's memory with a program stored on cassette.

To test this feature, see the test procedures under CLOAD.

Also See

```
PRINT, #, INPUT, CLOAD, LIST, !
```

The \ operator is used by a few computers to allow multiple statements in one program line.

For example, 10 A=10\B=5\C=A-B\PRINT C combines four statements in one line.

For more information see : (Colon).

Test Program

```
10 REM '\ OPERATOR' TEST PROGRAM
20 PRINT "THIS TEST ";\FOR X=1 TO 500\
   NEXT X\PRINT "IS COMPLETE"
99 END
```

Sample Run

```
THIS TEST IS COMPLETE
```

The \ (backslash) operator is used by some computers (e.g. those using BASIC-80) in the PRINT USING statement. It causes a string of characters to be printed whose length is equal to two more than the number of spaces enclosed by the backslashes. The computer also counts the backslashes, therefore no less than two characters can be specified. (To specify one character in the string, see the ! operator.)

For example, PRINT USING "\   \";"ABCDEFGHI" should print the first four letters "ABCD" because two spaces were included between the \ (backslashes) (2 spaces + 2 backslashes = 4 letters). For more information see PRINT USING and % operator.

Variations In Usage

The back-slash is sometimes seen separating letters and numbers as they are being deleted or "rubbed out" on some terminals. This is often done when correcting typing errors.

Also See

:(colon), PRINT USING, %

Operator

The ** (double asterisk) is used as an arithmetic exponentiation sign in some computers (e.g. the DEC-10, DEC-BASIC-PLUS-2, H.P. 3000, and those using the MAXBASIC) to compute the value of a base number to a specified power.

For example, 2**3 is the same as the cube of 2 or 2^3. For more information see ↑.

Test Program

```
10 REM '** (EXPONENTIATION)' TEST PROGRAM
20 PRINT "ENTER A BASE NUMBER";
30 INPUT B
40 PRINT "NEXT, ENTER THE EXPONENT";
50 INPUT E
60 A=B**E
70 PRINT "THE NUMBER";B;"TO THE";E;"POWER IS";A
30999 END
```

Sample Run *(using 4 and 3)*

```
ENTER A BASE NUMBER? 4
NEXT, ENTER THE EXPONENT? 3
THE NUMBER 4 TO THE 3 POWER IS 64
```

The ** (double asterisk) is also used by some computers (e.g. those using Microsoft BASIC) in the PRINT USING statement. An asterisk (*) can be printed in unused spaces to the left of a specified number's decimal point. The primary purpose for doing this is to prevent someone from increasing the size of a check printed by computer.

For example, PRINT USING"*******.##";456.25 will print ****456.25

The # sign represents the spaces set aside for the numeric value to be printed. The unused spaces are filled by a * sign.

For more information see PRINT USING.

Also See

PRINT USING, ↑ , !

400

The most common use of the + sign is in arithmetic addition. Example, `PRINT A+B` prints the sum of variables A and B.

ANSI

Test Program #1

```
10 REM '+' MATH OPERATOR TEST
   PROGRAM
20 PRINT "ENTER A VALUE FOR
   VARIABLE A";
30 INPUT A
40 PRINT "ENTER A VALUE FOR
   VARIABLE B";
50 INPUT B
60 C=A+B
70 PRINT "THE SUM OF";A;"+";B;"IS";C
99 END
```

Sample Run *(using 6 and 14)*

```
ENTER A VALUE FOR VARIABLE A? 6
ENTER A VALUE FOR VARIABLE B? 14
THE SUM OF 6 + 14 IS 20
```

Some computers use the + sign as a logical "OR" operator in an IF-THEN statement.

For example, `10 IF (A=8)+(B=6) THEN 80` reads: if the value of A equals 8 OR the value of B equals 6 the IF-THEN condition is met and execution continues at line 80.

Note that both (A = 8) and (B = 6) are enclosed in parentheses. Since there is no other apparent reason to enclose such simple equations in parentheses, they are the tip-off that the + is used as a logical OR.

Test Program #2

```
10 REM '+' LOGICAL OPERATOR TEST PROGRAM
20 PRINT "ENTER A VALUE FOR VARIABLE A";
30 INPUT A
40 PRINT "ENTER A VALUE FOR VARIABLE B";
50 INPUT B
60 PRINT "A =";A,"B =";B
70 IF (A=8)+(B=6) THEN 100
80 PRINT "NEITHER A = 8 NOR B = 6"
90 GOTO 999
100 PRINT "EITHER A = 8 OR B = 6"
999 END
```

Sample Run *(using 4 and 6)*

```
ENTER A VALUE FOR VARIABLE A? 4
ENTER A VALUE FOR VARIABLE B? 6
A = 4                 B = 6
EITHER A = 8 OR B = 6
```

Variations In Usage

Many computers use the + sign to join (concatenate) separate strings into one. For example, PRINT "H"+"I" concatenates the strings "H" and "I" to form the word HI.

Test Program #3

```
10 REM '+' CONCATENATION TEST PROGRAM
20 A$="PASSED THE CON"
30 B$="CATENATION TEST"
40 PRINT "THE + SIGN ";
50 PRINT A$+B$
99 END
```

Sample Run

```
THE + SIGN PASSED THE CONCATENATION TEST
```

The + sign is used by some computers in PRINT USING statements to automatically attach a + or − sign to a number being printed.

Also See

```
AND, *, $, PRINT USING, OR , &
```

The − symbol is used as an arithmetic subtraction sign to find the arithmetic difference between two numbers or numeric variables. For example, PRINT A-B prints the value of variable A minus the value of variable B.

The − sign is also used for negation in arithmetic operations. Negation simply means "changing the sign from what it is to the opposite".

Example, PRINT -(3-8) subtracts 8 from 3 which results in a negative 5. The first − (negation) sign reverses the sign within the parentheses and prints 5 (the + sign is implied).

Test Program

```
10 REM '- SIGN' TEST PROGRAM
20 A=3
30 B=6
40 C=B-A-(B-A)
50 PRINT "C =";C
60 PRINT "THE - SIGN PASSED THE TEST IF C = 0"
99 END
```

Sample Run

```
C = 0
THE - SIGN PASSED THE TEST IF C = 0
```

Variations In Usage

The − sign is used by some computers in PRINT USING statements to automatically attach a trailing − sign to a negative number being printed.

Also See

PRINT USING, +

Operator

ANSI

The / sign is used as an arithmetic division sign to find the quotient of two numeric variables.

Example, 8/4 is the same as $8 \div 4$

Test Program

```
10 REM '/ DIVISION SIGN' TEST PROGRAM
20 A=8
30 B=4
40 C=A/B
50 PRINT "C =";C
60 PRINT "THE / SIGN PASSED THE TEST IF C = 2"
99 END
```

Sample Run

```
C = 2
THE / SIGN PASSED THE TEST IF C = 2
```

Some Interpreters (e.g. Palo Alto Tiny BASIC) use only integer values so PRINT 15/4 yields a quotient of 3.

Variations In Usage

None known.

ANSI

The * symbol (asterisk) is used as an arithmetic multiplication sign (instead of the letter "X") to find the product of two numbers or numeric variables.

Test Program #1

```
10 REM '*' MATH OPERATOR TEST
   PROGRAM
20 A=5
30 B=A*6
40 PRINT "* PASSED THE TEST IN LINE";B
99 END
```

Sample Run

```
* PASSED THE TEST IN LINE 30
```

Variations In Usage

Some computers also use the * sign as the "logical math" operator for "AND". For example:

```
IF (A=8) * (B=6) THEN 80
```

reads, "if the value of A equals 8 **AND** the value of B equals 6 then the IF-THEN condition is met and execution continues at line 80."

Note that both (A=8) and (B=6) are enclosed in parentheses. This is the clue to look for when determining if an * is being used for multiplication or as a logical AND.

Test Program #2

```
10 REM '*' LOGICAL 'AND' TEST PROGRAM
20 A=8
30 B=6
40 IF (A=8) * (B=6) THEN 70
50 PRINT "* FAILED THE TEST AS AND OPERATOR"
60 GOTO 99
70 PRINT "* PASSED THE AND OPERATOR TEST"
99 END
```

Sample Run

```
* PASSED THE AND OPERATOR TEST
```

The * asterisk is used by some computers to specify a format for printing numeric values or strings in the PRINT USING statement. See PRINT USING for details.

Also See

AND, PRINT USING, OR, +

The = symbol can be used as an assignment operator. For example, A = 3 + 5 assigns the value 8 to variable A.

Test Program #1

```
10 REM TEST PROGRAM USING = AS
   ASSIGNMENT OPERATOR
20 A=4
30 B=6
40 C=A+B
50 PRINT "C =";C
60 PRINT "THE = SIGN PASSED THE TEST IF C = 10"
99 END
```

Sample Run

```
C = 10
THE = SIGN PASSED THE TEST IF C = 10
```

The = sign is also used by most computers as a relational operator to compare two numeric values for equality. For example, IF A=B THEN 100 tells the computer to branch to line 100 when the numeric variable A is equal to numeric variable B. If the condition of the = sign is not met (i.e. $A \neq B$), the test "falls through" and program execution continues on the next line.

Most computers also use the = sign for **string** comparisons. This feature allows one string or string variable to be compared, character-by-character, against another string or string variable. In the example, IF A$ = "ABCD" THEN 100 the interpreter compares the ASCII code of each character (from left-to-right) stored in string variable A$ against the characters enclosed in quotation marks. If the ASCII code of all characters is found to be equal, the computer branches or "jumps" to line 100. If the ASCII code of all characters is not found equal, the test "falls through" and program execution continues on the next line.

Test Program #2

```
10 REM TEST OF = SIGN AS NUMERIC COMPARISON OPERATOR
20 A=5
30 IF A-5 THEN 60
40 PRINT "= SIGN FAILED NUMERIC COMPARISON TEST"
50 GOTO 99
60 PRINT "= SIGN PASSED NUMERIC COMPARISON TEST"
99 END
```

Sample Run

```
= SIGN PASSED NUMERIC COMPARISON TEST
```

Test Program #3

```
10 REM TEST PROGRAM USING = FOR STRING COMPARISON
20 A$ = "ABCDE"
30 IF A$ ="ABCDE" THEN 60
40 PRINT "THE = SIGN FAILED THE STRING COMPARISON TEST"
50 GOTO 99
60 PRINT "THE = SIGN PASSED THE STRING COMPARISON TEST"
99 END
```

Sample Run

```
THE = SIGN PASSED THE STRING COMPARISON TEST
```

Variations In Usage

Different interpreters allow different length character strings to be compared. Some allow only one letter to be compared against another single letter, while others allow enough characters to compare an entire name and address, or more.

The combination of > or < with = is very common. Sometimes only numerics can be so compared, but in most cases the ASCII values of string characters are automatically derived and those numeric values are compared.

Also See

```
>, <, $, <=, >=, EQ, GE, GT, LE, LT, NE, <>
```

The ↑ (up-arrow) is used as an arithmetic exponentiation sign to compute the value of a base number to a specified power. Some computers use a ^ (carat or circumflex) instead of an ↑ (up-arrow).

ANSI

For example, 2↑3 is the same as the cube of 2 or 2^3.

Test Program #1

```
10 REM '↑(EXPONENTIATION)' TEST PROGRAM
20 PRINT "ENTER A BASE NUMBER";
30 INPUT D
40 PRINT "NEXT ENTER A POWER NUMBER";
50 INPUT F
60 P=D↑F
70 PRINT "THE NUMBER";D; "TO THE";F;"POWER IS";P
30999 END
```

Sample Run *(using 4 and 3)*

```
ENTER A BASE NUMBER? 4
NEXT ENTER A POWER NUMBER? 3
THE NUMBER 4 TO THE 3 POWER IS 64
```

The ↑ sign is also used to compute a number's root value by enclosing the inverse of the index number in parentheses (1/n).

For example, 8↑(1/3) is the same as the cube root of 8, or $\sqrt[3]{8}$

Test Program #2

```
10 REM '↑(USED AS A RADICAL SIGN)' TEST PROGRAM
20 PRINT "ENTER A BASE NUMBER";
30 INPUT B
40 PRINT "NEXT ENTER A ROOT NUMBER";
50 INPUT N
60 R=B↑(1/N)
70 PRINT "THE";N;"ROOT OF";B;"IS";R
30999 END
```

Sample Run *(using 64 and 3)*

```
ENTER A BASE NUMBER? 64
NEXT ENTER A ROOT NUMBER? 3
THE 3 ROOT OF 64 IS 4
```

Most computers having **PRINT USING** will print the exponential or 'E' form of a number when 4 ↑ s are placed in the format string. For example: PRINT USING "##.###↑↑↑↑", 12345 prints 12.345 E+03.

DIFFERENT OPERATOR FOR ↑

** is used by some computers. Others use ∧ to raise to a power.

IF YOUR COMPUTER DOESN'T HAVE IT

If the above all fail, substitute the following subroutine:

The subroutine programs found under LOG and EXP **must** be added to this one to make it work (saves space not to duplicate them here).

```
30000 GOTO 30999
30100 REM * EXPONENTIATION SUBROUTINE * INPUT X,Y;
      OUTPUT P
30102 REM ALSO USES A, B, C, D, E, F AND L INTERNALLY
30104 P=0
30106 IF X<>0 THEN 30112
30108 IF Y<0 THEN 30122
30110 RETURN
30112 P=1
30114 IF Y=0 THEN 30140
30116 F=X
30118 IF X>0 THEN 30130
30120 IF Y=INT(Y) THEN 30126
30122 PRINT "***";X;"TO THE";Y;"POWER IS UNDEFINED ***"
30124 STOP
30126 P=1-2*Y+4*INT(Y/2)
30128 X=-X
30130 GOSUB 30150
30132 X=Y*L
30134 GOSUB 30200
30136 P=P*E
30138 X=F
30140 RETURN
```

To use this subroutine in the TEST PROGRAM, make these program changes:

```
35 X=D
55 Y=F
60 GOSUB 30100
```

Variations In Usage

None known.

Also See

```
EXP, LOG, **, PRINT USING
```

The < sign is used as a "less-than" relational operator to compare two numeric values in IF-THEN statements. For example, IF A<B THEN 100 tells the computer to branch to line 100 if the value of variable A is less than the value of variable B.

ANSI

Test Program #1

```
10 REM '< RELATIONAL OPERATOR' TEST PROGRAM
20 A=10
30 IF A<20 THEN 60
40 PRINT "THE < SIGN FAILED THE TEST"
50 GOTO 99
60 PRINT "THE < SIGN PASSED THE TEST"
99 END
```

Sample Run

```
THE < SIGN PASSED THE TEST
```

Variations In Usage

The < sign can be used by most computers to compare strings. The < sign compares the ASCII code of each character (from left-to-right) in two strings. The first difference encountered determines their relationship.

For example, string "ABCDEF" is less than string "ABD" even though the first string has more characters. Since the ASCII code for C (decimal 67) in the first string is less than, or precedes, the ASCII code for D (decimal 68) in the second string, "ABCDEF" < "ABD" is true.

If each string has the same sequence of characters, the longer string is considered larger. For example, string "ABCD" is larger than string "ABC".

Some interpreters limit the number of characters which can be compared between strings.

Test Program #2

```
10 REM '< STRING OPERATOR' TEST PROGRAM
20 A$="ABC"
30 B$="ABCD"
40 C$="B"
50 IF A$<B$ THEN 80
60 PRINT "THE < SIGN FAILED THE TEST IN LINE 50"
70 GOTO 999
80 IF B$<C$ THEN 110
90 PRINT "THE < SIGN FAILED THE TEST IN LINE 80"
100 GOTO 999
110 PRINT "THE < SIGN PASSED THE TEST"
999 END
```

Sample Run

```
THE < SIGN PASSED THE TEST
```

< is frequently combined with = to make the < = operator and combined with > to make "not-equal" operators <> or ><.

Also See

>, <>, =, $, IF-THEN, <=, >=, EQ, GE, GT, LE, LT, NE

The > sign is used as a "greater-than" relational operator to compare two numeric values in IF-THEN statements. For example, IF A>B THEN 100 tells the computer to branch to line 100 if the value of variable A is greater than variable B.

Test Program #1

```
10 REM '> RELATIONAL OPERATOR' TEST PROGRAM
20 A=20
30 IF A > 10 THEN 60
40 PRINT "THE > SIGN FAILED THE TEST"
50 GOTO 99
60 PRINT "THE > SIGN PASSED THE TEST"
99 END
```

Sample Run

```
THE > SIGN PASSED THE TEST
```

Variations In Usage

The > sign can be used by most computers to compare strings. The > sign compares the ASCII code of each character (from left-to-right) between two strings. The first difference in equality encountered determines their relationship.

For example, string "ABD" is greater than string "ABCDEF" even though the first string has fewer characters. Since the ASCII code for D (decimal 68) in the first string is greater than, or follows, the ASCII code for C (decimal 67) in the second string, "ABD" > "ABCDEF" is true.

If each string has the same sequence of characters, the longer string is considered larger. For example, string "ABCD" is larger than string "ABC".

Some interpreters limit the number of characters which can be compared between strings.

Test Program #2

```
10 REM '> STRING OPERATOR' TEST PROGRAM
20 A$="ABCD"
30 B$="ABC"
40 C$="B"
50 IF A$ > B$ THEN 80
60 PRINT "THE > SIGN FAILED THE TEST IN LINE 50"
70 GOTO 999
80 IF C$ > B$ THEN 110
90 PRINT "THE > SIGN FAILED THE TEST IN LINE 80"
100 GOTO 999
110 PRINT "THE > SIGN PASSED THE TEST"
999 END
```

Sample Run

```
THE > SIGN PASSED THE TEST
```

> is commonly combined with = to make the >= operator and combined with < to make "not-equal" operators <> or ><.

Also See

<, <>, =, GT, LT, NE, $, IF-THEN, >=, <=, EQ, GE, LE

The <> sign is used as a "not-equal" relational operator to compare two numeric values in IF-THEN statements for inequality. For example, IF A<>B THEN 100 tells the computer to branch to line 100 if the value of variable A is not equal to the value of variable B.

ANSI

><
≠

Test Program #1

```
10 REM ' <> RELATIONAL OPERATOR'
   TEST PROGRAM
20 A=10
30 IF A <> 20 THEN 60
40 PRINT "THE <> SIGN FAILED THE TEST"
50 GOTO 99
60 PRINT "THE <> SIGN PASSED THE TEST"
99 END
```

Sample Run

```
THE <> SIGN PASSED THE TEST
```

Variations In Usage

The <> sign can be used by most computers to compare strings. The <> sign compares the ASCII code of each character (from left-to-right) in two strings. The first difference in equality encountered determines their relationship.

In the example, IF A$<>"ABC" THEN 100 the interpreter compares the ASCII code of each character (from left-to-right) stored in string variable A$ against the characters enclosed in quotation marks. If a difference is encountered, or one string is longer than the other, the condition of the <> sign is met and the computer branches to line 100.

Some interpreters limit the number of characters which can be compared between strings.

Test Program #2

```
10 REM '<> STRING OPERATOR' TEST PROGRAM
20 A$="ABCDE"
30 IF A$ <> "ABCD" THEN 60
40 PRINT "THE <> SIGN FAILED THE TEST IN LINE 30"
50 GOTO 999
60 IF A$ <> "ABCDE" THEN 80
70 GOTO 100
80 PRINT "THE <> SIGN FAILED THE TEST IN LINE 60"
90 GOTO 999
100 PRINT "THE <> SIGN PASSED THE TEST"
999 END
```

Sample Run

```
THE <> SIGN PASSED THE TEST
```

Alternate Spellings

Some computers use the operator $><$ or $\neq$.

Also See

```
#, <, >, IF-THEN, $, =, <=, >=, EQ, GE, GT, LE, LT, NE
```

The $<=$ sign is used as a "less than or equal to" relational operator to compare two numeric values in IF-THEN statements. For example, IF A<=B THEN 100 tells the computer to branch to line 100 if the value of variable A is less than or equal to the value of variable B.

A N S I

=<
≤

Test Program #1

```
10 REM ' <= RELATIONAL OPERATOR'
   TEST PROGRAM
20 A=10
30 IF A <= 20 THEN 60
40 PRINT "THE <= SIGN FAILED THE TEST IN LINE 30"
50 GOTO 999
60 IF A<=10 THEN 90
70 PRINT "THE <= SIGN FAILED THE TEST IN LINE 60"
80 GOTO 999
90 PRINT "THE <= SIGN PASSED THE TEST"
999 END
```

Sample Run

```
THE <= SIGN PASSED THE TEST
```

Variations In Usage

The $<=$ sign can be used by most computers to compare strings. The $<=$ sign compares the ASCII code of each character (from left-to-right) in two strings. The first difference encountered determines their relationship.

For example, string "ABCDEF" is $<$ string "ABD" even though the first string has more characters. Since the ASCII code for C (decimal 67) in the first string is less than, or precedes the ASCII code for D (68) in the second string, "ABCDEF" $<=$" ABD" is true. Also, if both strings have identical characters and are the same length, then they satisfy the $<=$ relationship.

If each string has the same sequence of characters, then the longer string is considered larger. For example, string "ABCD" is larger than string "ABC".

Some interpreters limit the number of characters which can be compared between strings.

Test Program #2

```
10 REM '<= STRING OPERATOR' TEST PROGRAM
20 A$="ABC"
30 B$="ABCD"
40 C$="B"
50 IF A$ <=B$ THEN 80
60 PRINT "THE <= SIGN FAILED THE TEST IN LINE 50"
70 GOTO 999
80 IF A$ <="ABC" THEN 110
90 PRINT "THE <= SIGN FAILED THE TEST IN LINE 80"
100 GOTO 999
110 IF B$ <= C$ THEN 140
120 PRINT "THE <= SIGN FAILED THE TEST IN LINE 110"
130 GOTO 999
140 PRINT " THE <= SIGN PASSED THE TEST"
999 END
```

Sample Run

```
THE <= SIGN PASSED THE TEST
```

Alternate Symbols

Some computers use the $=<$ or $\leq$ sign instead. Others allow $=<$ as an option.

Also See

```
IF-THEN, <, =, >, >=, <>, $, LE, LT, EQ, GT, GE, NE
```

>= is used as a "greater-than or equal-to" relational operator to compare two numeric (or string, when allowed) values in IF-THEN statements.

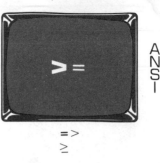

For example, IF A >=B THEN 100 tells the computer to branch to line 100 if the value of variable A is greater than **or** equal to the value of variable B.

=>
≥

Test Program #1

```
10 REM ' >= RELATIONAL OPERATOR' TEST PROGRAM
20 A=20
30 IF A >= 10 THEN 60
40 PRINT "THE >= SIGN FAILED THE TEST IN LINE 30"
50 GOTO 999
60 IF A >= 20 THEN 90
70 PRINT "THE >= SIGN FAILED THE TEST IN LINE 60"
80 GOTO 999
90 PRINT "THE >= SIGN PASSED THE TEST"
999 END
```

Sample Run

```
THE >= SIGN PASSED THE TEST
```

Variations In Usage

The >= operator is allowed by some computers for string comparison. It compares the ASCII code of each character (from left-to-right) in two strings. The first difference encountered determines the relationship.

For example, string "ABD" is greater than string "ABCDEF" even though the first string has fewer characters. Since the ASCII code for D (decimal 68) in the first string is greater than the ASCII code for C (decimal 67) in the second string, "ABD">= "ABCDEF" is true. Also, if both strings have identical characters and are the same length, then they satisfy the >= relationship.

If each string has the same sequence of characters, then the longer string is considered larger. String "ABCD" is larger than string "ABC".

Some interpreters limit the number of characters which can be compared between strings.

Test Program #2

```
10 REM '>= STRING OPERATOR' TEST PROGRAM
20 A$="ABCD"
30 B$="ABC"
40 C$="B"
50 IF A$ >= B$ THEN 80
60 PRINT "THE >= SIGN FAILED THE TEST IN LINE 50"
70 GOTO 999
80 IF A$ >="ABCD" THEN 110
90 PRINT "THE >= SIGN FAILED THE TEST IN LINE 80"
100 GOTO 999
110 IF C$ >= B$ THEN 140
120 PRINT "THE >= SIGN FAILED THE TEST IN LINE 110"
130 GOTO 999
140 PRINT "THE >= SIGN PASSED THE TEST"
999 END
```

Sample Run

```
THE >= SIGN PASSED THE TEST
```

Alternate Symbols

Some computers use the operator $=>$ or $\geq$ instead.

Variations In Usage

None known.

Also See

IF-THEN, >, <, <=, <>, EQ, GE, LE, LT, NE

The ' (apostrophe) is used by many computers as an abbreviation for the REMark statement.

For more information see REM.

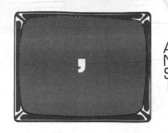

A
N
S
I

Test Program #1

```
10 REM '(APOSTROPHE) TEST PROGRAM
20 'PRINT "THE APOSTROPHE FAILED THE REM TEST"
30 REM THE APOSTROPHE FAILED THE TEST IF LINE 20 IS PRINTED
40 PRINT "THE APOSTROPHE PASSED THE REM TEST"
99 END
```

Sample Run #1

```
THE APOSTROPHE PASSED THE REM TEST
```

Variations In Usage

A few computers use the apostrophe in PRINT statements to enclose strings instead of using quotation marks.

Test Program #2

```
10 REM '(APOSTROPHE) * USED AS QUOTES * TEST PROGRAM
20 PRINT 'THE APOSTROPHE PASSED THE QUOTATION MARK TEST'
99 END
```

Sample Run #2

```
THE APOSTROPHE PASSED THE QUOTATION MARK TEST
```

Also See

```
REM, PRINT, !, "
```

Operator

The & (ampersand) is used by some computers as the "concatenation" operator, allowing two strings to be coupled together and stored as one string.

For example, if A$="SOFT" and B$="WARE" then C$ =A$ & B$ stores "SOFTWARE" in C$. (See +.)

Some computers (e.g. DEC-10) use & to indicate that the image allocations of a PRINT USING statement are insufficient to accommodate the number being printed. Example: PRINT USING "###"; -123 prints &-123 (see %).

CAUTION: Applesoft BASIC uses & internally but does not make it available to the user. Trying & with any of the following examples sends execution to address $3F5 and requires corrective action to regain control of the computer.

& is used by a few computers (e.g. PDP-11) to indicate that a statement which is too long for a single line is to be continued on the following line.

Example: IF (5-X) * (X-1) > 0 THEN &
               PRINT "THE VALUE OF X LIES BETWEEN 1 AND 5"

& is used by some of those computers having MAT INPUT capability (e.g. DEC-10) to indicate that additional input values will be entered on the next line (see MAT INPUT).

Example: when these program statements are executed

```
DIM C(25)
   .
   .
PRINT "PLEASE ENTER THE VALUES OF ALL CHECKS OUTSTANDING"
MAT INPUT C
```

the user can enter more values than will fit on one line by typing an & symbol before hitting the RETURN key:

```
?12.50, 55.00, 37.84, 163.00, 43.00, 100.00, 6.19&<cr>
?18.80, 25.00<cr>
```

(<cr> indicates that a RETURN key was pressed.)

MAX BASIC, on the other hand, uses an & to terminate the list of values being entered in response to a MAT INPUT statement.

Some computers use & as a prefix to a number to indicate a machine address and/or a hexadecimal number. For example, B5 is interpreted as a variable name but &B5 means B5 is a hex number equal to 181 decimal (see $).

422

A few computers (e.g. PDP-11 with BASIC-PLUS) accept & in place of PRINT.

```
10 & "THIS IS A PRINT LINE"
```

prints
```
THIS IS A PRINT LINE
```

Also See

```
PRINT, PRINT USING, MAT INPUT, +, $, %
```

Operator

The ⋈ (pronounced SOL, for the Sun), is the equivalent, for computer purposes, to the $ sign.

The Swedish ABC 80 computer uses SOL in the same way the $ sign is used by most other computers throughout the world.

String variables are formed with a ⋈ attached to a valid variable (i.e. A⋈ for A$). CHR⋈ is the equivalent of CHR$, MID⋈ is the same as MID$, SPACE⋈ the same as SPACE$, etc.

If a program contains any variable with a ⋈ attached, treat that word as if it were followed by $, and assume it is a string variable.

Also See

$, CHR$, LEFT$, MID$, RIGHT$, SPACE$, STRING$, NUM$

Special Section

Acorn ATOM

This special section is not intended to replace official ACORN ATOM documentation, nor serve as a tutorial. Its purpose is to provide a summary overview of special ACORN features for BASIC Handbook users.

The BASIC supported by the Acorn ATOM from Great Britain is highly non-standard and offers features that are not available on any other machine. Because of the rapid rise in Acorn's popularity, expect to see many programs written for the Acorn in computer publications. To assist you in understanding them, this brief summary of some of Acorn BASIC's most unique features is provided.

The most distinctive feature of Acorn BASIC is the naming of its variables. Integer variables are any of the letters A-Z. Arrays must be named AA-ZZ. So DIM AA(10) reserves room for 11 values of AA.

DIM A(10) does **not** do the same thing at all. It stores the address of the last byte used by the BASIC program in A and increases this address by 11 (the program now appears to be 11 bytes longer).

Floating point variables are formed by placing % in **front** of a variable or array name. %A, %B, ... %Z and %AA, %BB, ... %ZZ as well as %@ and %@@ are all available as variable and array names. String names are formed with $ placed in **front** of numeric variable names, i.e., $A, $B, ... $Z and $AA, $BB, ... $ZZ. The $ need not be used where there is no ambiguity.

The following statements are prefixed by the letter F to indicate they are key words used with floating-point expressions. Their use is similar, if not identical, to other key words described elsewhere in *The BASIC Handbook*. Variables used with these words must be declared to be floating point by the prefix % (i.e. %A).

This word	is a variation of	with these exceptions.
FDIM	DIM	array names must be of the form %AA to %ZZ
FGET	GET	Reads only **numbers** from a file
FIF	IF	AND and OR are not allowed with FIF
FINPUT	INPUT	does not allow strings to be input

FPRINT	PRINT	again, no string expressions
FPUT	PUT	writes only **numbers** to a file
FUNTIL	UNTIL	AND and OR not allowed with FUNTIL.

For additional information, ALSO SEE: DIM, GET, IF, INPUT, PRINT, PUT, UNTIL, %

The ! operator is used to indicate an address where a value is to be found or stored. !A=123456 stores the hexadecimal form of 123456 starting in location A with the two least significant digits and continues in location A + 1, A + 2, etc. until the entire value has been stored. Using A!6 instead would start storage 6 bytes after A.

Other operators and key words used by the Acorn:

′	*(apostrophe)* generates a new line in a PRINT statement; the next PRINT continues on the same line if an ' is not used.
@	specifies the numeric output field width
?	is used like ! but stores and recalls one byte at a time
#	is the prefix of a hexadecimal constant
&	is a hexadecimal prefix in the PRINT statement also the logical AND operator (i.e. bitwise ANDs two numbers. Example 6 & 12 = 4 because 0110 AND 1100 = 0100)
\	*(inverse backslash)* is the logical OR operator
:	is the logical exclusive OR operator
%	gives the remainder on division. Example 13 % 5 = 3. % is also used to convert an expression into integer mode.
BGET	gets a byte from a random file
BPUT	stores a byte in a random file
EXT	gives the length in bytes of a file
FIN	initializes a random file for input or update and returns a number used to refer to the file

FLT	converts integer expressions into floating point mode
FOUT	initializes a random file for output and returns a number used to refer to the file
LINK	calls a machine language routine
OLD	recovers a program after NEW has been typed (but before anything else happens to alter memory)
PTR	allows manipulation of pointers of random files
SGET	reads a string from a random file
SHUT	closes a file after use
SPUT	writes a string to a random file

Owners of an ATOM must study its reference manual carefully to become proficient in the use of the above. Most other words are similar to those of other BASICs and have been referenced on other pages in *The BASIC Handbook*..

NOTES

Special Section
ATARI

This special section is not intended to replace official ATARI documentation, nor serve as a tutorial. Its purpose is to provide a summary overview of special ATARI features for BASIC Handbook users.

The BASIC used on the ATARI 400 and 800 computers contains several key words not found in other BASICs.

ADR — returns the memory address (in decimal) of the string specified by the expression in parentheses. The address can then be passed to USR routines. ADR(A$) gives the address of the string stored in A$.

COLOR — determines the data to be stored in the display memory by the PLOT and DRAWTO statements. If COLOR N appears in a program in text mode (GRAPHICS 0, 1, or 2), N must be an integer between 0 and 255 and is interpreted as the ATASCII value of the character to be displayed. The first 2 bits (MSB) are used to determine the color of the character.

In graphics modes 3 thru 8, the value following COLOR only determines the color of the graphics block. In the 2-color or 2-brightness modes the MSB identifies the choice. In the 4-color modes the first 2 bits are needed to name which color is used (0, 1, 2, or 3). The actual colors used are **not** named by COLOR but are set with the SETCOLOR statement.

Examples: COLOR ASC("G"):PLOT6,4 will display an orange G in text mode.

COLOR 1 chooses the color associated with 1 that was selected by SETCOLOR if the computer is in graphics modes 3 thru 8.

DOS — is a command used to go from BASIC to the Disk Operating System (see Disk BASIC).

ENTER — reads a program from disk or tape into memory without erasing memory. ENTER can be used to APPEND or merge programs.

ENTER "D:DEMO.BAS" brings the program DEMO.BAS into memory from disk, replacing any lines in the resident program that have the same line numbers as the lines of the new program. This can be useful when a subroutine stored on disk or tape is to be incorporated into a program. ENTER is also handy for replacing one set of DATA statements with another set.

GRAPHICS

sets the GRAPHICS mode of the display to one of 9 choices. The mode chosen determines whether the screen prints text or graphics, how many colors are available, the resolution of the graphics points and whether a split screen with lines of text at the bottom will be used or not.

Mode	Screen Characteristics
0	Text mode of 40x24 character positions with 1 color (but 2 brightness levels). GRAPHICS 0 also clears the screen (CLS).
1	Text mode of 20x24 character positions with 5 colors and split screen. A PRINT statement puts characters in the 4 lower text lines and PRINT #6 writes to the upper text window.
2	Text mode of 20x12 characters. The screen is split 10 and 2. Otherwise the same as above.
3	GRAPHICS mode with 40x24 plot positions and 4 lines of text. Four colors are allowed.
4	80x48 GRAPHICS mode, split screen with 2 colors
5	80x48 GRAPHICS mode, split screen with 4 colors
6	160x96 GRAPHICS mode, split screen with 2 colors
7	160x96 GRAPHICS mode, split screen with 4 colors
8	320x192 GRAPHICS mode, split screen, 1 color (but 2 brightness levels)

The split screen can be removed in modes 1-8 by including +16 in the GRAPHICS statement. Example:

GRAPHICS 4 + 16

LOCATE

LOCATE X,Y,N is a command (or statement) used to place the invisible graphics cursor at a specified location (with coordinates X,Y) in the graphics portion of the screen, check to see what is displayed there, and store that data in the named numeric variable (N).

NOTE

is used to find the current disk sector number and byte number within that sector which it stores in two variables.

NOTE #2,S,B finds the current record on device #2 and stores the sector number in S and the byte number in B. These numbers can be used to build another file which is an index to the first file.

PADDLE

is a function which returns a number from 1 to 228 depending on how much the control knob on the designated game PADDLE has been rotated counterclockwise. As many as 8 game paddles can be connected to the ATARI.

POINT

is a command used when reading from a random access file. (See the section on Disk BASIC.) POINT places the "pointer" at the desired point in the file, ready for it to be READ.

100 POINT #2, A, B

is the form of the statement. A is the sector number on the disk and B is the byte number within the sector.

POSITION

is a command (and statement) used to POSITION the invisible graphics cursor at a specified location on the screen. POSITION X,Y is the form of the statement where X is the column number and Y is the line number of the POSITION. The maximum values allowed for X and Y depend on the GRAPHICS mode selected.

PTRIG

is a function which returns a 0 or 1 to indicate whether the trigger button on the game paddle is pressed. A 0 means the trigger is pressed.

PUT

outputs a single byte (one character) to a specified file. PUT #6, ASC("A") PUTs the character A on the graphics window (video screen). The position is controlled by the POSITION statement.

SETCOLOR

has 3 "parameters". SETCOLOR R, C, B chooses the particular Color and Brightness to be stored in a specified Register.

R names the register (0-4)
C names the color (0-15) and
B names the brightness (even number 0-14 with 14 being almost white.)

Available colors are:

0	gray
1	light orange (gold)
2	orange
3	red-orange
4	pink
6	purple-blue
7	blue
8	blue
9	light blue
10	turquoise
11	green-blue
12	green
13	yellow-green
14	orange-green
15	light orange

SETCOLOR can be used to set the color in each of the 5 registers. COLOR 1 then selects one of those registers (which one depends on which graphics mode is set) and that color is used in the display. *"This can be confusing"* — ATARI

SOUND

sends a specific note to the TV set. SOUND V, P, D, L specifies the 4 qualities of the sound.

V is the Voice selection (up to 4 simultaneous voices can be used)

P selects the Pitch. The frequency is approximately 32000/P. P can range between 0 and 255.

D is the Distortion factor. D is a number between 0 and 14. Each of the numbers causes a special effect.

L is the Loudness (volume) control. Loudness ranges from quiet (1) to **loud** (15). When more than one voice is used, the **total** loudness should be no more than 32.

STATUS   STATUS #1,Z calls the STATUS routine for the specified device (#1). The status of the STATUS command is stored in the variable (Z). It refers to the status of a printer or other peripheral.

STICK   is similar to PADDLE. The differences are that STICK gives information about the joysticks and only 9 numbers can result. The values are assigned to the direction the joystick is pushed as follows:

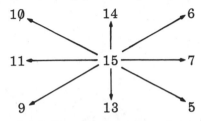

STRIG   is like PTRIG but applies to the joystick.

TRAP   is a statement like ON ERROR GOTO. It allows the program to remain in control even if an error occurs.

       100 TRAP 540

sends control to line 540 after an error has been detected. PEEK(195) gives the error code (similar to ERR) and 256*PEEK(187)+PEEK(186) gives the number of the line where the error occurred (ERL on other computers).

Each time the TRAP is sprung, it must be reset by another TRAP statement using a number between 32767 and 65535.

XIO   is a general input/output statement used for special operations, such as, filling an area on the screen between plotted points and lines with a color. The form is

       XIO C, D, B1, B2, F$

where   C is the command number

       D is the device number (#6 is the graphics window)

       B1 and B2 contain information needed by some of the commands, e.g., the sector and byte numbers of POINT, the row and column in DRAWTO, etc.

       F$ is a filespec needed in OPEN, RENAME, DELETE, etc.

The various commands performed by XIO are:

3	OPEN
5	GET record (INPUT)
7	GET character
9	PUT record (PRINT)
11	PUT character
12	CLOSE
13	STATUS of device
17	DRAWTO
18	FILL in an area of screen
32	RENAME file
33	DELETE file
35	LOCK file
36	UNLOCK file
37	POINT (set file pointer)
38	NOTE
254	FORMAT

Special Section

TEKTRONIX

This special section is not intended to replace official TEKTRONIX documentation, nor serve as a tutorial. Its purpose is to provide a summary overview of special TEKTRONIX features for BASIC Handbook users.

The TEKTRONIX 4050 series computers support an extended BASIC with many key words and capabilities not found in more standard BASICs. In most cases, it is not practical to try to adapt a program that uses these special-purpose statements on a word-for-word basis.

AXIS	draws X and Y axes with tic marks on graphics screen
BAPPEN	routine that adds a program in binary mode to the program in memory
BOLD	loads a program saved in binary mode from tape
BRIGHTNESS	sets 4054 display normal or bright, focused or defocused
BSAVE	routine that stores current program on tape in binary mode
CHARSIZE	specifies number of characters/line and number of lines/screen on 4054
COPY	makes hardcopy of screen image
DASH	sets dash pattern for lines on graphics screen
FIND	locates the beginning of a specified file on tape
FONT	selects one of several sets of special characters (e.g. Spanish, German, Swedish, etc.)
FUZZ	sets the number of digits to be compared and the closeness to zero for comparison (Example: FUZZ 6, 1E-5 causes two values to be considered equal if the first 6 digits are equal and causes a number whose absolute value is less than 1E-5 to be considered zero.
GIN	reads the cursor position and records the X and Y coordinates in specified variables

INIT	resets all parameters (e.g. FUZZ, CHARSIZE, etc.) to default values
KILL	removes reference to a file in the tape directory
LINK	loads new program into memory without resetting variables
MARK	prepares tape to receive data or program
MPY	creates the product of two matrices
MTPACK	adjusts tension and alignment of tape device
OFF	disables interrupt
OLD	loads ASCII mode file from tape into memory
PAGE	clears graphics display and homes cursor
POINTER	assigns coordinates of the joystick pointer to specified variables when a key on the keyboard is pressed. It stores the key entered in a third variable.
POLL	polls the devices listed and returns a number indicating the first one found requesting service, along with the value of its status byte
PRINT@	outputs values to physical and logical devices
RBYTE	reads one or more bytes from the General Purpose Interface Bus and stores it (them) in specified variables
RDRAW	draws a line from current position of the cursor (X,Y) to the point (X + H, Y + K) where H and K are given in the RDRAW statement
REP	replaces characters in a string similar to the MID$ function
RMOVE	is a Relative MOVE similar to RDRAW but doesn't draw the line, only moves the cursor
ROTATE	causes RMOVE and RDRAW actions to be rotated thru a designated angle
SCALE	sets the scale factor for the graphics display
SECRET	gives protection to a file by setting it in secret mode
SUM	calculates the sum of the elements of an array

TLIST	lists the names and sizes of the files on tape
VIEWPORT	defines the dimensions of the frame around the graph to be displayed
WBYTE	sends one or more bytes to a specified device on the General Purpose Interface Bus
WINDOW	defines the minimum and maximum data values to be included in the display window

Most other Tektronix BASIC words are similar to the more common BASICs which are covered elsewhere in *The BASIC Handbook.*

NOTES

Special Section
TRS-80 COLOR

This special section is not intended to replace official TRS-80 Color BASIC documentation, nor serve as a tutorial. Its purpose is to provide a summary overview of special TRS-80 features for BASIC Handbook users.

TRS-80 Extended Color BASIC has several key words that are either unique to this computer or are used for a purpose that is very remote from the usual usage.

AUDIO
: allows the computer to send sound through the TV speaker.

  Form: AUDIO ON
  : AUDIO OFF

CIRCLE
: draws a circle or portion of a circle with a specified center, having a given radius, drawn in a specified color. By giving the starting and ending points, any portion of the circle can be displayed.

  Also, the circle may be squeezed to make it out-of-round.

  Form: CIRCLE (X,Y),R,C,H,S,E
  : CIRCLE (128,96),35,6

  where (X,Y) names the location for the center of the circle, R is the radius, C specifies one of the available colors (0-8), H tells the height/width ratio (1 means a true circle, H>1 means it is taller than it is wide, or H<1 means it is wider than tall).

  S is a number 0-1 that gives the **Starting** location for a portion of the circle with 0 representing 3 o'clock, .25 at the 6 o'clock position, etc. E is also a number 0-1 specifying the **Ending** position. The portion drawn is the arc determined by tracing the circle in a clockwise direction from the Start position to the End position.

CLOADM
: loads a machine-language program from tape.

  Form: CLOADM "NAME",A

  where NAME is the program name and A (optional) represents the number to be added to the starting address to move the program to a desired memory location.

CSAVEM   saves a machine-language program on tape.

Form: CSAVEM X, 4E, 6F, 5F

COLOR   selects the foreground and background colors for the display. The color codes range from 0 to 8. Depending on the PMODE setting, either two colors or four colors are allowed in use at one time. The SCREEN statement chooses which two or which four colors to use.

For PMODE settings of 0, 2, and 4 there are two colors available. Selecting color set 0 (with SCREEN) gives (0) Black and (1) Green as the colors and color set 1 has Black and (5) Buff. With PMODE settings 1 and 3, there are four colors to choose from. Color set 0 has Green, (2) Yellow, (3) Blue, and (4) Red while color set 1 consists of Buff, (6) Cyan, (7) Magenta, and (8) Orange.

In text mode (selected by SCREEN also) the colors available are either Black and Green (color set 0) or Red and Orange (color set 1).

Form: COLOR 5, 7

causes Buff lines to be displayed (when drawn) on a Magenta background. If no COLOR statement is used, the highest numbered color in the current color set is the foreground color and the lowest numbered color is the background color.

DLOADM   is used to Down-LOAD a machine-language program from another computer.

Form: DLOADM "NAME", B

where B is either 0 or 1 specifying a baud rate of 300 or 1200. The "baud rate" is the transfer rate of data in bits per second.

DRAW   DRAWs one or more lines (even a whole figure) by following the instructions contained in quotes or in a string variable.

Form: DRAW "string"
       DRAW "S2;BM128,96;E50;L100;D100;R100;H50"

where "string" is made up of a combination of the following instructions:

     B   Blank - don't draw
     M   Move to specified position (default = 128,96 or the end point of the last DRAW

statement). A plus (+) or minus (−) following the M instruction means the numbers are to be **added** to the current position to locate the start of the next line.

U	DRAW Upward the specified number of points (default is 1 for U,D,R,L,E,F,G, and H)
D	Downward
R	to the Right
L	to the Left
E	45 degrees (half way between Up and Right)
F	135 degrees (half way between Right and Down)
G	225 degrees
H	315 degrees
X	eXecute another string of instructions and return Example: XA$
C	Color (default = foreground color)
A	Angle of rotation

        0 = no rotation (default)
        1 = 90 degrees clockwise
        2 = 180 degrees clockwise
        3 = 270 degrees clockwise

S	Scale factor where a factor of 1 means 1/4 scale, 2 means 2/4 or 1/2 scale, etc. (default = 4/4 or full scale)
N	No update, i.e., DRAW the next line from the previous starting point

EXEC   sends program control to a machine-language routine at the specified address. (See USR.)

Form: EXEC 24623

JOYSTK   is a function that returns a value between 0 and 63 to indicate the position of a joystick.

Form: JOYSTK(n)

where n is a number from 0 to 3 that determines which joystick is being checked:

    0 = horizontal position of the RIGHT joystick
    1 = vertical position of the RIGHT joystick
    2 = horizontal position of the LEFT joystick
    3 = vertical position of the LEFT joystick

JOYSTK(0) must be the first JOYSTK function used in any program.

LINE   draws a line, a box, or a filled-in box between specified points. The points are either the end points of the line or the opposite corners of the box.

Form: LINE (X1,Y1)-(X2,Y2),A,B
          LINE (20,10)-(150,100),PSET,BF

where (X1,Y1) is the starting point and (X2,Y2) is the ending point of the line or the opposite corner of the box.

A is either PSET which selects the foreground color for the line (box) or PRESET which selects the background color ("erasing" the figure by blending it with the background). B is optional and is either a "B" for an empty box or a "BF" for a filled box. If the starting point is omitted, the figure is drawn starting at the previous ending point (or from the center of the screen if no previous LINE statement was used). The hyphen (-) must not be omitted, however.

MOTOR   turns the cassette recorder ON and OFF

Form: MOTOR ON
          MOTOR OFF

PAINT   PAINTs the region with a selected color from a given point to a boundary of a specified color.

Form: PAINT (X,Y),C,B

where (X,Y) names a point within the region to be PAINTed, C selects one of the available colors (see COLOR), and B specifies the color of the existing boundary line.

PCLEAR   reserves the amount of memory to be used for graphics. Graphics memory is divided into 8 "pages" of 1536 memory locations each. If no PCLEAR statement is included in the program, the computer automatically reserves 4 "pages" of memory for graphics.

Form: PCLEAR 2

reserves only 2 "pages" making the rest available for larger programs.

PCLS   clears the graphics screen similar to the CLS usage in text mode.

Form: PCLS n

where n is one of the available color codes used to set the background. If n is omitted, the current background color is used.

PCOPY   copies one graphics "page" to another.

Form: PCOPY 3 to 5

PLAY   makes music using a string of instructions that can specify notes, tempo, volume, rests, etc.

Form: PLAY "music"
           PLAY "T2;L4;O3;A;L8;A;A;B-;A;G;F;L2.;A;P4"

where "music" is a string containing some of the following:

note	a letter from A to G or a number from 1 to 12 using - for flats and + or # for sharps
O	specifying which of the five Octaves to use (1-5)
L	names the Length of the tone (L1 = whole note, L2 = half note, L4 = quarter note, L4. = dotted quarter note, etc.)
T	sets the Tempo (1-255)
V	sets the Volume (1-31)
P	determines the length of a rest or Pause (1-255)
X	eXecutes another string of instructions (see DRAW)

PMODE   sets the resolution of the graphics screen, how many colors are available, and which graphics "page" is used first.

Form: PMODE R , P

where R is a number from 0 to 4 that establishes the resolution.

0   gives a 128x96 grid with two colors,
1   gives a 128x96 grid with four colors,
2   gives a 128x192 grid with two colors,
3   gives a 128x192 grid with four colors, and
4   gives a 256x192 grid with two colors.

P is a value from 1 to the value given in PCLEAR to specify which graphics page to start using.

PPOINT   checks the color of a specified point of the graphics screen. PPOINT returns the color code if that point is "on".

Form: PPOINT (X,Y)

PRESET   sets a specified point to the current background color.

Form: PRESET (X,Y)

PSET   sets a specified point to the current foreground color.

Form: PSET (X,Y)

SCREEN   places the computer in text mode or graphics mode and indicates which color set is to be used (see COLOR).

Form: SCREEN M, C

where M is a 0 (for text Mode) or a 1 (graphics) and C names COLOR set 0 or COLOR set 1.

SOUND   generates a tone at a specified pitch for a given length of time.

Form: SOUND P, T

where P is a number that determines the Pitch (1 is low, 255 is high, 89 is close to middle C on the piano) and T sets the duration (10 = .60 secs., 25 = 1.50 secs., etc.)

TIMER   is a function that measures time in "jiffies" (1/60 sec.) TIMER starts at power-up and resets to zero each time it reaches 65535. TIMER can be set to measure an event with

     TIMER = 0

(any number 0-65535 can be used to set TIMER) and can be "read" by

     PRINT TIMER

A Few Thousand Words About "DISK BASIC"

Many computers are capable of storing programs and data "externally" on rigid or floppy magnetic disks. A disk is referred to as a "mass external storage" medium since the amount of information it can store is many times what the computer can hold internally at any one time.

About the DOS

The Disk Operating System (DOS) is a "Master Control" software program. DOS is the "Operating System", and is concerned primarily with control and operation of the computer and its peripherals --- the Big Picture. It sees that the CPU (the heart of the computer), the BASIC interpreter (or compiler), and the storage and Input/Output devices work as a team.

It also tells the CPU where certain programs or data are stored and where space exists to store more. Some systems refer to the DOS as the "Executive", or the "Monitor".

We are usually aware of DOS because of its file handling features. It allows us to list directories of the programs and data files stored on disk (typically using a DIRectory type command). DOS commands are frequently confused with Disk BASIC statements and commands, since some of the same commands can be given either from DOS or from BASIC.

We use DOS commands to KILL (or DELETE) a file, RENAME a file, and COPY a program from one disk drive to another. It also allows us to load in the BASIC interpreter or compiler (which is just another software program). So-called "utility" programs usually accompany a DOS to do things like SORT a data file, RENUMBER program lines and help DEBUG a program.

Disk BASIC is NOT the Same

Disk BASIC, on the other hand, is ordinary BASIC with a few added capabilities, like storing and retrieving programs from disk.

"Plain old" Basic had to undergo some minor changes --- mostly additions, in order to control large data files. Disk BASICs have the "usual" BASIC language statements, functions, commands and operators, plus additional statements and commands for interacting with the files stored on disk.

The lack of uniformity of the added Disk BASIC features makes a thorough treatment of **all** Disk BASIC words impractical at its current stage of development. However, in order that you might recognize the nature of Disk BASIC as you read program listings, this summary treatment of the more common statements is included. It will help you recognize when a Disk BASIC is being used, and what it is being used for. You may then be able to rewrite it using your computer's version of BASIC.

Programs are usually written to interact with a disk drive because access is much faster and more convenient than writing to or reading from tape. Almost anything that can be accomplished on disk can also be done on tape. . . but **much** more slowly. If you attempt to convert a program written for disk to a computer that has only tape storage, it will require more than just substituting new statements for old. The program flow may have to be completely reorganized to minimize the impact of the slow tape, and human intervention is usually required.

"Bringing up" BASIC on a disk-based system is automatic for some computers. Others require a command such as RUN BASIC or just BASIC to move "down" from DOS into the BASIC interpreter/compiler.

Once in BASIC, getting back "up" to the DOS level requires one of a variety of commands. (Some computers give a choice.) Typically, BYE, DOS, EXEC, MONITOR, SYSTEM or CMD"S" do the trick. Sometimes we can return to DOS only by pushing the "reset" button.

Opening And Closing A File

Disk files consist of "records", clusters of letters or words which mean something to someone (or something), as in a DATA file. A "file" is a **group of records** to which we give a name. A file may be something more tangible, like a BASIC program being stored on the disk. Ordinarily we LOAD or SAVE an entire Program file at a time. DATA files on the other hand may be READ or altered a single record at a time.

To read or write (called accessing) information in a file, that file must first be OPENed. Disk files may be accessed **sequentially**, that is, each record in order, as on cassette tape, or **randomly**, as on a phonograph record where we can place the needle anywhere without spiraling thru the preceding grooves first.

An OPEN statement must be in the program to specify **which** access method, the **name** of the file to be OPENed, and what reference number to associate with the file. (That reference number will be used in the program's READ and PRINT statements.)

Disk BASICs are not at all uniform, but the following examples show what typical OPEN statements look like:

```
10 OPEN "I",3,"MYDATA"
```

opens a file named MYDATA for sequential INPUT, ("I"). The file can be read via a READ #3 statement. It is opened for READing only, and cannot be written into.

```
20 OPEN NEW "SCORES" AS 1
```

opens a NEW file named SCORES for sequential OUTPUT. PRINT #1 will put information from the computer into the file.

```
30 OPEN "DATA.FIL" FOR INPUT AS FILE 2
```

opens a sequential input file, DATA.FIL, which will be read by the program as file 2 with a READ #2.

Either of the OPEN statements in the last two examples could also open a random access file. The statement in line 10 above would need the "I" changed to "R" for random access. FILE is used in place of OPEN on some machines.

While a file is OPENed for use, it is vulnerable to having its data altered accidently, by a program error, power line glitch, or other unforeseen disaster. Therefore, as soon as a file is no longer needed by the program, it should be closed with a CLOSE 1 or similar statement. A file may be OPENed and CLOSEd any number of times during a program's execution.

Sequential vs Random

READ#, PRINT# and INPUT# statements are usually used with sequential files but must specify the device number associated with the file. Some Disk BASICs use WRITE# and PRINT# interchangeably. A few use WRITE# to place data in files with quotes around the strings, while others use WRITE# to insert line numbers before each DATA line.

Random files must have the contents of their records carefully formatted by the program. A FIELD statement defines what to expect, and typically reads like:

```
10 FIELD #1, 20 AS N$, 22 AS A$, 15 AS C$, 2 AS S$,
   5 AS Z$
```

That FIELD statement specifies that each of the records in file #1 contains the five items illustrated below. (Numbers are printed above the file contents here so we can visually measure the length of each entry.)

```
1234567890123456789012345678901234567890123456789012
JOHN A. EDMUND        3206 BEAL ROAD

          345678901234567890123456789012345678901234
          HARRISON        CA93888
```

The FIELD statement reserved the first 20 characters (including trailing blanks) for a name, the next 22 characters for a street address, 15 characters for the city, 2 for the state and 5 for the ZIP code. The BASIC program will now know how to interpret each record in this random file.

Is There Bufferin In The Buffer?

On its way to or from the disk, information is placed in a temporary storage area in the computer, called a buffer. LSET and RSET are used by many Disk BASICs to place data in the buffer before sending it to disk. LSET "left justifies" data in a string variable and RSET "right justifies" the data. For example,

```
10 LSET N$="JOHN A. EDMUND"
```

places the name in the record to be written as it is shown above.

```
10 RSET N$="JOHN A. EDMUND"
```

causes the name to appear in the record as

```
12345678901234567890 (reference scale)
      JOHN A. EDMUND
```

Random Strings

Some Disk BASICs require that all random file data be in string form (no numeric values allowed). In order to convert numbers to strings, and strings back to numbers, conversion functions are part of those BASICS.

The functions MKI$, MKS$ and MKD$ convert integers, single-and double-precision numbers to strings. CVI, CVS and CVD convert strings back into numbers. Other disk BASICs use CVT%$ and CVTF$ for converting integers and floating point numbers to strings and CVT$% and CVT$F to convert them back. They're simple to use. . . but treacherous.

Reading and Writing

Typical random Input and Output statements are GET#1 for Input and PUT#1 for Output. A few computers use INPUT:1 or READ:1 instead of GET#1, and PRINT:1 or WRITE:1 for PUT#1.

Scratching Where It Itches

On some computers, a sequential output file must be "SCRATCHed" before data can be written to it. Example:

```
10 SCRATCH #4
```

RESTOREing

After READing, some computers allow us to RESTORE data in a sequential file in order to READ it again. If RESTORE isn't available, CLOSEing then OPENing a file will automatically restore the pointer to the beginning of the DATA file, thus RESTOREing it.

EOF

When INPUTting data from a disk or other external mass storage device, it is necessary to detect when all the DATA has been INPUT and the end-of-file is reached. The EOF function is used in an IF-THEN statement to do the job. For example:

```
100 IF EOF #1 THEN 520
```

It reads "if the file is out of data, proceed to Line 520".

How Long?

Some Disk BASICs provide functions to determine the Length-Of-File (LOF) and (LOC)ation of the file pointer (i.e. which record is being accessed). A SET statement SETs the "pointer" (like setting the phonograph needle) to the exact record location where something is to be PRINTed or READ.

What's Ahead?

TYPE (or TYP) is used to detect what kind of data is in the **next** record of a sequential file. For instance, in North Star BASIC, if TYP returns a 0, End-Of-File has been reached. A 1 means the next record contains string data, and a 2 means it contains numeric data. Other computers using TYPE may give different meanings to the numbers returned.

```
EXAMPLE: 190 IF TYP(1)=2 THEN 220
         200 READ #1,A$
         210 GOTO 230
         220 READ #1,N
```

What's In A Name?

Finally, a word about file names. The **way** the name must be written is determined more by the computer's DOS than by its version of disk BASIC. Since OPEN and other statements need to specify the file name, however, it is appropriate to discuss them here.

Typically, a file name is composed of four items:

1. the number of the device on which the file is stored,
2. the name of the file,
3. the extension or group, and
4. a password, if any.

For example,

```
LOAD 1:COINS/DAT,PASS
```

LOADs a file on disk drive #1 named COINS, and it has the password PASS. The /DAT is the "extension" or group classification, and may indicate we're using it as a DATA file.

Where Are We?

Since no standards exist for **enhancements** to BASIC, disk BASICs have as much variety as is found at the San Diego Zoo. Either agreement must be developed as to what form disk statements will have, or we will continue speaking mutually unintelligible disk BASIC dialects at each other.

For more information of a tutorial nature, see CompuSoft Publishing's books dealing with Disk BASIC and Disk Operating Systems.

Index and Scorecard

This and the following pages are both an index to this expanded edition of *The BASIC Handbook* and a scorecard for your computer. As you run each test program record the results here. Later, a quick reference to these pages will reveal whether a particular word is accepted by your machine.

Word/Symbol	Page(s)	Test Runs Pass	Fail	Notes
A,	17,21,	____	____	_____
	32	____	____	_____
ABS	17	____	____	_____
AC,	19	____	____	_____
ACS	19	____	____	_____
ACSD	19	____	____	_____
ACSG	19	____	____	_____
ADR	429	____	____	_____
AND	21	____	____	_____
APPEND	25	____	____	_____
ARCOS	19	____	____	_____
ARCSIN	29	____	____	_____
ARCTAN	34	____	____	_____
ASC	27	____	____	_____
ASCII	27	____	____	_____
ASN	29	____	____	_____
ASND	29	____	____	_____
ASNG	29	____	____	_____
AT	32	____	____	_____
ATAN	34	____	____	_____

Word/Symbol	Page(s)	Test Runs Pass	Fail	Notes
ATN	34	___	___	_____
ATND	34	___	___	_____
ATNG	34	___	___	_____
AUDIO	439	___	___	_____
AUTO	37	___	___	_____
AXIS	435	___	___	_____
BAPPEN	435	___	___	_____
BASE	39	___	___	_____
BGET	426	___	___	_____
BOLD	435	___	___	_____
BPUT	426	___	___	_____
BREAK	41	___	___	_____
BRIGHTNESS	435	___	___	_____
BSAVE	435	___	___	_____
BYE	42	___	___	_____
C.	68	___	___	_____
CALL	43	___	___	_____
CDBL	44	___	___	_____
CH	45	___	___	_____
CHAIN	46	___	___	_____
CHANGE	49	___	___	_____
CHAR	51	___	___	_____
CHARSIZE	435	___	___	_____
CHAR$	51	___	___	_____
CHR	51	___	___	_____
CHR$	51	___	___	_____
CHR⋈	51	___	___	_____
CINT	53	___	___	_____

Word/Symbol	Page(s)	Test Runs Pass	Fail	Notes
CIRCLE	439			
CLEAR	54			
CLG	56			
CLK	58			
CLK$	58			
CLOAD	59			
CLOADM	439			
CLOG	56			
CLOSE	447			
CLR	54			
CLRDOT	61			
CLS	62			
CMD	446			
CO	68			
CODE	64			
COLOR	65,429, 440			
COM	66			
COMMON	66			
CON	68			
CONT	68			
COPY	435,445			
COS	69			
COSD	69			
COSG	69			
COSH	71			
COUNT	73			
CSAVE	74			

Word/Symbol	Page(s)	Test Runs Pass	Fail	Notes
CSAVEM	440			
CSH	71			
CSNG	75			
CUR	76			
CVD	448			
CVI	448			
CVS	448			
CVTF$	448			
CVT$F	448			
CVT$%	448			
CVT%$	448			
D	77			
D.	78			
DASH	435			
DAT	78			
DATA	78			
DEBUG	445			
DEF	80			
DEFDBL	83			
DEFINT	85			
DEFSNG	88			
DEFSTR	91			
DEG	93			
DEGREE	93			
DEL	95			
DELETE	95,445			
DET	97			
DIGITS	99			

Word/Symbol	Page(s)	Test Runs Pass	Fail	Notes
DIM	101			
DLOADM	440			
DMS	93			
DOS	429,446			
DOT	105			
DRAW	106,440			
DRAWTO	106			
DSP	107			
E	109			
E.	112			
EDIT	110			
ELSE	111			
END	112			
ENTER	429			
EOF	449			
EQ	113			
ERASE	114			
ERL	115			
ERR	116			
ERRL	115			
ERRN	116			
ERROR	118			
EXAM	119			
EXCHANGE	120			
EXEC	441,446			
EXIT	121			
EXP	123			
EXT	426			

Word/Symbol	Page(s)	Test Runs Pass	Fail	Notes
F.	137			
FDIM	425			
FETCH	125			
FGET	425			
FIELD	447			
FIF	425			
FILE	447			
FILL	127			
FIN	426			
FIND	435			
FINPUT	425			
FIX	128			
FLASH	129			
FLOW	130			
FLT	427			
FMT	131			
FN	134			
FNEND	136			
FONT	435			
FOR	137			
FOUT	427			
FPRINT	426			
FPUT	426			
FRAC	139			
FRE	140			
FREE	140			
FUNTIL	426			
FUZZ	435			

Word/Symbol	Page(s)	Test Runs Pass	Fail	Notes
G.	148	____	____	_____
GE	142	____	____	_____
GET	143	____	____	_____
GET#	448	____	____	_____
GIN	435	____	____	_____
GO	145	____	____	_____
GOODBYE	42	____	____	_____
GOS.	146	____	____	_____
GOSUB	146	____	____	_____
GOSUB-OF	147	____	____	_____
GOT	148	____	____	_____
GOTO	148	____	____	_____
GO TO	148	____	____	_____
GOTO-OF	149	____	____	_____
GR	150	____	____	_____
GRAD	152	____	____	_____
GRAPHICS	430	____	____	_____
GT	151	____	____	_____
HLIN-AT	153	____	____	_____
HOME	154	____	____	_____
I.	167,174	____	____	_____
IF	155	____	____	_____
IF-G.	156	____	____	_____
IF-GOT	156	____	____	_____
IF-GOTO	156	____	____	_____
IF-LET	157	____	____	_____
IF-T.	158	____	____	_____
IF-THE	158	____	____	_____

Word/Symbol	Page(s)	Test Runs Pass	Fail	Notes
LIN	182	____	____	_____
LINE	442	____	____	_____
LINEINPUT	184	____	____	_____
LINK	427,436	____	____	_____
LINPUT	184	____	____	_____
LIS	185	____	____	_____
LIST	185	____	____	_____
LLIST	187	____	____	_____
LN	190	____	____	_____
LOAD	189,446	____	____	_____
LOC	449	____	____	_____
LOCATE	431	____	____	_____
LOF	449	____	____	_____
LOG	190	____	____	_____
LOGE	190	____	____	_____
LOG1Ø	192	____	____	_____
LPRINT	194	____	____	_____
LSET	448	____	____	_____
LT	195	____	____	_____
M.	225	____	____	_____
MAN	196	____	____	_____
MARK	436	____	____	_____
MAT CON	197	____	____	_____
MAT IDN	199	____	____	_____
MAT INPUT	201	____	____	_____
MAT INV	203	____	____	_____
MAT PRINT	205	____	____	_____
MAT READ	208	____	____	_____

Word/Symbol	Page(s)	Test Runs Pass	Fail	Notes
MAT TRN	210			
MAT ZER	212			
MAT=	214			
MAT+	216			
MAT-	218			
MAT*	220			
MAX	223			
MEM	225			
MERGE	25			
MID	226			
MID$	226			
MIN	228			
MKD$	448			
MKI$	448			
MKS$	448			
MOD	230			
MONITOR	446			
MOTOR	442			
MPY	436			
MTPACK	436			
N.	232,233			
NE	231,232			
NEW	232			
NEX	233			
NEXT	233			
NOFLOW	235			
NORMAL	236			
NOT	237			

Word/Symbol	Page(s)	Test Runs Pass	Fail	Notes
NOTE	431	____	____	_____
NOTRACE	239	____	____	_____
NUM	240	____	____	_____
NUM$	242	____	____	_____
OFF	436	____	____	_____
OLD	427,436	____	____	_____
ON ERR GOTO	243	____	____	_____
ON ERROR GOTO	243	____	____	_____
ON-G.	247	____	____	_____
ON-GOSUB	245	____	____	_____
ON-GOS.	245	____	____	_____
ON-GOT	247	____	____	_____
ON-GOTO	247	____	____	_____
OPEN	446	____	____	_____
OPTION	250	____	____	_____
OR	251	____	____	_____
OUT	257	____	____	_____
P.	272	____	____	_____
P.A.	277	____	____	_____
PADDLE	431	____	____	_____
PAGE	436	____	____	_____
PAINT	442	____	____	_____
PAUSE	255	____	____	_____
PCLEAR	442	____	____	_____
PCLS	442	____	____	_____
PCOPY	443	____	____	_____
PDL	259	____	____	_____
PEEK	260	____	____	_____

Word/Symbol	Page(s)	Test Runs Pass	Fail	Notes
PI	262			
PIN	263			
PLAY	443			
PLOT	264			
PMODE	443			
POINT	265,431			
POINTER	436			
POKE	266			
POLL	436			
POP	267			
POS	269			
POSITION	431			
PPOINT	444			
PRECISION	271			
PRESET	444			
PRI	272			
PRINT	272			
PRINT AT	277			
PRINT USING	278			
PRINT @	277,436			
PSET	444			
PTR	427			
PTRIG	431			
PUT	431			
PUT#	448			
R.	298,303			
	308			
RAD	285			

Word/Symbol	Page(s)	Test Runs Pass	Fail	Notes
RADIAN	285	——	——	———————
RAN	287	——	——	———————
RANDOM	287	——	——	———————
RANDOMIZE	287	——	——	———————
RBYTE	436	——	——	———————
RDRAW	436	——	——	———————
REA	289	——	——	———————
REA.	289	——	——	———————
READ	289	——	——	———————
RECALL	291	——	——	———————
REM	293	——	——	———————
REMARK	293	——	——	———————
REN	294	——	——	———————
RENAME	445	——	——	———————
RENUM	294	——	——	———————
RENUMBER	294,445	——	——	———————
REP	436	——	——	———————
REPEAT$	297	——	——	———————
RES	299	——	——	———————
RESET	298	——	——	———————
REST.	299	——	——	———————
RESTORE	299,448	——	——	———————
RESUME	301	——	——	———————
RET	303	——	——	———————
RET.	303	——	——	———————
RETURN	303	——	——	———————
RIGHT	304	——	——	———————
RIGHT$	304	——	——	———————

Word/Symbol	Page(s)	Test Runs Pass	Fail	Notes
RMOVE	436			
RND	305			
ROTATE	436			
RSET	448			
RU	308			
RUN	308			
S.	314,327,			
	329			
SAVE	309,446			
SCALE	436			
SCR	310			
SCRATCH	310,448			
SCREEN	444			
SCRN	312			
SECRET	436			
SEG	313			
SEG$	313			
SET	314,449			
SETCOLOR	432			
SETDOT	315			
SGET	427			
SGN	316			
SHUT	427			
SIN	317			
SIND	317			
SING	317			
SINH	319			
SKIPF	322			

Word/Symbol	Page(s)	Test Runs Pass	Fail	Notes
SLEEP	321			
SNH	319			
SORT	445			
SOUND	432,444			
SPA	323			
SPACE	323			
SPACE$	323			
SPC	323			
SPUT	427			
SQR	325			
SQRT	325			
ST	327			
ST.	329			
STATUS	433			
STE	327			
STEP	327			
STICK	433			
STO	329			
STOP	329			
STORE	330			
STR	331			
STRIG	433			
STRING	331			
STRING$	331			
STR$	333			
STUFF	334			
SUB	43			
SUBEND	43			

Word/Symbol	Page(s)	Test Runs Pass	Fail	Notes
SUM	436	____	____	_____
SWAP	335	____	____	_____
SYS	336	____	____	_____
SYSTEM	336,446	____	____	_____
T.	337,345	____	____	_____
TAB	337	____	____	_____
TAN	339	____	____	_____
TAND	339	____	____	_____
TANG	339	____	____	_____
TANH	341	____	____	_____
TAPPEND	343	____	____	_____
TEXT	344	____	____	_____
THE	345	____	____	_____
THEN	345	____	____	_____
TI	346	____	____	_____
TIM	346	____	____	_____
TIME	346	____	____	_____
TIMER	444	____	____	_____
TIME$	348	____	____	_____
TI$	348	____	____	_____
TLIST	437	____	____	_____
TLOAD	349	____	____	_____
TNH	341	____	____	_____
TOP	350	____	____	_____
TRACE	351	____	____	_____
TRACE OFF	352	____	____	_____
TRACE ON	353	____	____	_____
TRAP	433	____	____	_____

Word/Symbol	Page(s)	Test Runs Pass	Fail	Notes
TROFF	354	———	———	———————
TRON	355	———	———	———————
TSAVE	356	———	———	———————
TYP	449	———	———	———————
TYPE	449	———	———	———————
UNTIL	357	———	———	———————
USER	358	———	———	———————
USR	358	———	———	———————
VAL	359	———	———	———————
VARPTR	361	———	———	———————
VIEWPORT	437	———	———	———————
VLIN-AT	363	———	———	———————
VTAB	365	———	———	———————
WAIT	366	———	———	———————
WBYTE	437	———	———	———————
WEAVE	25	———	———	———————
WHILE	369	———	———	———————
WINDOW	437	———	———	———————
WRITE	447	———	———	———————
XDRAW	371	———	———	———————
XIO	433	———	———	———————
XOR	372	———	———	———————
XRA	372	———	———	———————
" (quote)	374	———	———	———————
, (comma)	376	———	———	———————
. (period)	379	———	———	———————
; (semicolon)	380	———	———	———————
: (colon)	382,426	———	———	———————

Word/Symbol	Page(s)	Test Runs Pass	Fail	Notes
( ) (parentheses)	384	_____	_____	_____
[ ] (brackets)	384	_____	_____	_____
@ (AT symbol)	386,426	_____	_____	_____
# (number sign)	387,426	_____	_____	_____
$ (string)	391,425	_____	_____	_____
! (exclamation)	394,426	_____	_____	_____
% (per cent)	396,426	_____	_____	_____
? (question)	398,426	_____	_____	_____
\ (backslash)	399,426	_____	_____	_____
** (double asterisk)	400	_____	_____	_____
+ (plus)	401	_____	_____	_____
- (minus/hyphen)	403	_____	_____	_____
/ (slash)	404	_____	_____	_____
* (asterisk)	405	_____	_____	_____
= (equal)	407	_____	_____	_____
↑ (up-arrow)	409	_____	_____	_____
^ (carat)	409	_____	_____	_____
< (less than)	411	_____	_____	_____
> (greater than)	413	_____	_____	_____
< > (not equal)	415	_____	_____	_____
< = (less than or equal)	417	_____	_____	_____
> = (greater than or equal)	419	_____	_____	_____
' (apostrophe)	421,426	_____	_____	_____
& (ampersand)	422,426	_____	_____	_____
¤ (sol-Swedish string symbol)	424	_____	_____	_____

NOTES

Appendix A

ASCII to DECIMAL Conversion Table

In order to translate between binary computer numbers and English, a code number is set aside to stand for letters, decimal numbers and other characters. They are called "The ASCII Set". ASCII stands for the American Standard Code for Information Interchange.

Refer to the ASCII table as you read the following:

1. The characters represented by numbers between 32 and 90 are fairly uniform from computer to computer — but not 100%.

2. The numbers from 97 to 122 are also reasonably uniform, but since they are lower case, and many terminals print only upper case characters, they serve simply as duplicates of other numbers.

3. The numbers from 0 to 31 used to be uniform in the old days of slow and clunking printing terminals. With the advent of video terminals and different peripheral devices, this uniformity has pretty well disappeared.

4. From 123 to 255 is wide open.

Use this simple BASIC program to discover what character your computer assigns to each decimal code number. The delay loop in lines 40 and 50 gives you a little time to view them on a video screen. You may wish to change the numbers to match the speed of your computer.

```
10 FOR N = 0 TO 255
20 PRINT "ASCII NUMBER ";N,
30 PRINT CHR$(N)
40 FOR D = 1 TO 500
50 NEXT D
60 NEXT N
```

ASCII Number Code Chart (in decimal)

Decimal Code	ASCII Character	Decimal Code	ASCII Character
32	space	79	O
33	!	80	P
34	"	81	Q
35	#	82	R
36	$	83	S
37	%	84	T
38	&	85	U
39	'	86	V
40	(	87	W
41	)	88	X
42	*	89	Y
43	+	90	Z
44	,	91	↑ or [
45	–	92	↓ or \
46	.	93	← or]
47	/	94	→ or ^
48	0	95	–
49	1	97	a
50	2	98	b
51	3	99	c
52	4	100	d
53	5	101	e
54	6	102	f
55	7	103	g
56	8	104	h
57	9	105	i
58	:	106	j
59	;	107	k
60	<	108	l
61	=	109	m
62	>	110	n
63	?	111	o
64	@	112	p
65	A	113	q
66	B	114	r
67	C	115	s
68	D	116	t
69	E	117	u
70	F	118	v
71	G	119	w
72	H	120	x
73	I	121	y
74	J	122	z
75	K	123	{
76	L	124	\
77	M	125	}
78	N	126	~

NOTES

NOTES

NOTES

NOTES

NOTES

NOTES

NOTES

NOTES

Notice to Manufacturers
and
Software Houses

Each time *The BASIC Handbook* is revised for reprinting, the COMPUSOFT research staff makes every effort to incorporate the key features of new BASIC interpreters and compilers. To ensure that information regarding your new features is included, we urge you to send us exhaustive documentation of these features, including any and all literature you disseminate to BASIC customers. After receiving this information, we will contact you for details and verification.

A hearty "Thank You" to the many companies which have aided us in describing their BASIC treatments. The success of *The BASIC Handbook* is a direct function of our ability to accurately represent all manufacturers' BASICs.

Comments and suggestions from private readers and involved companies are actively solicited. Such correspondence should be sent to:

Editor, **The BASIC Handbook**
COMPUSOFT PUBLISHING
Box 19669
San Diego, CA 92119
U.S.A.

Notice to Readers

The research and editorial staffs of COMPUSOFT PUBLISHING have made every effort to insure that all information is correct, both in letter and in concept. However, it must be kept in mind that *The BASIC Handbook* is a reference work that must necessarily depend upon a wide gamut of private parties (commercial hardware and software makers). Though we have exhaustively checked the accuracy of all data sent us, we advise you that some data may prove to be obsolete by the time you read this.